7 2

# The Joy
# of Politics

## Also by Amy Klobuchar

*Uncovering the Dome*
*The Senator Next Door*
*Antitrust*

# The Joy of Politics

Surviving Cancer, a Campaign,
a Pandemic, an Insurrection, and
Life's Other Unexpected Curveballs

## AMY KLOBUCHAR

ST. MARTIN'S
PRESS
NEW YORK

First published in the United States by St. Martin's Press,
an imprint of St. Martin's Publishing Group

THE JOY OF POLITICS. Copyright © 2023 by Amy Klobuchar.
All rights reserved. Printed in the United States of America.
For information, address St. Martin's Publishing Group,
120 Broadway, New York, NY 10271.

www.stmartins.com

Designed by Steven Seighman

Library of Congress Cataloging-in-Publication Data

Names: Klobuchar, Amy, author.
Title: The joy of politics : surviving cancer, a campaign, a pandemic, an
    insurrection, and life's other unexpected curveballs / Amy Klobuchar.
Description: First edition. | New York : St. Martin's Press, 2023. |
    Includes index. |
Identifiers: LCCN 2022055881 | ISBN 9781250285140 (hardcover) |
    ISBN 9781250285157 (ebook)
Subjects: LCSH: Klobuchar, Amy. | United States. Congress. Senate—
    Biography. | Women legislators—United States—Biography. |
    Cancer—Patients—United States—Biography. | United States—
    Politics and government—2017–2021. | United States—Politics and
    government—2021–
Classification: LCC E901.1.K58 A3 2023 | DDC 328.73/092—dc23/
    eng/20230113
LC record available at https://lccn.loc.gov/2022055881

Our books may be purchased in bulk for promotional, educational,
or business use. Please contact your local bookseller or the Macmillan
Corporate and Premium Sales Department at 1-800-221-7945, extension
5442, or by email at MacmillanSpecialMarkets@macmillan.com.

First Edition: 2023

10  9  8  7  6  5  4  3  2  1

# Contents

# The Path

Life Lesson: *Sometimes when you don't quite make it to the top of the trail, you learn all kinds of things along the way.*

In July of 2020, just months after my presidential campaign had ended and five months into the pandemic, my husband, John, and I took a drive out west. Just four months earlier—way back when everyone thought you got the coronavirus from surfaces and that the sheer act of wiping down grocery bags could save your life—my husband had gotten really sick with COVID. He ended up in the hospital. He had pneumonia and his oxygen saturation levels fell below 70 percent. After six days in the hospital hooked up to oxygen and another few weeks of a lonely quarantine at home, he was fine save for one—and only one—long-haul symptom: he claimed the dust in our basement (and only that dust) prevented him from ever cleaning out the basement again.

In truth, John's illness had put a lot of things in perspective. This long driving trip was a time to finally talk about it.

You see, my husband had done everything and anything for me throughout my career in politics. From the beginning in 1998 when he meticulously typed in and individually verified permission for a thousand supporters to include their names on a newspaper ad ("More than 1,000 lawyers agree that Amy Klobuchar has the experience, judgment and integrity to be a great county attorney . . . who says lawyers can't agree on anything?") to the 2020 presidential run, when he traversed the country in an "Amy For America" T-shirt. From parades in Minnesota to church parking lots in South Carolina to casino basements in Nevada, he was always there for me.

You get way too used to that in my profession—the spouse sacrificing his or her own ambitions and time and life for you: urging you to run in the first place; patiently wading through your political slights of the day; bending at the knees in the family Christmas card photos so you don't look too short; stepping in when you are cornered by a long-winded political science professor and with a hand on the guy's back you say "Have you met my husband?" or "Have you met my wife?"; packing the school lunches; doing the day care pickups; giving up jobs and proximity to family and friends and moving across the country.

Being a congressional political spouse is a whole thing. And it's often a really raw deal.

That joke I just made in the first paragraph about the dust aversion and John not wanting to clean the basement and it being his only COVID long-haul symptom? It is actually Exhibit A. It is 100 percent true, and he said it to me in all seriousness to avoid cleaning the basement, and I laughed really hard because I knew how much he hated hauling stuff out of there. Now, in most marriages it would be a funny story to share at the Thanksgiving dinner table that gets exaggerated and larger than life over time. But for the political spouse—

and for that matter, the politician's kid[1]—it ends up as a cock-tail party fundraiser story, or in a speech, or worse yet, on TV. And just because he smiles at the event and laughs along with everyone else doesn't mean he likes that you brought it up—no matter how well-meaning. It's done. You said it. What is he supposed to do?

Twenty years into my life in politics, I remember a late night over beers at my husband's high school class reunion, when a woman I had never met before came up to me and said: "You know, it's so funny, it was always John who we thought would run for office. That's what we predicted. I guess in a way he ended up doing it anyway."

I wanted to say, actually, it isn't that funny. Yes, we did it, but in the end it was all about me. It was always me on the debate stage. It was always my name on the campaign signs. It was always my name on the ballot.

In any case, that year—2020—was the year I almost lost my husband: the greatest dad, the sweetest son, an accomplished author, law professor, and yes, the best husband. I almost lost him. Just like that. It was a year when a disease so utterly horrible came out of nowhere (actually, according to our scientists' best guess, it was Wuhan, China) and took so many people's lives. It was a year when we all knew some-one who lost their mom or dad or grandpa or grandma or husband or wife in a hospital and could never even hold their hand or say goodbye except on a cell phone or a laptop with nothing but tubes and beeps and hospital sounds on the other end of the line. It was a year when we were jarred into realiz-ing that your life could be ended by virtue of a single invisible

---

1. "MOM!" my daughter once said in a voicemail, "that story you told this

droplet. It could happen anywhere. You could get deathly ill just because you sat next to a guy at a coffee shop or stood by an office mate at the back of an elevator or danced next to the maid of honor at your niece's wedding. You could go for a walk and see someone on the street and a few weeks later you would hear they were in the hospital on a ventilator, and no one knew if they were going to make it.

Nothing could be taken for granted anymore.

That was why John and I decided to take the trip. We realized we could take nothing—including each other—for granted anymore. We embarked on the drive in early July 2020, when both the Midwest and the Western states were experiencing what turned out to be a brief and only temporary reprieve from the spread of the virus. Many people were beginning to wonder if it was finally over. It wasn't, but even wondering about it felt good.

A little over a month before our drive out west the horrifying murder of George Floyd had ripped apart Minnesota and our nation. Systemic racism had been talked about for years, but the time had finally come for a true reckoning. The prosecution of former Minneapolis police officer Derek Chauvin for the murder of Floyd was by then in the able hands of my friend, Minnesota Attorney General Keith Ellison.

Weeks before, and just over three months after I had

---

morning about me was from MIDDLE SCHOOL . . . you know the time I said you weren't a 'helicopter mom,' but instead you were a 'submarine mom' because you lurked beneath the surface and popped up unexpectedly? It was funny then but MOM, I'm in college now. And MOM it's trending. MOM the reporter used my name. MOM: NEVER tell that story again." (Exhibit B) ended my own presidential campaign, I had taken myself out of the running to be considered for Joe Biden's vice president. I knew the months stretching ahead would be much different than I'd ever thought they would be. I had that experience in common with . . . well, just about everyone, as so many people's plans were changed and canceled due to the pandemic. Weddings—and even funerals—were put on hold, and no one knew when or if there would be an end to the masks, the remote work, the chaos, and yes, the virus itself. I knew that when we returned from the ten-day trip I needed to go full-on back to my work in the Senate, as well as do everything I could to help the Biden campaign win in November. But that July, I needed to think. I needed to rejuvenate. I needed to spend some time with John.

We didn't have a grand plan for this drive. It was about as spur-of-the-moment as a politician's schedule could allow. My husband picked me up after I finished a meeting with local officials in Worthington, Minnesota, close to the South Dakota border. We drove west to the Black Hills, our arrival somehow exactly coinciding with Donald Trump's pre–Fourth of July rally in front of Mount Rushmore. Yes, that one. The one where they were worried that his post-speech fireworks amid the highly flammable ponderosa pines would set the entire national park on fire.

As we drove past ranches and farms and eastern South Dakota flatland, I listened to a radio station dissecting the appropriateness of the Trump administration's use of Mount Rushmore for the fireworks. That included the George Washington/Thomas Jefferson/Abe Lincoln/Theodore Roosevelt backdrop to what was in essence a campaign political rally, and, what's more, the decision to break with the ten-year ban on pyrotechnics at the historic spot. I tracked the fire-hazard risk level. I heard the alerts about the motorcade-related traffic and possibilities of road closures ahead. And I said to myself, "Well, there goes my 'getting away from it all' plan."

Our first stop that afternoon was the Badlands. As we filled up the car at a gas station just outside the park, my husband and I, clad in sunglasses and baseball caps (mine a pink "CAT" hat given to me by Caterpillar manufacturing workers, his a maroon and gold number, boldly advertising his University of Minnesota alma mater), quickly realized we were sharing the gas pumps and hot asphalt parking lot with legions of eager Trump supporters on their way to the Black Hills rally.

"Heard there are protesters up ahead," said one guy in a red MAGA hat and a "Build the Wall" T-shirt, elbow to elbow with my husband at the pump.

"Sounds like trouble," the guy added.

At this moment we realized he assumed we were heading to the same place.

"I heard it's going to be okay," I said, "unless of course everything catches on fire."

"Hope you're right," he said, quickly adding, "I mean about everything being okay."

In the end, months later, I turned out to be 100 percent right. The election results were in and everything WAS okay. At least until everything (in the form of the U.S. Capitol insurrection, our politics . . . and, eventually, our constitutional rights) caught on fire. And by the way, the peaceful Native American protesters outside of Mount Rushmore were the least of Donald Trump's worries that summer.

By that time he had already been impeached on charges of abuse of power and obstruction of Congress for soliciting Ukrainian authorities to influence the 2020 presidential election, and, in spite of his acquittal by the Senate, he remained deeply unpopular with the majority of voters.

After spending the night in beautiful Spearfish Canyon, South Dakota—where the Spearfish Canyon Lodge proprietors somehow decided that the most fitting room for me was one named after the well-known American frontierswoman and Black Hills legend "Calamity Jane"—we drove west to the Tetons, a park of spiritual renewal for our family. It was the place where my dad—a longtime newspaper columnist for the *Star Tribune* in Minneapolis, a sportswriter, an avid adventurer, and the author of twenty-three books—used to climb mountains.

Grand Teton National Park is also the destination where, when I was a college student, my dad and I once bicycled 1,100 miles in ten days. In fact, in the summer of 1981, the newspaper promoted the ride to their subscribers as a must-read daily adventure of the dynamic duo of Jim Klobuchar and his college-age daughter, Amy, riding through rattlesnakes and prairie dogs, and yes, up and over the Continental Divide. We never did see a rattlesnake. But the against-the-wind elevation gain, the multiple angry farm dogs, the two flat tires, and the one major tornado that downed acres of corn stalks were excitement enough.

Now, nearly thirty years later, I was back. After basically tracing that old bike route by car, John and I made it to Jackson, Wyoming, at the foot of the Teton mountains. Every night we ate COVID-era boxed take-out food with plastic forks in our hotel room, roaming the streets in the evening, walking and driving by all the landmarks that defined my family's camper-trailer trips growing up—the Silver Spur Cafe (where I used to get the pancakes with the blueberry syrup, quite exotic for the 1960s); the Snake River (where my mom had once taken my six-year-old sister and me on a rafting trip that to my mother's dismay was not the promotional brochure's promised riverbanks of loping deer, but instead a raftful of shirtless sunburned guys drinking Budweiser beer); the hotel formerly known as the Wagon Wheel (due to budget constraints, it was the only Jackson hotel we ever stayed in as kids, with the once-in-a-lifetime opportunity to sleep somewhere other than a campsite occurring only after my sister sprained her ankle on a hike down Death Canyon); the Chapel of the Transfiguration, with its beautiful view of the Tetons; Jackson Lake Lodge; herds of buffalo; the occasional bear; and of course, a moose slowly bobbing, antlers down, lapping at the creek, framed by the setting sun.

During the day John and I hiked. It was spectacular and, courtesy of the early days of the pandemic, there were fewer people than usual on the trails. One morning we set out on the 13.5-mile round-trip trek up to Lake Solitude and back, starting at Jenny Lake, climbing up to Inspiration Point, and walking through the serene Cascade Canyon, surrounded by what is known as the Cathedral group of mountains. These were the peaks my dad once climbed: Teewinot, Mount Owen, and the most famous of them all—the Grand Teton. And given that it was still relatively early in the season, as we ascended closer and closer to the lake, there was still ice and slippery snow on the top third of the trail.

Now, there was a personal health backstory to this trip, outside of my husband's bout with COVID. Only four months before we left for Wyoming, I had been in the hospital for a long-overdue hip replacement. I had delayed the surgery for nearly a year due to the presidential race, and the sore hip—caused by a condition called dysplasia—was the actual reason I was always clad in my signature flat shoes during the latter half of the presidential campaign.

Somewhere in the middle of the campaign the hip just went. I knew exactly what it was, since I'd had a similar experience ten years before with the other hip. Back then the surgery had completely fixed it. But there wasn't time for that in the middle of a presidential run, and the sorry truth was that I had to take at least six Advil in the hours leading up to each debate just to walk to the podium without limping. A few weeks after I left the presidential race, it was great to finally get the hip fixed, and the recovery from the surgery—in the middle of multiple votes on the first major pandemic legislation—had gone well. In the nonstop intensity of the Senate, no one ever even seemed to notice I was walking with crutches. Okay, maybe that says something about my work environment, but I was somehow able to pull off coming back to work on crutches five days after hip surgery with hardly a question from anyone. There was just too much going on for anyone to notice, including my colleagues.[2]

---

2. There were, of course, senatorial exceptions to every rule, including my friend and former Republican Senator Roy Blunt, who was then chair of the Senate Rules Committee and loaned me a room right off the Senate chamber so I could reduce the length of my walks on crutches for COVID legislative votes. And Virginia Senator Mark Warner, who risked COVID to visit me in my crutches/walker-bound room, and Tina Smith, my colleague who loaned me her apartment right after my surgery when my husband got COVID. More on Tina's generosity later.

In any case, four months later, I felt good enough to hike. Everything wasn't completely healed, but I wanted to feel normal again. The trip was part of that plan.

Around six miles up and about a half mile from the top of our hike to Lake Solitude, my hip and the top of my leg (still healing from the surgery) started to hurt and I didn't feel steady on the ice. I immediately realized that a major slide down an icy, rock-covered slope would not be the best idea. So instead of finishing the hike, I decided to rest. I plopped myself down on a big boulder smack in the middle of the trail.

I told John to go on without me. My husband—one of six boys who grew up in a mobile home in Mankato, Minnesota, and, as I explained earlier, the most supportive guy a woman could ever dream of—did all he could to get me to finish the hike. He knew how I always liked to make my goals, so he cajoled me to rest for a half an hour and finish the hike like I always did. I told him I could probably do it because I had done the trail before—and I would do it sometime in the future—but today I just couldn't make it.

Exhausted, I took out the crackers and salami and a bag of trail mix and told him I would be perfectly happy on this beautiful rock on a stunning part of the trail among slopes blanketed in wildflowers and mountains all around me.

"Take some pictures for me at the top," I said.

John was clearly unsettled by my sudden and completely uncharacteristic indifference to the charted goal at hand ("I mean it is just twenty minutes ahead," he kept saying), but he finally gave up and began climbing solo up the trail. After he rounded the curve and took his last possible glance back at me, I burst out in tears about all that had transpired to get me to that moment: not meeting my goal of finishing the hike, out of the presidential race, in pain, and in the middle of a pandemic.

But then I closed my eyes and thought, "There are others on much more difficult journeys than mine." People who had lost loved ones. People who had lost their jobs. I knew my travails were nothing compared to what so many were going through. I calmed down, grabbed the toilet paper roll out of the backpack to blow my nose, looked around at the joyful majesty of the mountains, said a prayer, and vowed to be thankful for all I had instead of focusing on what I'd missed out on. My husband had survived a bad case of COVID, my home city and state were going to find redemption one way or another, my country would bounce back, our democracy could be saved, and I was in a unique position to help make that happen. In other words, it was time to end the pity party.

At peace on that rock, soaking in the sun, my mind wandered to other hiking trips. Like the time our family went to Slovenia, the home of my ancestors. I remembered a story we heard on that trip of a writer who was dying of cancer and decided to write her own obituary to leave for her young children. In it she offered this wise advice: "[M]ay you always remember that obstacles in the path are not obstacles, they ARE the path."

The summer we heard that touching tale, our daughter would be college-bound in just a few weeks. As any good mom would do leading into such a momentous, life-changing event, I decided to keep sharing brilliant advice with her at every turn, and that dying writer's story provided me with the crux of it: the obstacles are the path; the obstacles are the path. Isn't that what parents are supposed to do when their kids go to college? Share wisdom? Yet it got—in our daughter's mind—so over the top that she later wrote a humorous essay for her college paper about the incident, noting that no matter what happened that week, from a room with a broken air conditioner and 100-degree heat to a delayed plane to an indecipherable menu, it was always the same answer: the obstacles are the path; the obstacles are the path.

Fast-forwarding to that moment on the rock on the Teton trail, my "obstacles are the path" reverie—including its obvious relevance to the moment—was suddenly disrupted by the distinct sound of ice and snow breaking from down the path, boots and poles rhythmically hitting the surface with astounding synchronicity. It wasn't one person—it was two. An older couple, equipped with the finest matching bright orange L.L.Bean jackets and ski poles, rounded the corner and came crunching up the ice slope.

"Are you okay?" they asked, noting I am sure the odd look of a lone woman with a blue bandanna dabbing her eyes with toilet paper perched on a boulder in the middle of a trail while tearing off pieces of salami and scarfing down a bag of trail mix.

"I'm good," I said, adding a feigned way-too-cheery explanation, "I'm just celebrating getting all the way up here four months after having my hip replaced."

"That is extraordinary," said the woman, "it truly is."

"I think so," I said, my spirits picking up as I contemplated how many OTHER people were up this high four months after a hip replacement.

Then, just minutes after the lake-bound older couple left me, coming down from the other end of the trail I saw two kids who had passed John and me about an hour back: a boy who looked around ten and a girl about fifteen.

"Hey, lady," yelled the young boy from a few yards above, "did you stop right there and not go up to the top?"

"I did," I said. "The view is actually much better from this rock."

"That is so cool," the boy said, coming down alongside of me, punctuating his words by kicking snow off his boots onto my boulder. "You know, it is SO overrated up there. The ice and snow are covering everything, including the lake. And you could never ever swim in that freezing Lake Solitude."

We both paused and looked up at the mountains around us.

"Cool," he said again.

"Cool," I said.

The chance encounter reminded me that life is too short to waste on regrets, what-might-have-beens, or negativity brought on by life's unexpected challenges. And what an important reminder that was.

You see, you need to start where you are. Your obstacles are your path. And sometimes when you don't quite make it to the top of the trail, you learn all kinds of lessons along the way.

# 1

# The Call

Life Lesson: *"Start where you are."*
— Reverend Claudette Anderson Copeland

On Monday, March 1, 2021, at around 4 P.M., the Piper Breast Center in Minneapolis called me about a test I had taken the Friday before. I don't remember the name of the woman who called. I don't even remember her job or title. I just remember what she said.

"I am calling with your test results from the biopsy you had Friday, which was a follow-up to the mammogram you had a week before at Mayo Clinic. The earlier test showed spots and calcification. The biopsy we just did shows us more. It turns out you have breast cancer. It is Stage 1A, which is better than some other stages, but it is still cancer. You need to find a breast cancer specialist and then they can map out a treatment."

"What will the treatment be?" I asked, vigorously writing everything she told me on a small yellow Post-it Note.

"Well, that you need to discuss with a doctor. It can be everything from surgery to radiation. You need to talk to a doctor right away."

"Okay," I said.

"Are you going to call a doctor right away?" she asked.

"Yes," I said, "I'm on it. Thanks for letting me know."

I pressed the "end call" button on my cell.

*"I'm on it"? "Thanks for letting me know"?*

What I really wanted to say was this:

*I have votes on the Senate floor in a half an hour.*

*I have to walk into the Senate chamber and pretend nothing is wrong in front of a bunch of guys.*

*Senator Durbin wants to meet with me about a bill. I have work to do!*

*A year ago I ended a presidential campaign and then devoted myself to helping someone else win. I have made it through an insurrection and have done everything I could to make things better. Why this? Why now?*

*My husband almost died of COVID. I have picked up the pieces of my life. It's just the wrong time in my life to deal with this.*

*We are in the middle of a pandemic. How am I going to get help?*

*I'm leading an investigation of what went wrong on January 6th with U.S. Capitol security. It isn't something I can just put off for another day!*

*Am I going to have this "treatment" and still be able to lead those hearings? I mean, these hearings are really important.*

*Where should I go to find a doctor?*

*What does "1A" mean? It sounds like an apartment unit.*

*Do I need chemo?*

*Am I going to have to wear a wig?*

*How bad is this surgery?*

*What are my chances?*
*My dad is dying. Can I be there for him?*

But all I said was, "I'm on it. Thanks for letting me know."

Shell-shocked, I called my husband in Minnesota and told him not to scare our daughter until we knew more. Fifteen minutes later I greeted the Senate elevator operator with a smile, went up a floor, walked into the Senate chamber, and voted for the confirmation of Education Secretary Miguel Cardona. All the while the Senate clerk monotoned through the alphabetically listed names of senators: ". . . Ms. Baldwin, Mr. Barrasso, Mr. Bennet, Mrs. Blackburn, Mr. Blumenthal, Mr. Blunt, Mr. Booker . . ."

This is something the clerk does—and has done—for decades: monophonically call out the list of all one hundred senators over and over again during the pendency of a vote (which can often last well over an hour), taking great care to be as evenhandedly boring as possible, showing no emotion or reaction to any individual name despite whatever scandal or skullduggery or abhorrent act any one of the senators might be involved in on that particular day: "Mr. Boozman, Mr. Braun, Mr. Brown, Mr. Burr, Ms. Cantwell, Mrs. Capito, Mr. Cardin, Mr. Carper, Mr. Casey, Mr. Cassidy, Ms. Collins, Mr. Coons, Mr. Cornyn, Ms. Cortez Masto, Mr. Cotton, Mr. Cramer, Mr. Crapo, Mr. Cruz . . ."

I waited for Senator Durbin, who'd let me know through his staff that he wanted to talk on the floor that afternoon. Dick Durbin is the chair of the Senate Judiciary Committee, and, as a member of that committee, I had asked him, as well as Democratic leaders Harry Reid and Chuck Schumer years

before, if I could join Dick as the lead author on the reauthorization of the Violence Against Women Act, also known as
"VAWA."

The VAWA bill meant a lot to me. But for eight years—
since 2013, when I first introduced it—I had also been trying
to pass a related bill closing what has been called "the boyfriend loophole," and in 2021 I stood a chance of including it in VAWA. My bill would stop domestic abusers from
going out and buying a gun after they had been convicted
of domestic abuse. The provision had actually made it into
the House-passed version of the reauthorization of VAWA.
Twenty-nine House Republicans had voted for it. Knowing that the NRA opposed the provision, I wanted to be in
on the negotiations—in the "room where it happens"—to
make sure some version of that provision stayed in the final
VAWA bill.

I had all kinds of other reasons for wanting to be one of the
leads on the Violence Against Women Act. I am one of the
few women on the Senate Judiciary Committee. I am a former prosecutor with an extensive record of taking on domestic
violence cases and overseeing a well-regarded domestic abuse
service center. And finally, one of my friends and mentors, the
late Senator Paul Wellstone of Minnesota, had championed
the original federal domestic violence legislation, along with
his beloved wife, Sheila.

Dick Durbin is a great guy and a true leader and someone
I trust. But when he came over with that "nice dad" look on
his face and just a touch of guilt in his eyes, I knew there was
more bad news on the way. He told me that despite my long-
standing request to lead the reauthorization of the Violence

Against Women Act, my experience as a prosecutor, the importance of my boyfriend loophole provision, and his full faith in me, I couldn't lead the Violence Against Women Act with him because Senators Patrick Leahy and Dianne Feinstein had dibs. We aren't in high school, and he didn't use those exact words, but "dibs" succinctly describes the seniority customs of the Senate. Senators Leahy and Feinstein were much more senior than me and they'd led the bill before and wanted to do it again.

Acknowledging that I had been making this request for a long time, he empathetically explained why it wasn't in the cards. He also noted the Senate Republicans' then long-standing objections to including my provision to close the boyfriend loophole. He thought that including my provision would face more opposition in the Senate than in the House.

As I listened to Dick, the clerk's repetitious recitation of the senators' names continued: "Mr. Daines, Ms. Duckworth, Mr. Durbin, Ms. Ernst, Mrs. Feinstein, Mrs. Fischer . . ."

I remember thinking at that moment that before I got the cancer call, Dick's news would have really pissed me off. But instead I basically conceded the inevitable: with the way the Senate works—at least the way it DOES work as opposed to how I think it SHOULD work—Durbin had no way around this one. Two respected senior members wanted to lead the bill, and that's how the seniority system works in the Senate.

Realizing I had much bigger problems that day, I responded . . . well, quite uncharacteristically, with a flippant "Whatever."

"Whatever?" Dick queried, obviously relieved at my response but puzzled at the same time.

"Whatever," I repeated, knowing full well that the result

would have been the same if I had put up a fight, and momentarily relishing the fact that even righteous indignation has its limits. I vowed to myself at that moment that despite this setback I would find one way or another to pass my domestic violence gun safety bill. Little did I know that the loophole would actually get closed, but that it would take two horrendous mass shootings in the spring of 2022 to create the impetus to finally pass my provision as part of the bipartisan gun safety legislation.

"Mrs. Gillibrand, Mr. Graham, Mr. Grassley, Mr. Hagerty, Ms. Hassan, Mr. Hawley, Mr. Heinrich, Mr. Hickenlooper, Ms. Hirono, Mr. Hoeven, Mrs. Hyde-Smith, Mr. Inhofe, Mr. Johnson, Mr. Kaine, Mr. Kelly, Mr. Kennedy, Mr. King, Ms. Klobuchar, Mr. Lankford, Mr. Leahy, Mr. Lee, Mr. Luján, Ms. Lummis, Mr. Manchin, Mr. Markey, Mr. Marshall . . ."

"Whatever."

It was all like a backdrop to a movie where something really bad is about to happen but everyday life keeps going on. You know, the scenes where people are out smiling, walking their dogs and driving shiny convertibles and going to three-year-olds' birthday parties—and then suddenly the bomb drops, or the sirens blare, or the lava comes rolling down the mountain. The list droned on: "Mr. McConnell, Mr. Menendez, Mr. Merkley, Mr. Moran, Ms. Murkowski, Mr. Murphy, Mrs. Murray . . ."

That cancer phone call only an hour before had changed everything. The natural progression of my year—and maybe even my life—had been seriously altered with a few sentences uttered by a complete stranger.

White spots. Calcifications. Biopsy. 1A. Surgery. Radiation.

But in fact nothing else had changed. No one—save for

my husband and "the cancer woman" who called me, whose name I didn't remember—even knew this was happening. It was my own private hell. And the only evidence that the conversation had even occurred was a Post-it containing my cryptic scribbled-down notes from the call.

"Mr. Ossoff, Mr. Padilla, Mr. Paul, Mr. Peters, Mr. Portman, Mr. Reed, Mr. Risch, Mr. Romney . . ."

As I later learned, what I experienced that afternoon—my freakish "life goes on without you" cancer story—isn't one bit unique. So many who have dealt with the scourge of cancer know exactly what I mean. In the end, when you get the call, they are your and only your white spots, your calcifications, your lumps, and your Stage 1A.

"Ms. Rosen, Mr. Rounds, Mr. Rubio, Mr. Sanders, Mr. Sasse, Mr. Schatz, Mr. Schumer, Mr. Scott of Florida, Mr. Scott of South Carolina . . ."

Listening to the roll call, I understood that the world would go on without me, whether I had cancer or not.

"Mrs. Shaheen, Mr. Shelby, Ms. Sinema, Ms. Smith, Ms. Stabenow, Mr. Sullivan, Mr. Tester, Mr. Thune, Mr. Tillis, Mr. Toomey, Mr. Tuberville."

The list would be read. The hearings would take place. The talking heads on the cable shows would comment. Dick and Patrick and Dianne would lead the bill. I wouldn't be in the room when they debated whether to include the boyfriend loophole. The senators would vote.

What also became apparent as the Gregorian-like chant of "Misters" and "Mizzes" and "Missuses" sounded over and over again was that I wasn't ready to tell any of them about the cancer. If I tell any ONE of them, I thought, in just a matter of days or even hours EVERYONE will know—my high school teachers, my staff, my daughter's friends, the guy who reads the paper every day at Cafe Alma on University Avenue. Because, to quote my staff, they were a "rando" group, those senators. Some I liked very very much, some I didn't but had to work with anyway. Some were my actual good friends and some in name only.[3]

It is human nature to tell people with whom you work when bad stuff happens. But around my workplace, all it takes is one word to the wrong person, even if it is inadvertent, to lead to an off-the-record call to a reporter, and it is no longer your story, your treatment, your future. It is theirs.

"Mr. Van Hollen, Mr. Warner, Mr. Warnock, Ms. Warren, Mr. Whitehouse, Mr. Wicker, Mr. Wyden, Mr. Young."

In less than an hour I made the decision to share the "news" with no one but my family. I was going to keep this cancer quiet until I figured it all out, and life—especially in the unforgiving "If you want a friend in Washington, get a dog"[4] fishbowl of D.C. politics—would go on as a constant

---

3. Here's a tip: when one senator says of another "my friend and colleague from the state of Florida . . ." don't be thinking it is necessarily true. It is a custom, a tradition, often a faux title of familiarity. As my Minnesota "friend and colleague" Tina Smith repeatedly tells people, "Amy and I REALLY are friends. She came to my kids' weddings BEFORE I was a senator. We aren't just Senate friends. We are really friends."

4. "If you want a friend in Washington, get a dog" is often attributed to former President Harry Truman. It turns out there is no record he ever said it, but that it was instead paraphrased from a line in the 1975 play *Give 'em Hell, Harry!* where Truman's character says, "You want a friend in life, get a dog." As pointed out in a March 17, 2016, PolitiFact check—in which the website sliced and diced the respected former Ohio Republican Governor John Kasich by giving him a "FALSE" rating for attributing the D.C. line to Truman during an Ohio town hall (see, I told you national politics is a tough

backdrop. In the end it was my problem. It was not the problem of my colleagues—many of whom were still fresh off the trauma of the insurrection—and it was not the problem of my constituents, who were dealing on multiple fronts with the pandemic, job and family losses, and the George Floyd murder trial, set to begin in just one week. I also knew that my then ninety-two-year-old dad, who had been in assisted living struggling with Alzheimer's over the last few years—was not going to live much longer. These next few months—coming as they did in the post-vaccine COVID era—were supposed to be about him, and a chance to say goodbye for me, our family, and his many friends.

I voted for both the Education and Commerce secretary nominees, attended our weekly Senate leadership meeting headed up by Senator Schumer, and, hours later, got back and started my search for next steps. I called a doctor at Mayo, where only ten days before they had seen the small white spots—the "calcifications"—during a routine mammogram as part of a routine physical.

The Mayo medical staff had actually insisted I stay for additional follow-up tests that Friday afternoon after they saw the spots. I told them I didn't have time for a follow-up, because I was doing a public event in Mayo's hometown of Rochester on COVID vaccines with their own doctors and then had to get back to Washington.

---

sport)—there is no evidence Truman even liked dogs. As PolitiFact noted, "History proves that Truman was no fan of dogs," based on his once giving away the White House puppy, Feller, to his doctor, which didn't play well in the press. When asked by a reporter whatever happened to Feller, Truman at first seemed to not even know what the newsman was talking about, and then later replied, "Oh, he's around."

"I'll do it later," I said. "I promise."

I still remember stripping off those double hospital gowns fresh out of the mammogram room and changing back into my work clothes and strapping on my watch. I put my lipstick on, squared my shoulders, suited up, and walked back into the real world.[5]

Like many women, my immediate reaction was this: they are just overreacting. I mean this mammogram exam was just routine. They call it "routine" for a reason, right? I feel fine. I don't have cancer. I couldn't have cancer. And besides that I have a plan for the day and I can't interrupt it.

But that is the thing about cancer: it has its own plans, and they never coincide with yours.

I wasn't completely in denial, though. I did schedule that follow-up biopsy in Minneapolis at the Piper Breast Center, for exactly a week later, when I returned home. And now—four days since the biopsy and ten days after the initial spots were discovered at Mayo—I had the results.

In retrospect, my one-week delay after the first indication of trouble wasn't that bad, but the previous year-plus of not going in for a routine exam was. Like so many Americans, because of the pandemic I had put off going in for my annual physical,

---

5. This call to action involving the suit and the shoulders and the lipstick was actually a favorite battle cry of one of my mentors, former Maryland Senator Barbara Mikulski, the first female Democratic senator to be elected in her own right (meaning she got her Senate seat "without some husband having to kick the bucket"). Barbara once stood on a historic Senate couch—all four feet eleven inches of her—with the women senators gathered around, giving us our marching orders before a vote. The funny thing is that I don't even remember what the vote was about, but I do remember the lipstick, the shoulders, and the suit part, with much fondness.

which at my age includes a scheduled mammogram every two years. At the beginning of the virus, that made sense. No one knew exactly how COVID was transmitted, there wasn't enough protective equipment, no vaccines existed, and a lot of people were getting really sick or dying. There also weren't enough hospital beds or even, for a while, any possibility for elective surgeries. But after a few months on the COVID front lines, medical care had changed. As the months went by it was just fine to go in for preventative care exams. The medical offices knew how to take precautions, and it was arguably a lot safer than going into a grocery store or a restaurant.

But still I waited.

I have since learned that during the pandemic one out of three Americans reported delaying or forgoing health care because of coronavirus-related concerns. In fact, Americans missed more than nine million cancer screenings during that time! Thousands of women who missed their mammograms were living with undetected breast cancer. And over and over doctors reported seeing patients who had to be treated for more serious conditions that could have been caught earlier.

In my case, after consulting with Dr. Karthik Ghosh, a breast cancer specialist at Mayo and the kindest of doctors, I realized that fortunately the tests had still caught the cancer early. They would have to do some additional procedures but if the Stage 1A classification held up without any additional bad findings, I could most likely get through this thing with a lumpectomy followed by a course of radiation. They would always keep open the possibility of a mastectomy as a game day decision in the middle of the surgery (lovely), but the stats supported a lumpectomy as the appropriate course of action.

A plan was hatched. I would go on with my regular work

(which at the time included chairing a major public hearing in Washington with Defense, FBI, and Homeland Security witnesses about security and intelligence failures leading up to and on January 6th, and also taking part in significant votes up to the Easter recess). Right when I could return home—a week before Easter—I would have the lumpectomy at Mayo, followed by a course of radiation two months later.

If I had needed immediate chemo or began missing days of work and votes in the then-perennially tied 50/50 Senate, I would have made a different decision. But for me at that moment, I wanted to deal with it with my family and my doctors in private. I also knew that I would ultimately share the story, because you don't hide things when you are a public official (at least I don't), and it was of course the right thing to do.

Sometimes I thought, "Well, I wish HE knew I had cancer," when someone brought me down at work. My favorite story at the time was dealing with a group of usually diligent male senators who had not yet read the draft of a document we needed to release to the public. I had gotten up at 4 A.M. so I could both do radiation treatment and edit the draft. When I found out they hadn't yet read it, and thus we weren't able to agree to any changes, I just wanted to scream, "And I am on a radiation table having this discussion?" But I didn't. And they are good guys. And if they had known, they probably would have read it earlier.

On March 30, I had the surgery. With my husband at my side, I headed to the big revolving doors and the lobby of the Gonda Building on the Mayo Clinic campus, a place near and dear to the hearts of many across the nation and the world, and a point of pride for my state.

Mayo Clinic began as a father-and-son medical practice

back in the late 1800s. Coordinated patient-centric care was its philosophy and its mission from the very beginning, when Dr. William Worrall Mayo (father of two doctor sons—Dr. Will and Dr. Charlie—who would later join him in the practice) advertised his medical practice in the *Rochester City Post* as being "over the Union Drug Store on Third Street." The ad promised, "All calls answered by day or night." With help from the Sisters of Saint Francis, the Mayo father and sons soon opened Saint Mary's Hospital after a tornado destroyed a third of Rochester, resulting in thirty-seven deaths and more than two hundred injuries.

Always with an emphasis on expertise, efficiency, and patient care, Mayo has long been known for its research, its top-notch medical care (rated number one in the country by *U.S. News & World Report* for the last seven years), and even its lawyers (which include the late United States Supreme Court Justice and *Roe v. Wade* author Harry Blackmun).

Taking a trip through Mayo is like being ushered through a day on a well-organized tour bus. At the beginning of the day you get your schedule, with each destination identified by floor and area. You wait for your appointment in serene, art-filled waiting areas. The records of your tests and visits with different specialists are shared with . . . well . . . "surgical precision" so that each department knows what the others have found. You can literally walk the hallways and pretend you are at an art museum or sit in those comfortable waiting rooms and imagine you are heading into a sales meeting at a major corporation. Yet when your name is finally called and you go through the swinging doors, you quickly realize that there is no mahogany conference table with swivel chairs awaiting you. Instead it's a jab in the arm or a pass with the ultrasound or an X-ray of your knee.

But no artwork, no efficiency, no kind smile or pleasant lilac-colored gown or reassuring hand on the shoulder can camouflage the stark nature of any medical procedure. Don't get me wrong—those amenities all make it better. But in the end you are still there with breast cancer. The pen drawing on your breast, the half-nude pre-op photos for the surgery, the warnings of what could go wrong, the paperwork, the prospects of more cancer and a potential mastectomy, the needles in the arm, the specter of COVID: it is all still there. And the most difficult part of all is knowing that only the surgeon (in my case my first-name namesake and excellent doctor, Amy Degnim), with advice from the oncologist (yet another excellent woman physician, Dr. Tufia Haddad), can see if it is worse than they thought. If it is, a mastectomy might be in order, but that bridge is crossed when you get there. Blanket permission given.

It was all so, so, so professional, yet part of me wanted to scream through my smile, "Everyone is so nice and calm, but you are going to take out a chunk of my breast, and you just drew a target on it!"

Having talked to other women who have been through breast cancer surgery, I know they have had similar experiences. But I did have one unique pre-op moment most likely not shared by others: I was about to head into surgery when someone recognized me and—as constituents have every right to do—used the minutes she had with her senior senator pinned down on a pre-op rolling bed with clearly no means of escape to make her case for the people of Burma.

It was of course legit: a lot of bad things were happening in Burma at the time and we had already helped a number of refugees.

"I promise," I said, my double hospital robes concealing the penned-in target on my breast, "I will look into it when I'm done here. I'd do it now but they won't let me have my cell phone."

As they put me under the anesthesia, I drifted away not to the calming count of pastoral sheep, but instead to the obsessive mantra "Don't forget Burma. Don't forget Burma."

Hours later I emerged from surgery, and John was there with a nice card from my kind primary doctor, Janet Vittone, and a plant. I felt a bit sick, but through the grogginess of the post-anesthesia fog I did manage to immediately focus our conversation on two critical things:

ME: Was it just a lumpectomy or did I need a mastectomy?
JOHN: It was just a lumpectomy!
ME: Could you get my phone so I can text the staff about Burma? There was someone I met before I had the surgery . . .
JOHN: I guess you're doing okay then.

The Burma moment was a precursor of things to come. During the week after the surgery I would continue with my public events in Minnesota, which—in hindsight—was really stupid. The doctors sagely told me not to do so much, but I did it anyway: a Lake Superior port expansion event in Duluth, a vaccine press conference in a suburban hospital, numerous staff meetings and Zoom calls.

Senatorial habits are hard to break, even following surgery.

For the most part, because of the pandemic, the events I did were outside and cold, with participants donning thick winter coats. COVID protocols meant that few people were greeting me with hugs, which would have been bad because they would have really hurt. We'll call that a pandemic silver lining.

As there are for many women after breast cancer surgery, there were all kinds of struggles and scares and painful moments in the days, weeks, and months after. I was always asking questions.

*Do I have a temperature?*
*Why is this scar suddenly hurting?*
*Is it an infection?*
*When can I ever wear the bra I like again?*
*Is this normal?*
*Does this mean something else is wrong?*

To keep my own dignity (not to mention the dignity of my office), I will spare you most of the details of the surgery and post-surgery experiences, except one that is so common among women with this kind of cancer that it would be an insult to all of us (and you know who you are, because I've talked to many of you) not to mention it.

For various reasons (which again we do not need to explore in nitty-gritty detail), the surgery and the medication decisions in its aftermath triggered months of hot flashes, which are inconvenient for any woman, but particularly vexing when you are right out of surgery and things you thought had ended are suddenly saying: "Surprise, surprise: I'm B-A-C-K!" Consider being a U.S. senator surrounded by men who have no idea what is going on. It is a recipe for hard times and dark thoughts: "These guys have no idea what I'm going through, and I wish it happened to them once. Like right now, when that guy is giving that obnoxious speech."

The hot flashes keep you up at night and drive you especially nuts during hot weather. I personally believe that if men experienced menopause and hot flashes, there would be a whole lot more research and potential solutions, but for cancer patients there are currently limited remedies outside of not very useful medications with side effects that made them not worth it for me. There were also organic remedies and homespun treatments that in my case had no effect (but go for it if they help you) and nightly visits to the freezer. For guys that can't relate, yes, I mean PUTTING MY HEAD IN IT.

Now one positive: my post-surgery hot flashes were invisible to nearly everyone but me.

Except once. I remember one amusing call from a fairly famous person in May, just a few months after the surgery. She called to tell me I had "looked really good on *Colbert*."

"Glowing," she said, repeating with emphasis, "glowing."

She added, "What is your secret?"

Wow. I recalled the Stephen Colbert antitrust interview, knowing immediately I would not share with her the cancer diagnosis. Instead I decided to break my vow to myself to keep everything quiet with one big reveal. I mean, how often do you get asked—after decades on this earth—what your fountain-of-youth beauty tip is?

"Hot flashes," I said. "Hot flashes."

"Because of the home pandemic-era ring light beaming on my head [I had done the Colbert interview by laptop from my D.C. apartment], I had not one, not two, but three of them during the ten-minute interview."

"Oh my," she said, "oh my."

"But it looked really good anyway," she gushed.

It was moments like those that kept me going, right through to radiation.

The radiation treatments started at the end of May.

*Five days only. Good!*

*Every morning really early. Bad!*

*Lie on a big silver table while this major machine radiates/ laser beams you and it doesn't hurt while they are doing it. Good!*

*Could make you really tired and hurt later. Bad!*

My husband was a trouper that week and the radiation specialists were amazing, including Dr. Kim Corbin, the radiation oncologist (you'll note I had nearly an all-women team). They warned me that the radiated area might get red and hurt, but they had solutions. They warned me that sometimes the symptoms don't show up for weeks. True. They warned me that radiation can make you tired for months. I never thought that was true for me, but now, looking back, and feeling the energy I had over a year later to cross-country ski in zero degrees in northern Minnesota or to run around the world and keep my eyes open in meetings with little sleep in Warsaw and Dubai, I think that I was pretty tired that summer. And all the swelling in my hands (who knows why) and other weird things made it all hard. But again, compared to so many women with breast cancer, I had it easy. I truly did.

One of the hardest parts about the whole thing was that the week of radiation coincided with losing my dad. On one horrible day I literally came back from radiation to pick out his tombstone. But the months leading up to it had allowed me and my family and all his friends and my uncle Dick and his family to say goodbye. My dad held court for months at the assisted living memory care unit, telling old stories (a few of them were even true) and sharing tidbits of wisdom and his faith in God to the very end.

The life perspective for me as I witnessed my dad slipping away with late-onset Alzheimer's while battling my own breast cancer? My dad had experienced a life well-lived, a life of service. There was so much to rejoice in, even to the end. If I found myself temporarily down over his inability to remember my name or even where he was at the moment, his singing of hymns, Christmas jingles, musical tunes, and yes, drinking songs would jar me into a smile no matter where my mind had wandered.

My dad grew up as the son of an iron ore miner in Ely, Minnesota, not far from the Canadian border. He spent the better part of his career as a columnist and sportswriter for the Twin Cities newspaper—the *Star Tribune*. When he retired in 1995, he had written eighty-four hundred columns and twelve million words. He went from that hardscrabble mining town to travel the country and the world. He was a finalist for the Journalist in Space Project and was voted the nation's "outstanding columnist" in 1984 by the National Society of Newspaper Columnists.

Throughout his time as a reporter, my dad wrote—as fellow journalist Dave Nimmer once said—about "people on the outside." He told the stories of "ordinary people doing extraordinary things." Through his columns, he kept fighting the fights of those who couldn't always do it for themselves.

So many of his columns were mailed to me in the United

States Senate, yellowed and folded, tacked up on people's refrigerators for years. There would be notes accompanying them. "Your dad helped my aunt get her job back." "Your dad wrote about my teacher." "This column is about me when I got married." "This story meant a lot to my grandpa before he died." My dad told their stories, and they carried them with them until the end of their lives.[6]

When Dad left the *Star Tribune*, he wrote a number of questions for himself about his career. The first one was, was it worth it? Was his job worth it? The "dead-of-night plane flights, writing against the clock, absorbing the jocks' screaming curses in the losers' dressing room, keeling over from the cops' tear gas in a Miami street outside the Republican convention"; "trying to keep the mother of a dead marine on the phone although she was crying and alone in the house while I struggled with my revulsion for doing this."[7]

Was it worth it? His answer? God yes.

And even through the Alzheimer's, somehow my dad's wit and insight never left him. In addition to John and Abigail and me, his many visitors during that last year included his brother Dick, my sister Meagan, and his many friends—including Pastor Mark Hanson, Rod Wilson, and Doug Kelley. Every one of us has joyful memories of our visits during those last few months of his life.

---

6. Many of these stories and more are detailed in my book, *The Senator Next Door: A Memoir from the Heartland* (New York: Henry Holt and Co, 2015).

7. This story is detailed in my dad's book: Jim Klobuchar, *Minstrel: My Adventure in Newspapering* (Minneapolis: University of Minnesota Press, 1997).

"What a nice day it is today," I would say, opening the shades to his little room in an assisted living facility in Burnsville, Minnesota.

"I'll second that f-ing motion," he would punchily reply as if giving the laugh line from a story well-told decades ago in the press box at a football game.

The immigrant nursing aides propped up a dictionary next to his single bed so they could look up the many new words he shared with them during that last year of his life.

Like us, they loved him. For all who knew him, my dad's farewell was sad but sweet. His zest for life and his resilience through his many struggles—including with Alzheimer's—were far from a source of angst for me during my cancer. They were a source of strength.

During that week of my dad's death and leading into the radiation, my colleagues were wonderful. Their help ranged from the small—Thom Tillis's nice staff letting me use his conference room for an hour after I ran out of a Commerce Committee legislative markup because I had just found out my dad died—to my Judiciary Committee colleagues easily passing out one of my antitrust bills. Calls and notes arrived from many. While they didn't know I had cancer, they truly rose to the occasion.

And then there was the medical staff at Mayo . . . the doctors and nurses and nursing assistants and technicians who allowed me to grieve for my dad, kept my story mine, and, through their good work and expertise, made my future mine, all at the same time. I still have the little red radiation pin the radiology techs gave me when I "graduated" and the red-white-and-blue-flag mask they found for me to wear for Memorial Day.

By the end of August I'd decided it was time to tell my story. As was confirmed again by tests I had a few months later, the doctors at Mayo told me that I was 100 percent cancer-free and that my chances of getting cancer again were the same as the average person's getting cancer in the first place. I don't know who that average person is, but it sounded good.

On September 9, 2021, I put out a simple statement explaining the diagnosis and my health status. I did an interview with Minnesota's *Star Tribune* newspaper. I went on *Good Morning America* with Robin Roberts; she too had been through a public bout with cancer. My message was simple: get your exams, and go in for the mammogram you may have delayed. I delayed mine but finally got it, and I still caught it early.

The outpouring of stories, tweets, posts, and calls to our office from women who had put off their exams and were now scheduling an appointment as a result of my news was unbelievable. Several women texted me from waiting rooms to tell me they were there for their mammograms. And then, sometime later, a letter to our office came from a woman in Maple Grove, Minnesota:

> *Just wanted to thank Senator Klobuchar for going public with her breast cancer diagnosis and reminding women to get their mammogram. Because of her reminder, I made an appointment. From that appointment, the mammogram found a lump and after several tests, I've been diagnosed with stage 2 breast cancer. I am thankful that we caught the cancer early and will fight to overcome it.*
>
> *Sincerely,*
> *Melissa*

I spoke at cancer forums and introduced new legislation regarding cancer screening with Senators Susan Collins of Maine and Mike Rounds of South Dakota, whose wife, Jean, had only recently died after a long struggle with cancer, during which Mike was with her day in and day out. Senators John Thune, Tammy Baldwin, and my colleague Tina Smith cosponsored the bill. My annual emceeing of the women's congressional softball game with CNN's Dana Bash and breast cancer survivor and longtime NBC reporter Andrea Mitchell was all the more meaningful that fall. The game is an annual match between the women of Congress and the women of the D.C. press corps, led by congressional team captains Kirsten Gillibrand and Debbie Wasserman Schultz (also a breast cancer survivor), and all the proceeds go to help young breast cancer survivors.

Through it all I learned one practical lesson: there is rarely a good time to go in for a mammogram or any other routine exam. People are constantly balancing their families, their jobs, and their health. It's easy to put off health screenings, just like I did. But I hoped my experience would be a reminder for everyone of the value of health checkups, exams, and follow-throughs. I am so fortunate to have caught the cancer at an early enough stage to not need chemotherapy or other extensive treatments, which unfortunately is not the case for so many others.

As often happens with anyone dealing with illness, this experience also gave me time to reflect on my life and those I love. It gave renewed purpose to my work. I have immense gratitude for my family, friends, colleagues, and the people of Minnesota, and I know that each day is a gift, a joyful gift. Perfect strangers who did not know I was sick helped me during those hard months. I would get on a plane from D.C. to Minnesota full of cranky mask-wearing passengers, knowing I wasn't supposed to lift up my luggage for three months but not wanting to explain why. I would pause for just a moment, and every single time a Good Samaritan I did not know—and who did not usually know me either (the then-mandatory masks make great disguises for politicians)—would jump up and push in the heavy suitcase filled with clothes and note-books and briefing papers.

The final lesson I learned?

You start where you are.

This one came out of a sermon I heard that summer of my recovery at the historic Ebenezer Baptist Church in Atlanta, Georgia, the one where the Reverend Martin Luther King Jr. preached, and where my friend (yes, truly my friend) Senator Reverend Raphael Warnock is the senior pastor.

That weekend Reverend Warnock was our host in Atlanta for the first Senate Rules Committee voting rights field hearing in decades. As the brand-new chair of the Senate Rules Committee, I felt we needed to take the committee on the road and hear testimony about state-passed obstacles to voting. My colleagues (Senators Warnock, Ossoff, Padilla, and Merkley) and I heard numerous witnesses testify in support of passing federal voting legislation.

Georgia—like a number of other states—had passed restrictive provisions into law aimed at making it harder for Georgians to vote. This happened right after Georgia had turned out in record numbers in 2020 in the middle of a pandemic, bringing Raphael Warnock and Jon Ossoff to the Senate, and surprising the nation with a Georgia victory for now-President Joe Biden. The Georgia laws that had been enacted after the record 2020 turnout were sadly geared to make voting arduous—from limiting the runoff period, to outlawing voter registration during the runoff period, to enacting a confusing requirement that voters put their birth dates (as opposed to the dates they fill out their ballots) on the outside of the inner ballot envelopes, to limiting the food and water volunteers could hand out while voters stood in notoriously long, sunbaked lines just to cast their ballots.

To sum up what all those post-2020 changes were about? In the simple words of Reverend Warnock, "Some people don't want some people to vote."

The visit to Reverend Warnock's historic church the day before the hearing was his idea, and I was honored to join him. That Sunday it was "Women's Day," and there was a guest minister preaching: Reverend Claudette Anderson Copeland, from a church in San Antonio, Texas. She herself was a survivor of serious cancer, something I did not know until she mentioned it at the tail end of the sermon. As I sat there next to Reverend Warnock, with no one in the church knowing that I was going through cancer treatment, her words stuck with me, and still do today.

"Start where you are. Begin. Commence. Get going. Crank up. Initiate. Mobilize. Start where you are."

"Never be intimidated by external indicators. The mortgage rate's too high. Weather too hot. Your body too sick. You think you're too young, too old, too black, too white. Some of us are so discouraged by where [we] want to be. It appears so distant and so far away and so unlikely. The dreams seem so expansive and the horizons seem so far. It feels like you won't ever get it done."

"But Jael told me to tell you start where you are."[8]

"You've gotten stuck in your reality at the expense of your possibility."

"Subversive shifts begin with one small beginning."

"Don't stay hamstrung by your yesterdays, harnessed and muzzled by who hurt you, who failed you and who dropped you and who quit on you and who cheated on you and who left you."

"Bust the move and start where you are."

I heard those words just a month after I'd gone through radiation. And in that moment, in that church filled to the brim with the joyful music of worship and the reverend's resounding voice, I felt like I was finally ready, five months after getting the call and finding out I had cancer, to find solace in my faith in God, to accept the setback, to take it as it was, and to start where I was. That moment in that church was it. I realized that the only way I could have the strength and the faith and the firm footing to move forward was to start where I was, not where I had wanted to be a year before. Not where I had planned to be before I got the call. But just where I was.

I realized then what I know now: everything would be okay. Start Where You Are. Don't get "stuck in your reality at the expense of your possibility."

Remember that "subversive shifts begin with one small beginning."

Begin!

---

8. Jael was a heroine in the Old Testament.

# 2

# Joy!

Life Lesson: *"I have enjoyed my life, its disappointments outweighed by its pleasures. I have loved my country in a way that some people consider sentimental and out of style. I still do. And I remain an optimist with joy, without apology about this country and about the American experiment in democracy."*
—THE WORDS OF VICE PRESIDENT HUBERT HUMPHREY, ETCHED ON HIS TOMBSTONE IN LAKEWOOD CEMETERY, MINNEAPOLIS, MINNESOTA

### Let It Snow

The day I announced my candidacy for President of the United States it was not supposed to snow. It was supposed to be cold, of course—hence the pop-up warming tents and stoked-up fire pits and hot cocoa and first aid kits. A cardinal rule of politics: you don't want to lose any of your supporters to frostbite at the campaign kickoff. Yes, we like ice sculptures in Minnesota, but not when they are made out of real people.

Against all odds and every weather prediction for February 10, 2019, it snowed. And it snowed. And it snowed. It started light and powdery in the morning, and then it got heavier and heavier and it just never stopped. The national cable news networks covered the announcement of my candidacy as if it were a train wreck about to happen. Is she taking it indoors? Will the sound system work? How can she even read a speech? And why are all those people just standing out there in the snow when it is freaking 16 degrees, and actually 7 degrees when you count the windchill?

In the end, it was pure joy. People came on skis. They pulled their kids on sleds. They wore snowmobile suits and ginormous mittens and boots and big wool stocking hats topped off with pom-poms. They cheered and stomped their feet. My dad was in the front, sitting in a lawn chair, covered with big white flakes, waving an "Amy" sign.[9]

I got to deliver the speech in a virtual snow globe—gold coat, no gloves, snow-covered hair on the aptly named Boom Island in the middle of the Mississippi River. That was, after all, our theme: crossing the river of our divides to get to a higher ground.

I began my speech with a salute to the river and its symbolism in American politics. The Mississippi River starts, you see, in my home state. Like so many Minnesota kids, I had once experienced the thrill of jumping across the Mighty Mississippi at its source, up north at Lake Itasca. The river then gets wider and wider as it flows through Wisconsin, where my mom was born, the daughter of Swiss immigrants Martin and Margaret Heuberger. It meanders through the Midwest to Iowa (where I noted I planned to "winter" for the caucuses); Illinois

9. Our campaign paraphernalia throughout the race simply said "AMY," and the "Amys" of America went wild, nabbing the signs, bumper stickers, and earrings. Whether they later voted for me or not was unclear, but they sure liked the "AMY" merch.

(the home of both Abraham Lincoln and Barack Obama); St. Louis, Missouri (with its arches honoring America's first pioneers); and Kentucky and Memphis, Tennessee, where Dr. Martin Luther King joined sanitation workers fighting for their dignity and preached about the mountaintop and ultimately gave his life. The river then finishes its mighty journey down through Arkansas and Mississippi, ending in New Orleans, where the spirit of our country's resilience abounds.

The Mississippi River—like all our rivers—connects us, across geography, across demography. The rivers are our shared story. On that blizzardy day, I told my story: On both my mom's and my dad's sides, my relatives came to this country with nothing but a suitcase, and made a home. It was cold. They didn't know anyone. But, like so many immigrants, they wanted a better life for their families.

My Slovenian American grandpa worked fifteen hundred feet underground in the mines of northern Minnesota's Iron Range. He never graduated from high school, but he saved money in a coffee can in the basement and sent my dad to college. My dad got a two-year degree from Ely Junior College, now called Vermilion Community College, and then finished up in another two years with a journalism degree from the University of Minnesota. He served in the army during the Korean War. His assignments included, among other things, writing anti-communist Cold War–era propaganda for a unit stationed in Germany called "the 5th Loudspeaker and Leaflet Company."

Later, as a young Associated Press reporter, my dad called the 1960 presidential race for John F. Kennedy. He covered the 1968 conventions. As a reporter and later a columnist for the Minneapolis *Star Tribune,* he interviewed everyone from Mike

Ditka to Ronald Reagan to Ginger Rogers. He didn't just tolerate the freedom of the press, he embraced it. He lived it.

My mom, a proud union member, taught second grade in the Twin Cities suburbs until she was seventy years old. Her favorite unit was the one on monarch butterflies. For days she would teach her students the science of metamorphosis as they watched the caterpillar form its chrysalis. With the kids' wide-eyed excitement building every hour, it all culminated on the big "release day," when my mom would take the class outside and, surrounded by thirty adoring second graders, release the glorious monarch to the skies.

"Fly, butterfly, fly," she would say.

To this day—years after we lost her—her students, now with kids of their own, still come up to me on the street and tell me she was their favorite teacher. And there are always so many great stories. At my mom's visitation, one mother, in between sobs, standing with her arm around her disabled son, told me how much her son loved having my mom as his second-grade teacher and how the monarch butterfly unit was his best school memory. She recalled how every year, on the day she released the butterfly, my mom would dress up as a monarch—in black tights, orange wings, antennas, and a sign that read "To Mexico or Bust." Then she would go grocery shopping after school in the same outfit. I had known about the shopping-in-the-outfit story but until that moment, I hadn't known why my mom went to that particular store. It was because the woman's son got a job at the store bagging groceries after he graduated. For years my mom would go to that store in her monarch outfit, just to stand in his line and give him a big hug.

My parents believed in public service. Like so many Americans, they were true patriots. They had friends and neighbors with varying political views, and they saw democracy and a love of country as our common bond—the defining principle that brought everyone together, just like the rivers.

But that sense of community was, as I put it that snowy day, "fracturing across our nation," and "worn down by the petty and vicious nature of our politics."

So many Americans were tired of the Ted Cruz–inspired government shutdowns and the constant Donald Trump putdowns. They were sick of the gridlock and the grandstanding.

This great nation must be governed, I said, "not from chaos but from opportunity." Not by "wallowing over what's wrong, but by marching inexorably toward what's right."

I laid out my plans for the country that day, with a major emphasis on bringing down the costs people have to pay for basic goods and services like health care and pharmaceuticals. I laid out my priorities on workforce training (including an impassioned plea for immigration reform), tax reform, and an increased investment in infrastructure. Infrastructure was especially meaningful given that we were standing on Boom Island, only a mile from where Minnesota's I-35W bridge had collapsed into the Mississippi River twelve years before, killing thirteen people and injuring so many others.

Near the end of the speech I got to the crux of it:

"So today, on an island in the middle of the mighty Mississippi, in our nation's heartland, at a time when we must heal the heart of our democracy, retake our nation's spirit, and renew our commitment to the common good, I stand before you as the granddaughter of an iron ore miner, the daughter of a teacher and a newspaperman, the first woman elected to the United States Senate from the State of Minnesota, to announce my candidacy for President of the United States."

The words were certainly lofty, but the snow fell heavier and heavier. Every paragraph, every sentence was blanketed in white stuff. At some point I had to start wiping the soggy flakes off the plastic-covered speech halfway down each page because the snow was literally covering the words.

But I kept smiling and didn't miss a beat. Why? Well, out there in the joyous crowd was my family—my husband John and our daughter Abigail, my dad and my in-laws. Out there were thousands and thousands of supporters who had braved the cold, the wind, and the snow. That included Rabbi Marcia Zimmerman, who gave the opening prayer, the incredible band Sounds of Blackness, and Mayor Emily Larson of Duluth, Minnesota who called the blizzard "the perfect Duluth day."

And out there, somewhere, was my hairdresser, Bea, who has cut my hair and tamed my bangs for thirty-five years. Bea, in her ever-wisdom, was concerned about the obvious that day: the dangerous intersection of a blizzard and a hairdo.

That morning Bea had decided to come out ahead of time and "touch up the hair" in the warming tent. But it turns out Bea didn't stay in that tent. Weeks later she told me she had gone into the snow-encrusted crowd to cheer me on. And then, she said, she started to pray.

"Oh, that's so nice, Bea," I said. "You didn't need to do that—you didn't need to stand out there in the cold just to hear what I had to say. But this will be a tough race, and I need all the prayers I can get."

"No!" she said. "I wasn't worried about the speech! The

prayers weren't for the campaign. They were for the hair! You didn't notice with everything going on but right before you went out on the stage I saw some gray coming in on your part, and I sprayed some brown stuff I had in my bag across the top, and the whole time I watched your hair getting covered with more and more wet snow I thought, 'This is it—that brown stuff is going to melt down and trickle down her face on national television.'[10] I was praying, 'Please God, don't let that happen.'"

And it didn't.

The snow at the announcement and my willingness to stand out there in the crazy blizzard—with no thought of taking it indoors[11]—was an unexpected gift that turned into the symbol of the grit and courage of our scrappy campaign. I was ready to take on the world and people were willing to stand with me, even in a snowstorm. As I said that day: "I HAVE GRIT."

That's a joyful way to start a campaign.

## The Chances

The speech in the snow and our initial presidential campaign events captivated the cable-watching class. Jennifer Rubin of *The Washington Post* declared that it had "the best visu-

---

10. Note that this blizzard announcement was well before the Rudy Giuliani televised hair-dye-dripping-down-the-face post-election block-our-democracy meltdown in front of the Republican National Committee (RNC) headquarters. Please also note that Giuliani's hair dye dripped without the benefit of any snow. He needed a Bea. Okay, he needed a lot more than that.

11. Honestly, even if we wanted to take it indoors, we didn't have the funding for a backup plan.

als of any presidential announcement." Former U.S. Attorney Preet Bharara noted that "if I ever announce running for something, I too will do it from the inside of a gigantic snow globe. That was pretty great."

Even Donald Trump noticed, tweeting out the very day I announced:

> Amy Klobuchar announced that she is running for President, talking proudly of fighting global warming while standing in a virtual blizzard of snow, ice and freezing temperatures. Bad timing. By the end of her speech she looked like a Snowman(woman)!

Now, I could have responded with intense facts and a lecture about the climate crisis. Yes, you do still have snow while the climate is changing (as it clearly is), but given he dubbed me "snowwoman," I felt another response was in order, and I wrote the tweet myself in the Twin Cities airport right after my campaign announcement before a flight bound for New York City to appear on *Good Morning America*:

> Science is on my side, @realDonaldTrump. Looking forward to debating you about climate change (and many other issues).
>
> And I wonder how your hair would fare in a blizzard?[12]

12. I don't think enough candidates use humor to point out the absurdity or hypocrisy of their opponents' attacks. But then again, it is an acquired art and only works when appropriate. When I was first running for the U.S. Senate, a Republican state legislative leader claimed I wore Gucci shoes

Trump's comments aside, the substance of the announcement speech—as often happens—got minimally covered. But we did get positive news coverage of our subsequent rollout events in Eau Claire, Wisconsin; at several great stops in Iowa, including Mason City (with a second overflow crowd event at the Southbridge Mall when the first one at the Lorados bar and restaurant reached capacity); at a CNN televised town hall in New Hampshire; and at a high school gym full of people in Greenville, South Carolina. There were big exuberant crowds everywhere we went and a lot of questions about where I got the gold coat I'd worn in the snow, since honestly, except for South Carolina, everywhere we went it kept snowing.

Despite the memorable launch the pundits didn't give me much of a chance, based in part on my low national name recognition. As Chris Cillizza of CNN reminded his Twitter followers:

Most people didn't know Amy Klobuchar's name prior to this weekend. They still may not know the name, but they've seen the announcement in the snow. That's a win for her.

Fair.

*New York Times* columnist David Leonhardt wrote that while I wasn't a front-runner like Biden or Harris, I was part of

---

(which was hilarious from the get-go, because I always had inexpensive and arguably not very stylish shoes . . . Let's call them "sensible" instead). My response? I would overtly bring it up: at every campaign stop I would take off one of my sensible shoes, show the American brand, and pound it on the podium. It really worked.

a "strong next tier" with Warren and Booker and a few others. *Vanity Fair* noted (quite correctly, I would add) that our campaign would have an "uphill battle." I was ranked on "chances of winning" lists of candidates somewhere between seventh and eleventh.

Given the large number of people running for the Democratic nomination (by the first debate there would be more than twenty), and the presence of nationally known heavyweights like Joe Biden, Bernie Sanders, and Elizabeth Warren, I knew my chances seemed slim. But if I didn't think there was a chance, I wouldn't have done it. After all, the winner of the Kentucky Derby in 2022, Rich Strike, was given 81–1 odds, and I was doing a whole lot better than that.

I had actually discussed the "slim chances" factor with none other than Barack Obama a few weeks before my announcement. He separately met with a number of the candidates (of course remaining neutral, until he endorsed Joe Biden on April 14, 2020). We had an excellent talk. I remember how cool he looked in his leather jacket at his coffeemaker as he told me how he put his chances of winning at less than 50 percent when he launched his 2008 primary campaign against Hillary Clinton. He then paused and said with a smile, "Now some people around me put it at even less."

President Obama warned me that I had to be ready to steel myself against attacks and that things would go wrong every single day. Mistakes, he noted, would happen all the time. He gave me multiple examples of what had happened to him and how he dealt with it. He reminded me to be firm in my purpose but to have fun while I was doing it.

That discussion with Barack Obama was one of the best talks I had ever had with him—or with anyone, for that matter—about the pluses and minuses and risks and benefits of a political decision. It guided me throughout the campaign.

What President Obama was getting at was this: whenever you run for president or any other office or put your name in for any job or promotion, you must both acknowledge the possibility of failure and wrestle with the fears that go with it. This isn't just failure in the ultimate win-loss column, but, in the context of campaigns, embarrassing mini-failures, like not knowing something or screwing up and answering a question wrong. It also includes gut-punch failures like finding yourself shut out by people who you once thought were with you or just being flat-out rejected by an audience or an activist group or a major political player. And if it makes you feel any better, all of that DOES happen to anyone in a big race at one time or another.

Running for office also includes unrelenting attacks, especially if someone thinks you might win. I have been attacked for being liberal, conservative, fat, short, young, old, stern, frivolous, dumb, nerdy, ambitious, brassy, mousy, too tough, and yes, too nice. And that was just one day on Twitter.

My answer to all of this?

Whatever you are running for, you have to expect red-in-the-face moments and that bad stuff will happen and you could lose. Duh. But then you have to ask yourself, "Do I have something to say and a true purpose for doing this?" "Would I be good at the job?" "Would I be better than my opponent?" And, "If I don't win, do I have a plan B?"

When you think that way, any fear is surmountable, because you can always see the upside and you allow yourself to be guided by the joy in pursuing your goal. That's what gets you through the bad days. Remember that even for experienced leaders—both in and outside of politics—there is a bit of a gulp or an adrenaline rush or a "pinch myself because I can't believe I am walking out into . . ." you name it: a presidential campaign announcement; Stephen Colbert's show; a launch of a new product; the boardroom; a speech before your fellow workers; your first sales pitch; your first meeting with your boss; an event in John Legend's living room; a stadium filled with five thousand people; a nationally televised debate. Honestly, no matter the setting, you won't get anything done at all until you have taken that first step grounded in Franklin Roosevelt's timeless adage: "The only thing we have to fear is fear itself."

Yes, I would sometimes step back from all of it and wonder how I could have gone from that grade-schooler who started to cry after getting sent home by the much-feared principal Mrs. Quady simply because I had the audacity to wear flowered bell-bottom pants to school, to going head-to-head with the former vice president in a nationally televised presidential debate. Or, yes, when I stepped out on a big rally stage to multiple lights and cameras, I would close my eyes and remember my favorite teacher, Miss Kalionen. As I gulped my words for my fourth-grade science presentation, she would stand in the back of the class and say with much authority, "Talk louder, Amy, I can't hear you." "Talk louder, Amy, I can't hear you."[13]

Anyone who thinks it is no big deal to just waltz out for a presidential debate in which you know you are going to get

---

13. How fun was it years later when I got elected to my first office and I got a note from Miss Kalionen in that same vintage report-card scrawled handwriting in which she said: "You really learned how to talk louder."

hammered about something or other, or to go on a prime-time Fox town hall (which I did twice . . . and yes, they always offer eyelash extensions on Fox) without saying a few prayers or inhaling a deep breath or crossing your fingers ahead of time, is not telling you the truth.

There were lots of reasons NOT to run—the lack of name recognition, the many opponents, the inevitable attacks, the endless fundraising. Yet, for reasons that I still don't completely understand, I didn't seem to care about all the obstacles. First, I find campaigning joyful. Yes, there are bad days, but overall I love it. I am happiest when I am with people. Meeting with people all over the country was exhilarating.

Second, I felt in my heart I had a North Star purpose for running—to move our country forward with ideas, action, spirit, and yes, joy.

No matter the challenge, once I decided to stand in the snow and put myself out there, I never looked back. To paraphrase what Senate Majority Leader Mitch McConnell infamously said in 2017 and unfairly directed against Elizabeth Warren on the Senate floor, "Nevertheless, I persisted."

## Without Fear or Favor

The thing about announcement speeches is that you look back at them years later, and, with the benefit of hindsight, you can see if your purpose for running—your plans and message and theme—meet the test of time. In my case, I can look back at that snowy day through the rearview mirror of so many miles traveled—the 2020 election, Donald Trump's ever-exploding land mines, the pandemic, the insurrection, the continued Washington divisiveness, the soul-crunching Supreme Court reversals, the war in Ukraine, and the 2022 midterms—and feel that, measured against all of that, the themes of my speech still mean something.

As I noted that day in the snow, throughout my political career I have been willing to take on tough issues "without fear or favor." That means recognizing and acting on things that you know are important that a lot of people don't want to deal with because it may make them unpopular.

I believe the core purpose of politics should be, in the words of one of my mentors, the late great Minnesota Senator Paul Wellstone, "improving people's lives." Because if you can't do that, what good are you? And for all the talk about authenticity and gaining trust in politics today, in the end one of the major ways you get and hold your constituents' trust is to actually tackle tough problems—without fear and without favor—and get things done for them.

It matters to people when you are not afraid to pursue goals that they actually care about—even if you don't succeed the first time, or the second time, or even the third. Passing the gun safety legislation to close the boyfriend loophole? That took me nine years and I failed again and again and again before it finally got done.

When I got to Washington as a brand-new senator, I immediately started taking on the big special interests. Ethics reform in Congress was my first goal. A number of the new senators were part of that effort, including then-Senator Obama. We got it done. As a member of the Senate Commerce Committee, I then joined a bipartisan group to work on landmark consumer legislation for safer children's products. My provision to limit lead in toys passed as part of the legislation. From there I introduced the bill to get rid of the pharma-lobbied-for provision banning Medicare from negotiating less expensive drugs for seniors. Part of that FINALLY passed in 2022, but there is still a lot of work to be done. As I said in my presidential campaign TV ads, the big pharmaceutical companies may think they own Washington, "but they don't own me."

Doing my job without fear or favor has also meant, at times, being willing to take on the biggest companies in the world. The purpose is not to destroy them. The purpose is to make sure monopolies aren't taking over and limiting choice, destroying capitalism and taking a wrecking ball to competition through the sheer power they wield. As members of Congress, we have a duty to protect our constituents from monopoly-driven price gouging. We must preserve our economic system and individual entrepreneurship and innovation from what Adam Smith—the "godfather" of capitalism— once called "the unbridled power of the standing army of monopolies."

One way in which my work in the Senate has been . . . let's call it "unique" . . . compared to many of my colleagues has been my willingness to address technology issues. Yes, that means net neutrality and high-speed broadband available to every household and business in America (something we are close to attaining with the bill South Carolina House leader Representative Jim Clyburn and I led that was later incorporated into the Biden-signed bipartisan infrastructure bill). But it also means proclaiming the end of the "just trust us" era of Big Tech. Congress needs to promote and protect competition by putting digital rules of the road into law and guarding people's private data, as well as stopping disinformation online. As I noted in my presidential announcement speech, we must make our laws "as sophisticated as the people who are breaking them."

From the very beginning of my time in Washington, I decided to advocate for the causes of those who couldn't afford the big lobbyists or the big megaphones. I took on the NRA, which has repeatedly thwarted efforts for gun safety legislation. I took on the hard right on immigration reform, which meant getting attacked on the airwaves in my first Senate race, as well as many times since. I took on climate change deniers by introducing clean energy legislation. And—by leading major federal voting rights legislation—I directly confronted those who were trying to make it harder for people to vote.

In the presidential race, my "without fear or favor" campaign also meant facing some tough issues on which I had a unique perspective: chemical dependency treatment (my dad, while sober for the last decades of his life, had struggled with alcoholism through most of my childhood); criminal justice reform (having served eight years as a prosecutor); rural issues (representing a state that is first in the country for turkeys and sweet corn and having visited all of Minnesota's eighty-seven counties over and over again); antitrust (I had long led the subcommittee); health care (our daughter's birth did not go as planned and I was kicked out of the hospital after only twenty-four hours); and long-term care (having had both my parents in assisted living).

And for those who don't see the "joy" in all of this, believe me, there is joy in accomplishment. There is joy when you finally win, even if it's sometimes—like in the case of Medicare prescription drug negotiation—more than a decade later.

But there is also joy in the doing—the simple joy of knowing that while others may shirk from the challenge, you are actually willing to take on the fight (e.g., me and my two lawyers against Facebook, Amazon, Google, Apple, and their thousands of lawyers and lobbyists).

I will never forget the story of the late Minnesota Senator Paul Wellstone, who, after losing a Senate floor amendment battle, went back to his office in the Hart Building, grumbling and mad. When he walked inside, he saw that his staff all had their heads down, looking gloomy. They'd watched the whole thing. Paul, still mad, but self-aware enough to poke fun at himself and at the same time boost their spirits, stood as tall as he could in his five-foot-five frame and barked in his gravelly voice, wildly gesticulating while he spoke, "OK, WE LOST, BUT WHERE'S THE JOY IN THIS OFFICE? WHAT HAPPENED TO THE JOY?"

I love that story, not only because Paul was such a character, but also because it illustrates how it is never easy. The answer to Paul's question, of course, is that the joy is in doing the right thing. And sometimes when you do that, you even win.

## Don't Back Down

Now, I was never satisfied to simply TALK about taking on these fights, to simply identify, critique, and admire the challenges facing America. That's why the focus of my work in office—and the way I laid out my plans in the presidential race—has been about real results. In our ads and from the debate stage, I would repeatedly note that I had passed more than a hundred bills in Washington, D.C., and that in 2019 a Vanderbilt University study had rated me the most effective Democrat in the Senate. I believe in turning ideas (and things people clap for in speeches) into action. That means lists and road maps with both short-term and long-term goals. That means not backing down.

When you don't back down and you get results, you bring people with you.

I learned that results matter in politics way back in high school. The first office I ever ran for was actually in middle school—not a lot of memories of that one except a great photo of me and some guys with bad haircuts. But after that campaign I went for the big time. In my junior year I ran for—and won—the position of secretary-treasurer of my high school class. As a candidate for this admittedly inconsequential high school post, I nevertheless promised I would meet a significant and seemingly unreachable goal: a better prom. And I delivered. Big time. Along with my fellow council members, we found a way to buy Life Savers lollipops at discount from a local store, sell them at a significant markup at tables outside of the cafeteria, and finance a very nice prom at a fancy Minneapolis hotel.

Never mind that the next administration (meaning the class of juniors that followed us) failed miserably at their job of raising money for our senior prom. We ended up having it at the Ridgedale Center mall, under the after-hours but still glaring lights of the Woolworths and Orange Julius signs. And, yes, my date ended up dancing in the mall fountain with another girl because I refused to do it on the grounds that I didn't want to ruin my pink polyester prom dress and matching shawl. And yes, as the class cheered the sopping-wet couple on, the chief chaperone—the vice principal—asked me if I needed a ride home. But—as I still tell high school classes today—in the end it all turned out pretty well for me.

Later runs for office were a bit more serious. After college and law school and thirteen years of working as a lawyer in the private sector, I ran for Hennepin County attorney—the chief prosecutor and legal officer for Minnesota's largest county. I won a tough race in part because I put out new ideas for reforms, with a focus on goals and results. I was willing to take on the common orthodoxy about how the office should be run based in part on my experience in the private sector. I beefed up our white-collar-crime division, prosecuted a once-popular judge who we discovered had stolen money from the trust fund of a child with disabilities, worked directly with the Innocence Project on videotaped interrogations and DNA reviews, and set clear goals for the office.

During each of my eight years on the job as DA, I would put out public 100-day and year-end goals[14] and always publish follow-up progress reports to show where we were in meeting them. I still recall the immediate negative reaction from the chief district court judge when I announced the first 100-day goals: "You need to start viewing your time as county attorney as more of a marathon than a sprint," he said.

Knowing the gargantuan task before me of managing over four hundred employees in an office that handled more than ten thousand cases a year, I responded in kind. I told him

---

14. The goals included things like getting through a backlog of uncharged property crime cases; speeding up the handling of child protection, foster care, and adoption cases; prioritizing felon in possession of a gun crimes; and saving taxpayer money by reducing our reliance on outside counsel for lawsuits against the county hospital.

that to succeed and get results "you have to do *both* sprints and marathons!"

In fact, when I ran unopposed for re-election four years later, parade volunteers donned T-shirts that couldn't have been more direct. On the front: "Re-elect Amy Klobuchar." On the back: "Real results."

After eight memorable years as county attorney, I decided to throw my hat in the ring for the U.S. Senate in 2005, when then-Senator Mark Dayton announced he wasn't seeking re-election. I surprised national party leaders by defeating several worthy primary opponents and gaining their support along the way. That first Senate campaign featured parade units of volunteers with brooms sweeping the road along the parade route. The signs declared, "It's time to bring sweeping change to Washington." My crew danced down the street with their sweeping brooms to the Tom Petty song blaring over a boom box from the back of a pickup truck: "I Won't Back Down."

As my former mentor Walter Mondale would remind me as I practiced my thirty-second "elevator speech" with him for my initial run for the Senate, inspiration and results work best when they are tied together. For many people, it is inspiring to have an elected official who is willing to take on special interests on their behalf. They are 100 percent right about that. The imbalance of power and disparities in this country are irrational, unethical, and completely unacceptable. But just speaking truth to power is ultimately meaningless unless you can do something about it by bringing pharmaceutical costs down or making it easier for people to afford child care or housing or getting a tech company to be more responsible in its dealings with its customers. You also have to be willing to take on government bureaucracy when it fails. Helping a family stranded abroad trying to adopt a child or getting a veteran his or her rightful benefits? There's nothing more rewarding and inspirational than that.

The importance of not accepting defeat in order to push for results has truly defined my work in the Senate. There was the time as a freshman senator when I refused to leave my seat in the Senate chamber until I secured the funding to pay for the rebuilding of Minnesota's I-35W bridge. That bridge, which became a tragic symbol of our nation's then-decaying infrastructure, was only eight blocks from my house. On a beautiful summer day in 2007, the bridge suddenly collapsed, killing thirteen people and injuring so many more.

"A bridge just shouldn't fall down in America," I said the day of the disaster, "but when it does, we will rebuild it."

Six weeks after the bridge collapsed—on the morning of September 11, 2007—Senate Majority Whip Dick Durbin found me ensconced in my chair at my Senate desk, refusing to leave. "Somehow I think you're here to do more than pray," he said.

The Senate had started that day with the traditional morning prayer, with only one senator in attendance: me. I explained to Dick that during floor speeches the previous week the senators were getting themselves worked up in a lather about the tragedy of my bridge collapse, yet there was no money to fix the I-35W bridge in—get this—the bridge bill. I told Dick I wasn't leaving my chair until my amendment to include the funding for my bridge got done. With Dick's help—and after being shot down a few times that morning—my sit-in-my-chair-and-don't-leave protest prevailed, and we won.

My persistence paid off. With the help of the Bush administration and a major bipartisan effort, we got the full federal funding and rebuilt the bridge in less than thirteen months.

I also learned that results matter when I passed one of my first consumer protection bills. The legislation was designed to make swimming pools safer after a little Minnesota girl, Abbey Taylor, died a year after being severely maimed by a malfunctioning swimming pool drain. It turned out that a number of kids were dying in similarly tragic—and gory—accidents each year. Yet every time Congress came close to doing anything about it, the swimming pool/residential and commercial property lobby would stop the improvements in their tracks, even though the better drains cost less than $100.

Abbey's intestines were literally ripped out in a suburban kiddie wading pool by a malfunctioning drain, and, after visiting her in the hospital at the urging of my longtime friend and mentor former Republican Congressman Jim Ramstad, I vowed to her and her parents that I would get it done. With her big smile, little Abbey said to me, "I don't want this happening to any other kid." I remember thinking at the time in that hospital room that I had no idea how I would do it, but I promised I would.

Getting the swimming pool bill done turned into another protracted fight in the Senate, but in the end the family of former George H. W. Bush Chief of Staff James Baker was an enormous help. Virginia Graeme Baker—James Baker's granddaughter—had died in a similar accident. With my urging and theirs, Majority Leader Harry Reid and Minority Leader Trent Lott found a way to put the provision in an energy bill.

To date my proudest moment in the Senate is calling Abbey Taylor's dad, Scott, from the cloakroom and telling him that our bill had passed and that it was going to be signed into law by President Bush.

Time and time again I took on the odds and got bills passed, often with unlikely allies: Senator John Cornyn and I passed the pandemic-era Save Our Stages bill, which amounted to the biggest investment in the arts in the history of America and kept so many music venues and theaters alive; with help from former Republican Representatives Sean Duffy of Wisconsin and, yes, Michele Bachmann of my state, I passed a much-needed but controversial provision to allow what is now one of the most beautiful bridges in Minnesota to be built between Wisconsin and our state; Senator Thune and I passed a major bill to take on the foreign shipping conglomerates when they were fleecing American manufacturers, farmers, and consumers of their hard-earned profits; Senator Roy Blunt and I led the legislation to completely overhaul the sexual harassment rules of the Senate; Senator Collins and I passed a bill to take on the pharmaceutical industry on drug shortages; Senator Chuck Grassley and I passed multiple bills, including one to make sweetheart deals between doctors and various medical industries public and another to greatly increase funding to our antitrust enforcers.

To me, goals and results are not just a way of governing; they are also part of running for office and campaigning. Why run if you don't have a plan and the determination to get things done?

Like my other campaigns, the presidential race would also focus on the theme of results. Thanks to a crack policy team headed up by my deputy chief of staff and later campaign policy director Rosa Po, we came out with a detailed first 100-day plan for America, heralded by many of my opponents (at least to me privately) as first-rate. Our issue positions were well reasoned. And the immediacy of action—meeting the challenges I'd outlined without fear or favor—was a major campaign promise to remedy years of gridlock and temper tantrums. People needed results.

I believe that having a higher purpose, combined with reaching compromise and getting concrete results, is what really matters. I never wavered from that positive theme in the presidential campaign. When you have a purpose—and when you keep your eyes focused above on that North Star—you find common ground and you bring people with you. When you find common ground and bring people with you, you get results.

## Sisters in the Brotherhood

One of the most groundbreaking and inspiring aspects of the 2020 Democratic presidential primary was the number of women in the race. While Hillary Clinton's run for president broke many glass ceilings, the 2020 Democratic primary shattered even more. In fact, in two nights in June—on the combined consecutive-evening Democratic debate stages in Miami—we exceeded the number of women to ever appear on any presidential debate stage in the history of America.

This was the first presidential primary ever where America could see in blazing color that women leaders look different, dress different, come from different parts of the country and, YES, even have different views, and can even DEBATE each other about them!

At the June 26 NBC/MSNBC/Telemundo debate and the June 27 debate (the candidates were divided into two nights because there were so many of us), six women appeared on the stage: Kamala Harris, Elizabeth Warren, Kirsten Gillibrand, Tulsi Gabbard, Marianne Williamson, and me. Before that, in the entire history of U.S. major primary debates—on both the Republican and Democratic sides—only five women had ever appeared on stage: Hillary Clinton, Shirley Chisholm, Carly Fiorina, Michele Bachmann, and Carol Moseley Braun.

The number of women running in the 2020 Democratic primary was certainly groundbreaking, but it came with some headwinds. Okay, let me correct that. We had one big category 4, 150-mile-per-hour, close-down-the-hatches, hurricane-force headwind, and that was this: many people didn't think a woman could beat Donald Trump. It was an insidious challenge that hit all the women candidates, but particularly those of us left standing by the fall—Elizabeth, Kamala, and myself.[15]

Since the main goal of our party was to beat Donald Trump, the notion that a woman couldn't beat Donald Trump was definitely a problem. Polls actually showed that a number of our voters felt like the best candidate to take on Trump was a man. This was based in part—unfairly, of course—on Hillary's 2016 loss[16] to him, as well as the fact that Donald Trump, was, well, just so macho.

Sometimes people even said it aloud. "How can a woman beat a guy like that?" But since this wasn't a playground brawl,

---

15. Highly recommended book on this topic? *Electable: Why America Hasn't Put a Woman in the White House . . . Yet,* by Ali Vitali, NBC journalist who covered the 2020 presidential primary.

16. She actually won the popular vote, which in many countries would have meant something.

I always thought the answer could have been: "A woman is the perfect foil to that guy." But whether whispered or voiced aloud, the idea that a woman couldn't beat Trump clawed away at our support and hurt the women candidates, including Kamala, Elizabeth, Kirsten, and me. By the way—unlike most of the guys left standing by the fall—all four of us were undefeated, having never lost a race in our lives.

Time and time again the women candidates on that stage had shown they could meet a bar and clear it, and then meet another bar and jump over that too. Kirsten Gillibrand entered politics by winning a congressional seat in New York that no one thought a Democrat could win. She raised the bar again when she went into labor with her second son following a twelve-hour workday in the House. Eight months later she was appointed to the U.S. Senate to fill Hillary Clinton's seat, and within two years she successfully ran in a special election to complete the term. She took on sexual assault in the military, benefits for 9/11 first responders, and work/family leave with what can fairly be said was a vengeance (in a good way).

Elizabeth Warren had led a major government agency to take on financial sector regulation, and when the Republicans denied her their support to permanently lead the Consumer Financial Protection Bureau, she turned it around on them. She challenged one of their golden boy U.S. senators—Scott Brown—and beat him. Brown then later ran for the Senate in New Hampshire and lost to the formidable Jeanne Shaheen, leaving Brown—whom I worked with just fine—to become, in Jeanne's words, "the first man in the history of America to lose to two women in two different states."

And then there was Kamala Harris, the first woman

attorney general of the biggest state in the union, the first Black and Asian American senator out of California, and the daughter of immigrants. Needless to say, you don't get where she has gotten without being tough and knowing how to win and get things done.

But in the end—and the 2020 primary obviously didn't change this—we have never had a woman president. There's a reason I picked "The Bullpen"—written and sung by Minneapolis rapper Dessa—for my walk-on music at every campaign rally. Of course I love Dessa and her music, but the lyrics to this song—which she wrote to honor women rappers in a man's world—couldn't be more perfect for women in politics:

> *It's been assumed I'm soft or irrelevant*
> *'Cause I refuse to downplay my intelligence*
> *But in a room of thugs and rap veterans*
> *Why am I the only one*
> *Who's acting like a gentleman?*

So when I was asked during the campaign if women are held to a higher standard in politics than men, I answered, "Yes; otherwise we could play a game called 'Name Your Favorite Woman President,' which we can't do, because it has all been men."

A lot of women out there know exactly what I mean. We have to work harder than men to get ahead.

When the presidential primary campaign concluded, the women's campaign group EMILY's List told me that the three most common kinds of attacks used against Kamala, Elizabeth, and me were the ones that are particularly virulent against all women candidates for any office: dumb, ambitious, or too tough. They told me that those kind of hits tend to go absolutely viral (thanks Facebook algorithms) against all women candidates, and never mind that our male counterparts say all kinds of bad things and flub up and make mistakes. Ambitious? Dumb? Too tough? To me they are all aimed at one thing: you are not worthy to hold this office.

Running for office is hard for all candidates, but the ambitious/dumb/too tough three-cornered attacks seem to particularly affect whether women candidates decide to even run for any elected position in the first place. I have heard numerous stories of political party leaders trying to recruit qualified women to seek local political office only to be told: "I don't know enough about how politics works, so I won't do it"; "I don't want to get smeared and put my family in that position"; "I don't want to hurt my reputation."

My favorite story is of the woman who told a senior legislator who was recruiting for swing state legislative districts, "I can't run because trade issues are huge in my district and I don't know anything about them." A less-qualified man immediately responded when asked by the recruiter about this very issue: "I drive a Volvo with some American parts, so I can talk directly about the nuances of the trade issue, no problem."

In my early days of running for Senate, sexist "dumb" or "imply you are dumb" attacks were the norm. Looking back at it now, I realize that being called a "prom queen" (yes, a former opponent's campaign manager actually once said that, but sadly it wasn't true) and "Miss Congeniality" probably helped me more than hurt me, but they said it, and in a U.S. Senate race no less!

Condensing my whole image down to beauty queen titles[17] with a dash of "dumb" and "too nice" just never seemed to stick. I wonder why. I always thought it was really odd, given how intensely competitive I am and always have been.

In fact, right out of the gate in the presidential campaign, the main attacks lodged at me—and the subject of a *New York Times* story—were focused on me being too tough and demanding on my staff. I acknowledged in several interviews and town halls that I could in fact be tough and demanding. I made clear that I loved my staff but that I had made mistakes. I apologized. I also explained that I pushed and drove people in part because I had high expectations for getting things done, and that meant high expectations for them and myself.

Our staff on our presidential campaign was also amazingly consistent and cohesive and positive, and that was fairly obvious for all to see. That being said, criticisms always hurt, and while some of them were off base, I knew I was far from perfect. I knew I had said things in anger that I shouldn't have said and that hurt people's feelings. There were many people who made the case that some of the criticisms directed at me were sexist, and I certainly got asked that question by the media. Yet I never once conceded that they were based in

---

17. The closest I ever got to an actual royal title was when I was named "Ms. Skyway" of March 1988 by downtown Minneapolis's *Skyway News*. This honor was only bestowed twelve times a year and the only qualification was that a recipient work in a building connected to the city's famous second-story glassed-in building-connecting skyway system, once described by then–*Prairie Home Companion* host and author Garrison Keillor as a "human Habitrail." While my title did not come with a tiara, I did get a dinner for two at a fancy downtown restaurant, a free aerobics class, and twelve helium balloons.

sexism because that is a murky argument to make when some of the stuff was true, some false, and some in between. But it wasn't as if I didn't think about it.

Did I want to point out some of the scenes I had witnessed of male colleagues directly rebuking staff? Of course I did. But in the end that didn't excuse me for whatever mistakes I had made.

Now for anyone who watched the presidential primary town halls or debates, the women candidates tended to be the best prepared and—to my mind—all handled themselves in an impressive and professional manner. In fact, I would argue that one of the reasons we are sometimes considered "too tough" or just "cold" is because we are held to such high standards that we have to constantly worry that we will be labeled "dumb" for not knowing an answer. Hence, perfectionism runs higher among us than it may for a male candidate.

In the end you have to simply learn to deal with the attacks, the unfairness of much of it, the fact that you may be the very best candidate but you aren't the very best candidate for that moment in history, or that people just don't see you the way you see yourself. You admit your mistakes and flaws and apologize, you ignore the things that are completely untrue or exaggerated, and you move on.

So why is it worth it? Well, as of 2023, women hold just twelve of the nation's governorships (an all-time record) and only one-third of the seats in the House and one-fourth of the Senate. And as Liz Cheney noted in 2022, it's not like all these guys have done a particularly stellar job anyway.

As I once told talk show host and comedian Trevor Noah, in the history of the U.S. Senate, there have been nearly two thousand senators, and less than sixty have been women. His answer? If a nightclub had numbers that bad, they'd shut it down. Since that isn't really a possibility here, my answer? We need to get more women to run. For those who are still not convinced to do it (or to get someone else to do it), here are my top five ways to make a run for any office—from school board to state legislator to Congress to President—worth it:

1. **Have a North Star purpose and confidence that you can run and win regardless of the fear factors.**

   You have to believe in your heart that you are advancing a cause or a case and you can truly make a difference, win or lose. You also have to know that if you do win, you can do a really good job. Finally, you can never forget WHY you're running for office, because you have to make decisions all the time (as in what you say and do and how you treat your opponents) that could knock your actual purpose for running right out of the roller rink.

2. **When the expectations are low, think of it as a gift because you can surprise everyone. (Clue: it isn't that hard to do.)**

   If there's never been a woman mayor, or a woman police chief or a woman manager or a woman union leader, all the more reason to go for it. If people think you aren't going to be a great candidate or great in office, that's a low bar and you can more than meet it. You can jump right over it.

3. **Remember that overcoming the fear of failure and the ability to withstand attacks or setbacks is a plus in itself.**

Enough said on that. Just don't let it define you or your campaign.

4. **If you surround yourself with fun people, it is actually fun. Don't forget the JOY.**

To this day, when we have reunions with campaign staff or when someone gets married or has a child, there are such great campaign stories, so much joy, so many fond memories. Like the time staff members Mitch Perry and Hannah Hankins and I were supposed to have a simple car pick me up at the Las Vegas airport and the company sent a white bachelorette limo with flashing disco lights because it "was all they had left" (let's just say we had a few drinks in that car); or our Iowa post-dinner Prince cover band where we did dramatic renditions of "Purple Rain"; or the steak fry in the pouring rain; or the close run-ins with hibernating gophers (as in the University of Minnesota mascot) in research labs and angry beef cattle at the Minnesota State Fair; or the many times they "lost the candidate" (as in me) in parades and various festivals. "I was just getting a corn dog," I would say.

Joy in winning. Joy in doing. And, yes, sometimes, even joy in losing.

5. **Knowing you are making history is a cool thing.**

The fact that you are willing to even put yourself in the arena can make a difference. Perhaps no one who looks like you or has your background has ever sought the office before and then that makes everyone else realize that they can do it too. Think Shirley Chisholm in 1972. Or Margaret

Thatcher or Angela Merkel or Madeleine Albright or Hillary Clinton or Condoleezza Rice or Nikki Haley, or the head of state you may never have heard of—Jacinda Ardern, former prime minister of New Zealand, who became the world's youngest female head of government at thirty-seven and also made history as the world's second elected head of government to give birth while in office. Immediately after the Christchurch mosque shootings, she was the one who had the courage to ensure that strict gun laws be immediately put in place.

Don't focus only on national or international figures. Look for the local firsts for inspiration in your own town or state. Just in my own home state of Minnesota: in 2007 I was the first woman elected to the U.S. Senate in the history of our state, standing on the shoulders of two incredible women who had valiantly tried before me—former Minnesota Secretary of State Joan Growe and former Senate Majority Leader Ann Wynia. There's Minnesota's former State Senator Mee Moua, a previously little-known candidate who in 2002 became the first Hmong American woman in the U.S. to be elected to a state legislature. There's Betty McCollum, the dean of Minnesota's congressional delegation and the longest-serving female member of Congress in our state; Ilhan Omar, who came to Minnesota as a refugee and is the first Somali American to serve in the United States Congress; and Angie Craig, the first openly LGBTQ member of Congress from Minnesota. There's Minnesota's Lieutenant Governor Peggy Flanagan, only the second Native American woman to serve in statewide office in the country. And there's Andrea Jenkins, the current Minneapolis City Council president who is the first Black trans woman elected to public office.

I remember when these women got elected. I remember all of these historic moments—all of these firsts—but what most stands out is Mee Moua's State Senate victory on election night in 2002. Mee's dad was a U.S.-trained medic in Laos, and the family fled to a refugee camp in Thailand when the communists took over. Mee was nine when her family was allowed to come to the U.S. She went on to go to college and get a law degree.

Mee hadn't been expected to win a special election in her first run for office—all the odds were stacked against her. But she did it. I was there to witness the moment. There she stood on the stage on her joyous election night and just couldn't stop crying. She later explained that she couldn't speak that night because there was "a ball of tears" in her throat.

Mee said her grandmother—who had fled Laos with the family—once said, "Take all the time you need. Those tears represent the thousands of voices who've never been heard. Take your time, then speak loud and clear for all those voices."

That's what I mean about making history. That's what I mean about speaking loudly and remembering that the only thing to fear is fear itself. Letting your voice be heard—that's joy all on its own. From the time my fourth-grade teacher Elsie Kalionen stood at the back of our classroom and declared as I made my science presentation, "I can't hear you, Amy. Speak up. Speak up," to the first walk down the aisle of the U.S. Senate chamber, to the rigors of a presidential campaign, I have learned the lesson loud and clear: don't let fear stop you.

## Frenemies

In the crowded field that was the Hunger Games of the Democratic 2020 primary, I spent an amazing year crisscrossing the country, taking part in multiple nationally televised debates and sparring with my opponents, many of them ending up as my friends.

Our campaign was at its core a scrappy, happy crew of staff and volunteers. And we were clear-eyed about it all. None of the pundits expected us to last through the spring or the summer of 2019, much less to March of 2020. In the end we were never actually voted off the island until we chose to do it ourselves on our own terms, right before Super Tuesday.

But a lot happened along the way. Of course, there were the debates and parades and forums and multiple town hall meetings (Bernie, Pete, and I all did two on Fox). CNN made a ritual out of individual candidate town halls, often the night before the debates. I was asked about everything from opioids to tax policy to ethanol to trade agreements.

It might not have shown up all the time on stage, but throughout the primary there were moments of unexpected kindness and understanding between candidates. Like the time John Delaney and Andrew Yang were willing to trade their NAACP Iowa times with me on Martin Luther King Day because I decided to do both South Carolina and Iowa in one day. Or Kamala inviting me and my family to get together with her, her husband, Doug, and her extended family the night before Thanksgiving in a hotel lobby restaurant in Iowa. I remember that that night she went to bed a little early. I remember her sitting with her grandniece on her lap.

But what I didn't know then was that she was in the process of making her own decision to get out of the presidential race—something she would do just a few days later. That made her invitation to hang out the night before the holiday all the more impressive.

I remember candidates giving each other tips on how to deal with bad microphones and buzzing sound systems and surly crowd members. Or candidates acknowledging another candidate's good performance or even giving them a tip on how to make it better. Joe Biden boosted my spirits after numerous town halls with kind words about an answer I had given or a point I had made. He did it during debate breaks. He even did it on stage. In fact, Joe Biden repeatedly reached out with words of kindness. That's a quality in politics that is vastly underestimated.

Then there was the time at the Los Angeles PBS/Politico debate at Loyola Marymount University when I quickly realized that the pen they had given me to write things down at the podium ahead of the debate didn't work. In fact, it exploded ink on my paper, putting me at an obvious competitive disadvantage vis-à-vis my opponents, who were all madly scribbling down their talking points. In the arc of political debates, this pre-debate podium time period is always critical as candidates are allowed to crazily write down their thoughts in the three to five minutes before the debate goes live so they don't miss a key point or a stat or a joke. It was a stark disadvantage to have no working pen, and the debate rules forbade you from bringing out your own. And going backstage for a pen would have lost me precious minutes.

The solution? First, Bernie, who was standing to my

right (okay, that alone is funny), noticed and handed me his officially supplied pen and used his own instead (that's when I learned that most of the men were surreptitiously tucking a spare pen in their suit jacket inner pockets just in case the debate-supplied pens didn't work). Then when the pen Bernie gave me ALSO didn't work, Tom Steyer, on the podium to the left of me, took out his stashed pen and gave me my third official pen, and yes, the third time was a charm.

Now, years later, I would like to thank those two guys for sneaking in the pens, as it was one of my best debates.

Overall, Bernie and I had many good-natured and amusing exchanges. We get along, and are always on the lookout for common ground despite our differences. We had long worked together to take on outrageous health-care costs and had valiantly teamed up for years to get rid of the pharma-backed provision banning Medicare from negotiating on behalf of fifty million seniors for less expensive prescription drugs. In fact, two years before the presidential race, we joined forces to debate Republican Senators Lindsey Graham and Bill Cassidy on an hour-long CNN televised town hall on the Affordable Care Act, hosted by the intrepid Jake Tapper and Dana Bash.

My most amusing moment during the presidential campaign with Bernie was of little historical note but hilarious all the same. It happened during the New Hampshire debate—a key one for both of us. I consistently made the point that I came with "receipts" to both govern and win.

EXHIBIT A: I was the only one on the stage at that point who had won in extremely red congressional districts.
EXHIBIT B: Every time I led our state ticket the statehouse had flipped in our favor.

EXHIBIT C: I noted that the capacity to win and govern was one of the reasons I had gotten the endorsement of *The New York Times*[18] and three of the major papers in New Hampshire—the *Union Leader*, the Seacoast papers, and *The Keene Sentinel*.

On the last point, Bernie replied with a wry smile and in his always forceful voice, "I must confess, I don't get too many newspapers' editorial support. Must confess that."

I immediately tracked in my mind which newspapers' endorsements he had obtained and remembered the paper in Conway, New Hampshire. I had interviewed with their editorial board, as had a number of other candidates, and they had asked me great questions, including one on UFO research.

I responded: "Well, you got the Conway endorsement."

I imagine Bernie was really thinking at that moment, "OMG, enough," but instead he said, "I did. We're very proud of that."

And I ended it with a smile: "Well there we go."

Another debate factor that weirdly brought the candidates together was the temperature. That's because many of the debate stages were notoriously cold, as debate planners tried to overcompensate for the crowd and the TV lights with way too much air-conditioning.

But of all the cold stages, nothing compared to the debate stage in Atlanta. That one was extreme. Think long-underwear cold. Think the kind of place where you can't remember what you are saying because all you can think

18. Actually, it was a co-endorsement I shared with Elizabeth Warren. The newspaper made history that year by endorsing two women simultaneously.

about is that your feet are freezing. Rachel Maddow, one of the Atlanta debate moderators, later told me that that Atlanta stage was one of the most brutally cold places she'd ever encountered on TV, describing it as "cold as a meat locker." Pete told me his husband, Chasten, who was out in the crowd, wished he'd brought extra socks.

We later learned that the converted Atlanta studio (which was, by the way, otherwise beautiful[19] and made for a great debate) included cold air vents that were . . . well, gusty, later leading to a hilarious quivering-bangs depiction of me by Rachel Dratch on *SNL*.[20] But by the time we figured out the source of the cold air we didn't have the luxury of studying the air trajectory of the vents and registering a complaint with the debate commission (if there ever was one). Instead we had exactly four minutes during the first debate break to do something about it.

Kamala and I cared the most, and huddled together backstage during the entire coveted four-minute debate break. We explained to the harried stage manager that, yes, women perform worse than men when it's cold so this just isn't fair. We have the studies to prove it, we told him. Look at the female

---

19. Thanks to the extraordinary Atlanta businessman and movie producer Tyler Perry, who owns the complex and was a wonderful host.

20. Note to mean internet trolls and *SNL* producers: the quivering bangs were not caused by a neurological disorder. No, the shaking bangs were caused by the cold air vent directly over my head. The clue to solving this crime: when Kamala and I approached the stage manager during the debate break, he kept saying to me, "I realize I have to turn off that vent right above your head because people are complaining about what is happening, and I will." I didn't know what he was talking about until I saw the memes. That vent. Those bangs!

vs. male math scores[21] in warm vs. cold rooms, we said. Find a way to turn off the cold air!

We may not have won the primary, but we sure won that debate with the stage manager.

There were many other amusing moments throughout the debates. Never noted or detected? I once wrote funny notes back and forth to Cory Booker live on the debate stage in Houston when the moderators weren't calling on us very much. I mean what else were we going to do? I will never reveal what the notes said, except for one. It came at a debate juncture when Andrew Yang—to illustrate his universal basic income proposal—offered to give a "freedom dividend" of $1,000 a month from his campaign funds to ten random families who won a campaign lottery: "BOOKER," I wrote, "DO NOT DO THAT WITH CAMPAIGN FUNDS. I think it may be illegal. You can't buy votes."

Julián Castro once nearly tripped over the forlorn extra pair of shoes I kept offstage (just in case the pair I was wearing grew too painful). Sorry, Julián. Elizabeth Warren and I shared a number of mid-debate discussions in the women's bathroom (and of course we NEVER talked about our male opponents). And during one lengthy back-and-forth on prison reform between Joe Biden and Tom Steyer in South Carolina, Tom—with his overly exuberant hand gestures—nearly belted me off my two-inch-high debate perch (a wooden box

---

21. As reported in a May 22, 2019 *New York Times* article entitled "Battle of the Thermostat," a 2019 study found that at colder temperatures men scored higher than women on verbal and math tests. But as a room grew warmer, women's scores rose significantly . . . in fact, by 27 percent on math tests if the temperature rose from 70 to 80.

necessitated by the fact that Mayor Pete and I were the only people of average height left standing[22] and Elizabeth[23] and I were the only women). I remember thinking as I later looked at a hilarious photo of me holding on to the podium for dear life as Biden and Steyer went after each other on either side: if Steyer had accidentally pushed me off that box, at least he has deep pockets![24]

Finally, my debate matches with Mayor Pete were, well, memorable. They were often focused on how much experience should matter in a presidential candidate, and post-debate our supporters would sometimes carry on against each other on Twitter for days.

But in the end debates are just debates. And no one ever knew all the equally positive moments Pete and I have shared. I have been to his and Chasten's place, I have had dinner with him several times, and yes, I even invited him to Minnesota in 2022 to speak at our big state Democratic event—the annual Humphrey-Mondale Dinner. I am still amused when people are surprised to learn that Mayor Pete (now Secretary Pete) and I are truly friends, despite the fact that our supposed rivalry continues. Okay, maybe it still sometimes does. Here's one: shortly after Pete published his post-primary election book—entitled *Trust*—I came out with my own book. It is entitled *Antitrust*. True story.

All that said, our campaign—led by Justin Buoen, my campaign confidant and excellent manager going way back to the first Senate race (where he started right out of college

---

22. Pete never used a debate box.

23. Elizabeth is five-foot-eight and never used a debate box.

24. Tom Steyer's estimated net worth is $1.4 billion.

carrying signs on the parade routes)—was on so many levels joyful. What you never see on stage? The prep sessions with the pizza, and yes, sometimes beer; the young people so excited to nab a seat for the debate; the pre-debate rallies and the post-debate parties; and the next morning after a good debate when your daughter tells you she was proud of you.

## On the Trail

While the debates were the most public-facing part of the campaign, they were actually in sum total only a couple hours every few weeks. There was a lot going on in the meantime.

The first four states in the 2020 Democratic primaries/caucuses—Iowa, New Hampshire, Nevada, and South Carolina—would be a key measure of any presidential candidate's success, even though I also longed to run in some of the states in what would be the next "Super Tuesday" round and beyond: Colorado, Wisconsin, Michigan, and Minnesota—to name a few!

First up was Iowa.

With Abigail and John at my side, I made it my goal to visit all of Iowa's ninety-nine counties, something similar to what I have done in Minnesota for years. At one point—with a crunched schedule set in anticipation of the first Senate impeachment hearing—we flew straight from the Los Angeles debate to visit some of the last twenty-seven of the ninety-nine Iowa counties in just three and a half days, including a visit to "Albert the Bull" in Audubon; a 10 P.M. tour with bleary-eyed delegates at a planetarium in Cherokee; a county wax museum; and a Casey's "breakfast pizza" stop with local northwest Iowa residents on our big green "Amy" bus, all just two days before Christmas.

Outside of the incredible number of sights I saw and food I ate and miles I traveled, many people touched me on those journeys. There was the Vietnam vet who was so horrified by what Donald Trump had said about John McCain that when I even brought up McCain's name at a town hall he started sobbing. When I approached him later, he told me he loved McCain, he hated Trump, and he had just lost his son to suicide.

There was the grandma and retired U.S. foreign service officer Janice Weiner, who later got elected to the Iowa City Council, standing in the back of one rural town hall, her granddaughter in a front baby pack. She raised her hand and told the group how her daughter had struggled with drugs, leaving her to care for the child. Everyone at that event wanted to help her.

There was the stoic Fran Parr near the Iowa/Nebraska border, whose entire house was flooded when a levee broke. She stood unflappable in the freezing sleet pointing out across the highway to a field in which only her roof jutted up above the massive flood. "I am just going to miss my kitchen the most," Fran said. "I just loved the way the light came into the kitchen window at breakfast."

And then there were all the young people who put their hearts and souls into our campaign. I still have the cherished photo of our hardworking volunteers and campaign staff, led by the inimitable Lauren Dillon, all gathered with our family for one memorable Thanksgiving dinner at the big and welcoming Des Moines house of our campaign chairwoman, Andy McGuire.

Despite all the travels and fun, during the very last month

leading up to the Iowa caucuses there was one glaring challenge for three of the six of us who had qualified for the Iowa debate—Elizabeth, Bernie, and I, along with my friend Senator Michael Bennet, who was also running. The four of us had a constitutional duty to sit as jurors in the U.S. Senate for the impeachment trial of one Donald Trump. As someone who loves grassroots campaigning and retail politics, the thought that I was chained to my desk for two weeks leading right up to the big day was a political strain. Yet, for me, there was no question of where I should be. Holding court over Donald Trump's first, and later over his second, impeachment trials was my constitutional duty: as history has since made quite clear, the case against Trump had to be brought.

Donald Trump had put our democracy, our Constitution, and our country's standing abroad in peril. And our duty to do something about it was growing clearer every day. But my political reality was this: as Joe Biden and Mayor Pete and others traversed the state of Iowa, Bernie, Elizabeth, Michael, and I were in the Senate chamber taking notes on legal pads, sitting demurely in our matching brown leather chairs day after day after day after day.

The impeachment trial went from January 22 to the final vote on February 5, with little break in between. In the end, Trump wasn't convicted, with only one Republican—Mitt Romney—voting with Democrats to convict. You needed two-thirds of the Senate, or sixty-seven votes, to convict and there were only forty-eight, with fifty-two voting "Not guilty." But as the months went by and the nation saw Trump's continued assault on our democracy both leading up to and after the U.S. Capitol insurrection, there was only one indisputable conclusion: Senate Democrats (and Mitt Romney) were more than on "the right side of history" in voting to impeach and convict.

Our daughter Abigail was a star during this time—yes, I'm biased. But actually, she's been a star throughout her whole life. During the impeachment trial she and John each went solo with our staff and filled in for me at numerous events. At age twenty-four, she spoke for me as well as anyone could have. A winner of her college's standup comedy contest, she hosted her own series of campaign events: Minnesota-style "hotdish[25] house parties" throughout Iowa and New Hampshire and many other states.

It isn't easy being a politician's kid. And especially when her own story of being born with a swallowing problem was a central part of my getting involved in politics in the first place.

When Abigail was born, she couldn't swallow. She was in intensive care, and I got kicked out of the hospital only twenty-four hours after she was born, since the insurance rules back then were that you could stay in the hospital only that long. Months later I went to the state legislature as a mom—not as an elected official—and testified in favor of changing the limit. Minnesota became one of the first states in the country that guaranteed new moms and their babies a minimum forty-eight-hour hospital stay.

Growing up, Abigail had a lot of health issues related to

---

25. Hotdish is a meal of choice in my state. Its ingredients invariably include tater tots and some kind of canned soup. To much fanfare, former Minnesota Senator Al Franken inaugurated a bipartisan Minnesota-delegation annual hotdish contest when he came to the Senate. The first year I won, and I've included the not-so-secret recipe at the end of this chapter. We always served this hotdish at the presidential hotdish parties and guests would also bring their own!

the swallowing problem—including depending on a stomach tube for nutrition during her first two years—and allergies, but she was always so strong that no one would know it today. She graduated from Yale *magna cum laude*, won an award for her senior political science essay, worked as the legislative director for a Manhattan city council member, and now attends law school.

In the end, despite my hard work, my family's devotion, our excellent staff, and key supporters (including so many Iowa elected officials), when the caucus results were finally tallied, Pete—who had run a stellar campaign—eked out a historic victory in Iowa, followed closely by Bernie.

But win or lose, I made a lot of good friends in Iowa whom I will cherish forever.

And all was not lost. Heading into Iowa I had enjoyed a series of good debates in Ohio and Atlanta and Los Angeles and gotten a lot of buzz. Though that had not translated into the caucus votes I needed to win Iowa, I was still standing and in the mix. Unleashed from my Senate impeachment desk, I could now head to New Hampshire. While in Iowa I had had only a few days to make my final case, in the Granite State I would have an entire week. And, more important, I would finally be able to campaign on an equal playing field, at the same pace as my opponents.

We had by far, in my view, the best arrival of any campaign in New Hampshire that year. We took off from Des Moines the very evening of the caucuses and arrived with press in tow at the Manchester airport. It was 3 A.M., and dozens of cold volunteers were awaiting us with signs, cheering like we'd actually won Iowa. I gave a speech AND press interviews.

The minute we landed, I knew something was up in New Hampshire. Now, it didn't just happen overnight. While I had spent significantly less money on staff and ads in the state than my rivals, we were seeing larger and larger crowds, going from dozens in backyards and living rooms to high school gyms with hundreds and hundreds of people. I gave substantive speeches on foreign policy and addiction and Medicare and senior policy. I was indefatigable, regardless of the weather. In one raging nor'easter featuring pummeling rains and straight-line knock-you-off-your-feet winds, I completed visits to all ten of New Hampshire's counties in thirty-one hours. I once drove with staff in a near-whiteout blizzard from an event in Connecticut to Manchester, arriving at 1:20 A.M. so I could make it to a discussion on the Constitution at UNH Law School in Concord the next morning and a town hall in Portsmouth later in the day.

We had already held town halls across the state from Dover to Wolfeboro to North Conway, Gotham to Littleton, Claremont to Keene. The Keene town hall was actually on New Year's Eve in a snowstorm, since during the impeachment proceedings we'd gotten used to always wedging things in at crazy times. We still drew hundreds of people.

At the New Hampshire Institute of Politics, I hobnobbed at "Politics and Eggs," a timeless New Hampshire tradition where candidates address the crowd but also sign wooden eggs that are ultimately given to the audience members. That was the event where I accidentally introduced my New Hampshire campaign manager Scott Merrick's girlfriend, Mikayla Foster (daughter of former New Hampshire Attorney General and supporter Joe Foster), as his fiancée (okay, they weren't yet engaged, so wishful thinking). Fortunately, they got engaged shortly thereafter, and John and I attended the wedding in the fall of 2021.

I always love a parade, and we had covered a lot of ground in the Granite State leading up to the primary. New Hampshire's Amherst, Merrimack, and Franconia Day Fourth of July parades had not disappointed. We had even spent a precious four days off on a rainy family spring break in the state. Highlights included touring the Mount Washington Hotel, where the Bretton Woods conference was held; visiting Chutters in Littleton, which contains the world's longest candy counter; dinner with the esteemed filmmaker Ken Burns at his Restaurant at Burdick's; attending Easter church service in Walpole; and hiking up Pack Monadnock on some really slippery rocks, where we were greeted at the top by a group of senior citizens who looked much less exhausted and more fit than we did. They shared with me some typical New Hampshire common sense as our family scrambled over the last rock: "Why would you take the trail when there is still snow on the rocks? Try the road next time."

But in the end, with the primary approaching, our many travels were helpful. I knew the state. I knew the issues. And, most important, I could flawlessly pronounce all of New Hampshire's idiosyncratic towns and places—from BER-lin to Lake Winn-eh-paw-SAU-kee to, yes, Pack Mah-NAD-knock.

New Hampshire primary voters historically thrive on debates, and the February 7, 2020 Democratic debate in the Sullivan Arena at Saint Anselm College in Manchester did not disappoint. I personally loved it. Maybe it was the location—it was held on top of an ice rink, giving me a kind of home-field advantage. It was not for the fainthearted, but of course, it was just fine for a Minnesotan. Maybe it was because my two friends who had stayed neutral in the race but whom I respect so much (Senators Jeanne Shaheen and Maggie Hassan) were sitting in the front row. Or maybe it was simply because I was energized by the fact that I finally had an open shot to campaign like everyone else.

It is fair to say it was a defining debate for me. I was one of the few candidates who raised my hand when asked by ABC's George Stephanopoulos if anyone was concerned about having a socialist head up the ticket. I was direct in my support for a public option plan for the Affordable Care Act, asking why, when the Affordable Care Act was nearly 10 points more popular than the President of the United States, were we talking about "blowing it up"?

But most of my wrath was focused on Donald Trump. I noted that after signing the Republican tax bill, the president had literally gone down to Mar-a-Lago and looked at all his friends and said, "You just got a lot richer." I also went after Trump on his position on abortion, arguing strenuously (and now presciently, in light of the U.S. Supreme Court's appalling 2022 decision in *Dobbs v. Jackson Women's Health Organization*) that *Roe v. Wade* should be codified into law.

I talked climate change. I was one of the first to state my support for the USMCA trade agreement between the U.S., Mexico, and Canada. I made a point of opposing isolationism and gave a full-hearted endorsement of the importance of NATO and working with our allies.

The last few days in New Hampshire were a whirlwind of activity, with my campaign zipping from one location to another. We had long lines at every event, and people were energized. The debate performance had landed and the money was pouring in. We used much of it for ads, and we literally cut an ad the day after the debate, which featured only the debate closing. We kept going up in the daily polls, and started to surpass Elizabeth and the vice president. I won't lie: It was a lot of fun to finally have all the pundit doubters come to our events and see the big crowds and the rally speeches. In the end I came in a close third, not far behind Bernie and Pete, both of whom had been expected to do well with their post-Iowa momentum. I was the sleeper candidate of the evening.

As I noted from the stage that night, surrounded by enthusiastic staff and workers, "I cannot wait to bring our green bus around the country. I cannot wait to build a movement of fired-up Democrats, independents, and moderate Republicans."

And then I reminded them once again: "Tonight is about grit."

And no one could dispute that.

With a solid third place in New Hampshire—which the pundits would have guessed was impossible way back when we started in the snow—our campaign could finally claim some momentum of our own. But there was one major problem: we did not have the necessary time left or the resources in the bank to truly capitalize on the momentum when the February 22 Nevada caucuses were only eleven days away, the February 29 South Carolina primary seven days after that, and then the mother of all primaries only three days later. Yes, March 3 was Super Tuesday, the fourteen-state blockbuster primary day featuring Alabama, Arkansas, California, Colorado, Maine, Massachusetts, Minnesota, North Carolina, Oklahoma, Tennessee, Texas, Utah, Vermont, and Virginia.

The money kept pouring in. But with only those few weeks left and minimal staff in each state (although we did quickly hire into the Super Tuesday states, having already had some staff on the ground in South Carolina and Nevada), we had no choice but to put most of our newfound cash into ads. Yet on the airwaves we were competing—at least in Nevada—with billionaire and environmental advocate Tom Steyer, who, among others, was running tons of ads. Former New York City mayor and businessman Michael Bloomberg—the other billionaire in the race—was already blanketing the airwaves in the fourteen Super Tuesday states.

We would have really liked to use our money to put even more staff on the ground. But there simply wasn't the time to build the necessary infrastructure—staff, multiple offices, etc.—in the short period we had available to us. It was the classic chicken-or-the-egg problem in presidential primary campaign politics. It was like trying to build a plane during takeoff.

I loved Nevada. I lead the tourism caucus in the Senate. I am good friends with the two senators from the state—Catherine Cortez Masto and Jacky Rosen—both of whom had remained neutral in the race. I had helped out there many times, even before running for president, including keynoting their state convention at the invitation of former Senate Majority Leader Harry Reid.

It soon became clear that our New Hampshire momentum just wasn't enough, especially in a caucus situation with so many candidates. Yet when Bernie won Nevada hands down, I wasn't about to fold up our tent. I knew so many of those Super Tuesday states could be good for me. I also knew that the next state—South Carolina—would be Biden's.

I had truly enjoyed the visits we made to South Carolina,

which included Jim Clyburn's "World Famous Fish Fry" in 2019 in Columbia (an event I had keynoted in 2008 when Obama was running), with all the candidates steaming hot in matching Clyburn T-shirts; the 143-year-old Galivants Ferry Stump—the oldest and largest political "stump speaking" event in the country, held in front of a general store on the banks of the Pee Dee River in northeastern South Carolina; the overflow group we had in Democratic stalwarts Don and Carol Fowler's house; the Martin Luther King march where Elizabeth and I wore mittens and huddled in the cold.

The South Carolina debate went well, but it wasn't the game changer I needed. The very powerful majority whip Jim Clyburn, a longtime friend of Joe Biden, the dean of South Carolina politics, and the highest ranking African American in Congress, endorsed the vice president at the perfect moment for maximizing the impact of his support (just days before the primary). Biden won.

We next headed for an intense schedule of Super Tuesday states.

## Begin with Joy; End with Joy

We were getting bigger and bigger crowds in Super Tuesday states like North Carolina, North Dakota, Virginia, Oklahoma, Arkansas, and, yes, Maine. While I was far from dominating or even winning most of these states, I was going to win in Minnesota, and clearly do better in many of these states than I had in Nevada and South Carolina. There was an argument that once the field cleared even more (in addition to there being more debate opportunities), and with the upcoming primaries in Wisconsin and Michigan, we could gain more New Hampshire–type momentum, and stay in for the long haul to a brokered convention. How many times did I point out that Bill Clinton had never come in first in his 1992 race until Georgia—the same day he failed to place first in Idaho, Maryland, Minnesota, Utah, and Washington, and after losing big-time in Iowa and coming in second in New Hampshire, third in Maine, and third in South Dakota? While it was really a long shot, a lot of things were still up in the air. We also had such loyal supporters and a devoted staff.

It was a heady time, but it was also a time when as a candidate you have to step back and ask yourself, "What is my purpose here?" In the end I knew the purpose was pretty straightforward: it was to put someone in as our candidate who could beat Donald Trump, bring decency back to the White House, and get stuff done for the people of America.

My purpose was *not* to hold on to the very last gasp and hope I had the numbers at a brokered convention. It was not to show the world I could continue to do better than anyone had thought I could.

Every time I did the math, it seemed harder and harder. I had to make a decision. Should I take the long odds and try to catch on and seek to beat Joe Biden in a few remaining smaller candidate debates where I could really shine so I could MAYBE catch on in numbers in a massively brokered convention? Or should I put the ambitions aside, embrace what was most likely the inevitable, and use my power at that very moment for good? I had maximum power at that moment, because at the very least I could help Joe Biden—whom I really liked personally and thought could beat Trump—

win Minnesota, where he was badly trailing behind me (first) and Bernie (second). I also knew that most of my support would go to Biden in other states, with a smattering to Elizabeth (there were, of course, still people out there who really wanted a woman to lead the ticket) and Pete.

A visit to Selma on March 1 only two days before Super Tuesday crystallized all of it for me. Alabama was one of the Super Tuesday states, but with so many delegates in other states at stake, it turned into a day trip for most of the candidates. Everyone was there. Like many of the others, I had been to Selma for the "Faith and Politics" trip two other times to commemorate the historic 1965 civil rights march of John Lewis and the Freedom Riders across the Edmund Pettus Bridge.

The march came to be known as "Bloody Sunday," because state troopers and police attacked the marchers, including then-twenty-five-year-old Lewis, whose skull was fractured, the scar forever visible. Lewis was a true hero. In fact, during the weekend of one of my earlier visits in 2013—more than fifty years after the 1961 Montgomery march and forty-eight years since the march in Selma—the white police chief of Montgomery, Alabama, actually gave Congressman Lewis his police badge and publicly apologized to him for his predecessors' not protecting the marchers.

Fifty years was a long time to wait for that apology, but it happened.

This visit was much more somber. John Lewis was very sick, having been diagnosed with Stage 4 pancreatic cancer a few months before. This would be one of his last public appearances; only four months later we would lose him.

There was a Sunday service first thing in the morning

at Brown Chapel AME Church where Joe Biden and Stacey Abrams and the Reverend Al Sharpton spoke. After the
church service we all headed to the bridge and marched to
"We Shall Overcome" and "This Little Light of Mine." There
were reporters and cameras everywhere, and many people
were pressing to get in the front of the march. Somewhere in
the middle of the bridge the crowd stopped, seemingly para-
lyzed by the sheer number of people. Then suddenly the line
parted as everyone craned their necks to see who was coming up over the other side of the bridge toward us . . . yes, it
was . . . Congressman Lewis, accompanied by Stacey Abrams
and national religious leaders.

Congressman Lewis's visit was a surprise, as it had been
reported that he had been getting sicker and sicker. He
looked frail, but was still clear and resolute in his purpose. It
was incredibly emotional as he climbed up to the top of a little step stool with Stacey's help. People encircled him. It was
hard to hear his words, but I was close enough to not miss a
single thing he said.

John Lewis reminded us that day of the horror the marchers encountered fifty-five years before and exhorted us to vote:
"We must go out and vote like we never, ever voted before." He
passionately called out for voters to use the ballot box as "a non-
violent instrument . . . to redeem the soul of America."

I looked over at Pete and I knew he was as moved as I was,
and I also knew, without him saying a word, that he knew
exactly what he had to do at that moment.

I thought of Lewis's words. I thought of him describing how
he had been beaten on that bridge and how he thought he was
going to die and that somehow "God Almighty helped me."

He said, "We should keep the faith and keep our eyes on the prize."

"Our eyes on the prize . . . ?"

How could I best keep my eyes on the prize?

How could I best seek redemption for our country after the four years of havoc and corruption Donald Trump had wrought on America?

It was my decision to make. No one had called me and asked me to get out of the race. No one had called our staff and told them I should get out. In fact, my team—still energized by our showing in New Hampshire—was running on all four cylinders, full speed ahead.

It was my call and only my call. At that moment—first in the church, and then, with John Lewis confirming on that bridge what I thought was right—I decided to end the campaign and do all I could to fulfill my purpose that year. It would just be in a different way than I'd hoped. I remembered the words of John McCain . . . the last thing he'd told me a few months before he died. Because he couldn't speak like he used to, he had simply pointed to the words in one of his books: "There is nothing in life more liberating than fighting for a cause larger than yourself." This cause was larger than me. It was larger than delegate counts and debates. I knew that.

In the end, I made the decision in Selma that while I could have remained in the race for weeks and maybe months more, won Minnesota on Super Tuesday, and participated in additional debates, endorsing Joe Biden was the best way to use whatever strength my supporters had generously given to me to help Joe win the election and beat Donald Trump.

I respected all the candidates, but I truly believed that besides me, Joe Biden had the best chance to beat Trump. I also believed that with the uncertainty of what appeared to be a dangerous virus coming our way, and with Trump still maintaining support among the MAGA crowd, we had to unite. We couldn't continue to extend this fight. The consequences were just too grave.

Of course it hurt to lose and withdraw from the race. Abigail had just finished up a visit to a church in Tennessee. Our campaign staff was scattered all over the country, fighting for every last vote. Ads were running. Delegates were being courted. When I called my husband to tell him, he grew quiet and then said: "But I just spent a half an hour in Owls Head, Maine, getting a lobsterman to support you, and he said yes!"[26]

But despite all of the blood, sweat, and tears, and yes, disappointment, I can honestly say that it was likely the most celebratory end to a presidential campaign in recent American history.

When most people end their national campaigns, it is pretty glum. I wanted to end my campaign in a different way. I wanted to end my campaign as it started—with joy—and use my power for good.

Right after the Selma event we checked Joe Biden's schedule and realized he was going to be in Dallas the next day. That seemed to me like the perfect larger-than-life place to make this announcement. It was, after all, the day before Super Tuesday. We quietly took down rallies we had set up

26. If you are that lobsterman or you know who he is, could you call my office so I can write a nice note?

throughout the West the very next day, doing only the early morning one in Salt Lake City. I spoke to the vice president. He was kind and grateful. I called some of my opponents: Pete (who had announced he was out of the race the night before), and Bernie and Elizabeth (who had been good friends throughout all of it). They were all really sweet.

John and Abigail met me in a hotel room in Dallas, and I gave them both hugs and returned to working on my speech. There frankly wasn't a lot of time for much emotion. When we got to the event, Joe and Jill Biden joined John, Abigail, and me in a room behind the stage to commemorate the moment. The only other person in that room was Cam, our long-time campaign photographer. As she was taking the photos of the five of us talking, I noticed that the camera was shaking. Behind that big lens she had just broken down crying. I thought, "I am going to let Cam be my alter ego tonight. She can cry for me."

The vice president and I went over to Cam together and gave her a big hug, with both of us telling her it was going to be okay. She later got a great job taking photos in the White House. Joe Biden was good on his word.

Then there was the practical. That's something I kind of love about politics. Despite all the emotion, the delegate counters had work to do. Marc Stanley, a major Biden supporter and now the ambassador to Argentina, had to come in and have me sign over my pledged delegates in a number of states. He was there to notarize the documents. "No looking back," I thought, and I signed them.

The rally was incredible. It was one of the last really big things I got to do before COVID hit. Elected officials and leaders joined us from all over Texas, including Beto O'Rourke, who had gotten out of the presidential race months before in Iowa, but was a key endorsement in Texas.

When Joe and Jill and John, Abigail, and I went out on stage, the crowd went wild. Then came the time for me to give my speech. Joe stood right next to me. I noted the incredible beginning of my campaign in the blizzard, and how it was now coming to a close in the heart of Texas. I thanked our tremendous staff and spoke to how we had beaten the odds. I touched on all we had done, and when I mentioned the debates, Joe chimed in, "And she won every one of them." Not quite true, but still.

I directly addressed my supporters: "If you feel tired of the noise and the nonsense and our politics, and if you are tired of the extremes, you have a home with me. And I think you know you have a home with Joe Biden."

I noted the importance of unity, since, in my words, we were never going to out-divide "the divider-in-chief."

I talked about how Joe Biden understands that service is not about self-interest, it is about sacrifice.

I looked over and saw tears streaming down Jill's face.

And I ended with the practical: "Tomorrow is Super Tuesday. Texas, you are one big Super Tuesday state. But there are fourteen Super Tuesday states and one of them is my home state of Minnesota. So, what I want you to do is 'Vote for Joe.'"

I had told the vice president that saying that directly to the camera would mean something in my state. He laughed and said, "I know we are going to do well tomorrow, but I am way behind in your state."

"No," I said. "I will deliver."

After walking off that rally stage one last time, and noting that it was the most joyously upbeat end for a presidential campaign ever, I realized I had about twelve hours to make good on my promise.

With the vice president's then-senior adviser, Symone Sanders, at our side, Joe Biden and I did joint and separate interviews with Minnesota TV stations. We cut radio and TV ads that started running first thing the next morning in Minnesota. They got me on a plane and shipped me out to New York, where I did both the *Today* show and *CBS This Morning,* as well as Minnesota early morning media call-ins.

That's what I did with my twelve hours. And then I went home.

That night, the results started coming in. And yes, Joe Biden won across the country, but most important, he won in Minnesota. One of the more amusing telltale indicators that those twelve hours mattered was that I still won a number of the Minnesota counties that got predominantly Canadian and North Dakota TV! They just didn't get the news! Joe won most of the other ones.

From the stage in Los Angeles that evening, Joe Biden called me out and thanked me for winning Minnesota for him. He also phoned me personally and said the same thing.

Our campaign had begun with joy in an unexpected blizzard in Minneapolis, and it ended with joy in that hot, people-packed arena in Dallas. For me, what mattered the most is what I learned in between the blizzard and Dallas. I learned about myself, my convictions, my flaws, and yes, my faith. I was constantly tested, and when it counted I had shown grace under pressure. I learned about the strength of the people around me—my family, my friends, and our incredible team. I saw perfect strangers take the leap to help me out.

But what I was most proud of in the end is that I had used my power—which was truly given to me by the people who were always at my side on our journey—for good. Joe Biden won the 2020 general election, and we sent Donald Trump—albeit kicking and screaming—packing.

## Recipe for Amy Klobuchar's Award-Winning Taconite Tater Tot Hotdish

### Ingredients

Ground beef (1–1.5 lbs)
Cream of mushroom soup (1 can)
Cream of chicken soup (1 can)
Onions (1 small)
Garlic (a couple cloves)
Salt and pepper
Pepper Jack cheese, shredded (8–12 oz)
Tater tots (1 package)

### Instructions

Preheat the oven to 450 degrees F.

Brown ground beef, drain off fat. Sauté onions and garlic.

In a large bowl, mix together beef, onions, garlic, both cans of soup, salt, and pepper. Spread evenly into the bottom of a 9×13 baking dish. Cover with about half of the shredded cheese.

Place tater tots in one layer over the entire pan. Bake at 450 for 30 minutes, or until tater tots are crisp. Cover with remaining cheese and bake until cheese melts.

# 3

# The Plague

Life Lesson: *"I have no idea what's awaiting me, or what will happen when this all ends. For the moment I know this: there are sick people and they need curing."*
—ALBERT CAMUS, *THE PLAGUE*, 1947

## "Yes, it is that bad."

In 1947, Albert Camus, an Algerian-born French author, wrote *The Plague*, a novel about how the residents of a town in Algeria cope with a deadly epidemic. The book—entitled *La Peste* in French—is set in the 1940s as the bubonic plague hits Oran, Algeria. The first sign? A massive number of rats die on the streets right in front of the town's residents. Soon the people get it too. Leaders are at first in denial, hoping it will just go away, not heeding the advice of doctors. As journalist Steve Coll describes in a recent *New Yorker* look-back at the novel, the Algerian town's "[a]dvisers can't bear to initially acknowledge the catastrophe or even to speak aloud the name of the disease that is its cause."

Hmm.

For those doubting the adage that truth can be stranger than fiction, it feels like a good moment to time-travel seventy-five years forward from the novel's publication and peek in on a real-life 2020 White House discussion between our nation's then-top medical adviser, Dr. Anthony Fauci, and then-President Donald Trump. As recounted by Dr. Fauci to *The New York Times* years later, the following exchange occurred in the White House in the early days of the coronavirus pandemic:

> TRUMP: "Well, it's not that bad, right?"
> FAUCI: "Yes, it is that bad."

From there Trump went on to minimize the risk of the disease for months, failing to disclose much of what he was learning about how contagious the virus truly was, spinning dangerous and fanciful stories of miracle treatments—from bleach drinking (don't do that) to ultraviolet rays. While privately revealing to reporter Bob Woodward that the coronavirus was "deadly stuff" ("It goes through air, Bob. That's always tougher than the touch."), he continued to tell Americans that the virus was "under control," repeatedly sharing with the public what he portrayed as his definitive insight that the pandemic would "go away by spring."

But the nation soon had to come to grips with the truth: "Yes, it [was] that bad." The American death toll by the end of 2022 was well over one million people. And for those of us who had a loved one who got seriously sick or died from the virus in those early deadly months, the President's failure to share the truth—including about how the disease was actually transmitted—was not just a political footnote in history. It was the difference between life and death.

The relevance of Camus's seventy-five-year-old novel

doesn't end there. In the fictional plague, the authorities ultimately order a quarantine. Yet certain Oran leaders continue to spout falsities about the town's epidemic in order to aggrandize and expand upon their own power (this one is just too much of a softball to do the leap to the future Trump time travel bit again). Camus describes one town priest who preaches with much fervor that the plague is a scourge sent by God to punish those who have rejected him, thereby castigating those who have died from the plague as sinners. (At least this was the priest's mantra until a friend's child dies and the preacher must admit the boy was innocent.) The preacher himself eventually gets sick, refuses to call for a doctor, and dies.

Ultimately the citizens of Oran bind together to fight the plague and see that their destinies—and in fact their very lives—are inextricably tied together. The hero of the story—a doctor, the novel's truth teller—warns the townspeople early on about the scourge of the disease and works around the clock to save lives while running an auxiliary hospital.

Camus eventually received the Nobel Prize in Literature for *The Plague* and other works. At a very young age he wrote about isolation, estrangement, evil, and the ultimate triumph of human dignity. He was anti-fascist, anti-Nazi, and anti-communist, and many of his works, including *The Plague*, were seen as allegories on those topics, written as they were in the lead-up to, during, and after World War II. In granting the prize to Camus, the Nobel Committee praised his "clear-sighted earnestness." His work, they said, "illuminates the problems of the human conscience in our times." Camus was forty-four when he received the prize in 1957. He died in a car accident three years later.

I read *The Plague* during the worst of the pandemic. I

thought about how one of its themes—the difficulty of sticking with the truth when a lie is so easy to exploit as a path to political power—is now ubiquitous in our politics. While the practice of lying and dividing one's way to the top was stoked by Donald Trump, it didn't start with him. And while a deliberate disregard for truth was magnified during our two-year-plus pandemic, it didn't begin or end there.

When leaders in positions of trust repeatedly make stuff up, a societal breakdown of an agreed-upon set of institutional facts follows. And this problem has gotten worse and worse. The embers of false premises and constant discord were flamed by dueling radio and cable TV talk shows, brought to an art form by Sean Hannity, Tucker Carlson, and Trump, and fanned into a full-fledged forest fire by social media, where both exploitive and explosive disinformation runs rampant.

Progress on so many of our existential challenges—from climate change to global public health; from immigration to income disparities; from monopoly power to online disinformation, gun safety, and civil rights—has been slowed or severely set back by the lack of trust and faith in our government officials. Real progress on hard issues is hard to come by when politicians hide behind lies to further their own power.

I believe that finding a way for people to believe again in shared facts and actual truths is the only way out of our political morass. As the former and beloved New York Senator Daniel Patrick Moynihan once said, "You are entitled to your opinion. But you are not entitled to your own facts."

So, yes, the pandemic was our own modern-day global

plague, starting as it did in Wuhan, China, and then indiscriminately killing so many in its path—from grandmas and grandpas to the hospital ER intake worker to the bus driver at your kids' school. Yes, scientists and researchers and medical personnel saved the bulk of us. But we all know that many of the people who died did not need to.

Innocents get hurt when people who know better choose to traffic in disinformation in order to either pad their profits or further their destinies. How many news stories do we have to see with a widower telling the story of how his now-dead wife refused the vaccine after reading an internet post that said it would plant a microchip in her arm before we admit that our modern-day plague was not just a medical plague, but also a disinformation and misinformation plague? As the widower mourns, we know the truth: his wife died because she believed someone who was lying to her.

## The Empty Chair at the Table

Like many who struggled through COVID over the past few years, for me the pandemic was deeply personal. But my stories of my husband who was stricken with a serious case early on and my dad who contracted the virus in an assisted living facility at age ninety-two simply pale in comparison to those whose loved ones died alone or the many Americans whose jobs went away or whose lives were disrupted forever. There are many people still coping with long-haul COVID symptoms and trauma and mental illness. There are millions with preexisting conditions and autoimmune diseases for whom the consequences of getting sick from the virus are exponentially worse. They are worn down after spending years protecting themselves and their family members from the highly contagious virus—constantly balancing their work and health, living with the day-in and day-out fear that doing their jobs or going on simple errands will mean they themselves die, or, worse, that they may kill someone they love.

As often happens with plagues, the coronavirus hit the medical frontline workers first. One of the very first medical workers to perish? Dr. Li Wenliang, a thirty-three-year-old Chinese ophthalmologist working in a hospital in Wuhan. In December of 2019, Dr. Li advised his fellow doctors to take additional safety measures to avoid the illness. The immediate reaction from the authorities? Wuhan police accused the doctor of spreading a baseless rumor. Tragically, Dr. Li later died from the very disease he had presciently warned Chinese authorities about, leaving behind a child and a pregnant wife.

Within weeks the virus started spreading around the world, arriving on our shores and sickening doctors and nurses and medical workers as patients streamed through hospital doors. One of the early losses was Dr. James Mahoney, a much-loved doctor at a hospital that primarily served Brooklyn's Black community. Dr. Mahoney, who had cared for patients throughout the 9/11 terror attacks and the AIDS crisis, delayed his retirement and refused to leave the front lines during the coronavirus pandemic. In April of 2020 he died from the virus in the very hospital where he had spent four decades saving lives.

Other heroes soon followed. Josh Obra of Anaheim, California was a registered nurse working at a 147-bed elder care facility that specialized in memory care. In addition to attending to the needs of the residents, he mentored his sister Jasmine, who was studying to be a nurse. Josh and Jasmine tested positive for the coronavirus on the same day in June of 2020. At a time when so many families grappled with the unpredictable nature of the disease—with one family member experiencing minor symptoms while another became seriously ill—Jasmine recovered, but sadly, her big brother Josh did not.

In the life-or-death lottery unleashed by the coronavirus, there was also the heart-wrenching story of Dr. Lorna Breen, the energetic, empathetic medical director of the Emergency Department at New York-Presbyterian Allen Hospital in Manhattan. For Dr. Breen, the onset of the pandemic meant excruciating shifts surrounded by health-care workers rationing their protective equipment and desperately ill patients outmatched by the virus. Admitted patients would die alone, with only medical personnel at their side holding phones set to "speaker" mode and loved ones sobbing on the other end. According to Dr. Breen's friends and family, she was shattered by her inability to save more patients, and on April 26, 2020, she died by suicide. In her final days, as reported by *The New York Times*, she told a friend, "I couldn't help anyone. I couldn't do anything. I just wanted to help people, and I couldn't do anything."

Then—unsurprisingly—COVID hit more frontline workers: grocery clerks and drugstore employees, Uber and Lyft and cab and bus drivers, plumbers and electricians, EMTs, firefighters and police officers.

Twenty-seven-year-old Leilani Jordan died in April of 2020. She worked at a Giant Food in Largo, Maryland, and when the pandemic began she insisted on working because she wanted to make sure older people could still get their groceries.

Sonny Quitlong—a Filipino immigrant in Seattle—held down two frontline jobs. He worked at a grocery store and was a mail handler at a United States Postal Service distribution center. His seventy-year life was marked by hosting enormous Thanksgiving dinners and having countless joyful conversations with grocery store customers. He died in April of 2020.

Sergeant Clifford Martin was the second police officer in Chicago to die of COVID, with tragically many more to follow. He started his life in a housing development and went on to become, as a colleague described him, "one of the most respected detectives in the Chicago Police Department." He had two children who followed in his footsteps and joined the department. He died after working twenty-five years as a police officer.

Jason Hargrove, a Detroit bus driver, posted a viral video in March of 2020 venting his frustrations about disrespectful passengers who put others at risk by coughing without covering their mouths. "We're out here as public workers, doing our job, trying to make an honest living to take care of our families," he said before adding, "Some folks don't care." Eleven days after sharing the video, Hargrove died from coronavirus complications.

Marny Xiong, the child of Hmong refugees and the chair of the St. Paul, Minnesota, school board, was only thirty-one when she died in June of 2020. The month before her death her dad had experienced trouble breathing but was afraid to go to the hospital alone, so she went with him. By May 7 they were both in intensive care and on ventilators. While her father finally got home at the end of May, Marny continued to spend weeks on a ventilator, never able to speak to her family again, dying on June 7.

That funeral was one of the saddest memorials I have ever attended. With her dad and mom and the rest of their tight-knit family sitting in the front row, those who knew Marny best mourned the loss of their once-vibrant daughter and sister with such grief. The slides and the videos of Marny with her young friends and the schoolkids she helped played throughout the service. Marny's whole life was in front of her. She had talked about being the city's first Hmong mayor. And, just like that, she was gone.

Early on, the pandemic hit impoverished neighborhoods and communities of color particularly hard. The disease put one big magnifying glass on what were already unacceptable levels of racial and income inequalities in America and across the world. The closed-in public housing projects, the crowded public transportation, the prevalence of preexisting conditions, the lack of access to health care and good nutrition—all these factors contributed to higher transmission of the virus as well as higher mortality rates in our nation's minority communities.

A study published by the Kaiser Family Foundation in February 2022 showed that Hispanic, Black, and Asian Americans were roughly two times more likely to die from the coronavirus than white Americans.[27] And while the coronavirus

---

27. During the height of COVID when most deaths occurred, these numbers held true. But as COVID deaths greatly declined with the advent of the vaccines, the death rate among white Americans eclipsed the death rate of minorities. With regard to the health system's response to the post-surge

reduced the average life expectancy of white Americans by 1.2 years, according to the National Center for Health Statistics the life expectancy of Black and Hispanic Americans fell by three years.

And then it hit the seniors, creating wretched stories of our elders dying alone. In the early months between May and August of 2020, for example, Centers for Disease Control data showed that there were 114,000 COVID deaths in the U.S. Seventy-eight percent of those who died were sixty-five and older. As of February 2022—about two years into the pandemic—CDC data showed that while people over sixty-five accounted for only 16 percent of the U.S. population, they totaled a tragic 75 percent of deaths from COVID-19. That doesn't even count the older people who may have died from loneliness, illness, or unrelated causes simply because they were forced into isolation. Every time elderly people get the virus, their chance of dying is exponentially higher than that of the rest of us. In fact, anyone who gets it over age eighty-five is 630 times more likely to die from the virus than someone who is between eighteen and twenty-one.

That's why when I got the call from the Burnsville, Minnesota, assisted living community where my dad lived with the news that he had come down with the virus, I was really scared. He was ninety-two. It was June of 2020 and there was no vaccine and no known treatment. And he had Alzhei-

---

numbers, a Harvard professor of epidemiology was quoted by *The Washington Post* as saying that officials must figure out how to connect with "communities who are ideologically opposed to the vaccine" while also contending with "the cumulative impact of injustice" on communities of color. "Whites Now More Likely to Die from COVID than Blacks: Why the Pandemic Shifted," *Washington Post*, October 19, 2022.

mer's. The majority of the twenty-some people living in his memory care home got the virus, with three of them dying in just a few weeks.

When the word got out to his longtime friends in the Twin Cities that he had COVID, several called me to ask why we didn't take him out of the assisted living facility and place him in a hospital. Looking back, I am sure many adult children of people in assisted living had the same experiences we did, trying to explain the hard truths to family and friends. This is what I told them: First, there was really no place for him to go. Hospital beds were hard to come by, and harder still when the person already had a place to stay to receive care, even if it was the place where he or she had gotten the virus. Second, he was in a familiar place, with people who knew him well taking care of him. Moving patients with Alzheimer's to unfamiliar settings can be confusing, and really set them back. Third, like many families with a loved one with advanced Alzheimer's, we had to remember our number one goal: minimize his pain, keep him close to people who loved him, and make sure he was as comfortable as possible despite the disruptions to his normal routine. Having spoken with the doctors and nurses visiting the home daily, I felt they had a good plan as to how they would handle his care if he got sicker.

All of that didn't make it easier when the moment came and we thought it could be the last visit. The three of us— John and Abigail and I—were there, standing outside his assisted living window on a beautiful summer day feeling like kids dressed as astronauts, covered in gloves and double masks with plastic face protectors ringed around our heads. We peered through a closed window and saw Dad in his pullover sweater in the middle of summer, looking so small and scared, as an assisted living aide held up a phone so he could communicate with us.

My dad couldn't figure out why we couldn't come in and give him a hug. He didn't understand the masks and the astronaut getups. He tried to open the window to join us outside. I remember biting my lip and working so hard not to cry, and John finally resorting to playing some of my dad's favorite songs on the phone, including an old favorite: a Slovenian drinking song. In the end—through the coughs and the confusion—Dad boisterously broke into the Notre Dame fight song all on his own, one of the treasured tunes for Catholic boys growing up in Ely, Minnesota, in the 1930s.

We all smiled through our tears, and sure enough, despite losing three of his next-door neighbors to COVID over the next week, he somehow bounced back. He lost weight, but he never needed oxygen. Thanks to his loving nurses and caretakers, the high-protein banana/peanut butter shakes they made him, and perhaps his years of high-altitude mountain climbing and crazy-long bike rides and marathons, he made it through.

Months later, when we would visit him outside on the patio, he would continue to exuberantly declare, "I'm POSITIVE."

"No, you aren't positive anymore, Dad," I would say, "you are now testing negative."

"No, I AM POSITIVE," he would assertively answer back.

Finally, as so often happens in families coping with a loved one's memory loss and confusion, you adapt to the virtual reality of the moment: "Yes, Dad," I nodded, "you are the most POSITIVE person I know."

He was no longer infectious, but his positive attitude brought smiles to everyone he greeted.

But I will never forget staring through that window, unable to hold his hand.

## John Gets Sick

Those first six months were still the hardest. There were no vaccines and no magical cures. Ambulance sirens were wailing down the streets of every major city. People were still wearing bandannas for masks (I know I did) and the idea of bulk-purchasing what we would soon learn were the truly protective masks—the N95s—was eons away. It would be nearly two years before there was readily available in-home testing. Vaccine deniers and mask mandate protesters were only a blip on the news back then. It was a time when everyone thought you mainly got coronavirus from surfaces and that it could live on those surfaces for an indeterminate amount of time. In the earliest weeks, people still thought you could hang out at a crowded bar as long as you wiped down your wineglass and didn't touch the door handle.

That's when my husband got it. It was at a bar. And it was at the very worst time: mid-March of 2020. There were no Paxlovid pills to treat it, tests were hard to find, and not many doctors had even adopted the hospital protocol to place seriously ill COVID patients with respiratory issues on their stomachs, as they later realized that it could result in a higher survival rate than letting them rest on their backs. Back then there were only overrun hospitals and shortages of beds and ventilators and, yes, doctors. Your treatment and ultimate survival were for the most part out of anyone's control, but your chances could well depend on your underlying health, where you lived, and if there was the time—or the space—to truly help you.

My husband was in that first wave of people who got really sick from COVID. As best we know now, he caught it when he had drinks with a good friend of ours at an outdoor bar in Washington, D.C. The friend had no temperature, and only a slight cough, which he attributed to an old cold. He felt fine otherwise, and they shared a bowl of peanuts. Our friend's very limited cough with no temperature and no flu symptoms just didn't fit the initial profiles of the disease.

Months later, when the antibody tests were available, the friend called and told us that he had tested positive for the antibodies and that the week he saw John was the only time he had been at all sick. Tracing his own steps, he figured out that a few other people he had seen that week had gotten sick. Our friend may have in fact been an early super-spreader, but between there being no guidance about how the virus was truly transmitted and no available testing, he had absolutely no idea—nor could he have—that his friendly invitation to go out for drinks would almost kill my husband.

Meanwhile, I was off to the Mayo Clinic in Minnesota to get my long-awaited hip replacement, delayed as it was during the presidential campaign. I still remember that when I got to Rochester, the orthopedic surgeon told me that his Orlando orthopedic conference had just been canceled. I told him that I had just received a Senate briefing about the virus and I thought it was going to get much worse. I remember telling his young medical residents who sat in on the initial pre-surgery consult that they wouldn't be orthopedic residents for very long, as everyone would be pitching in to care for coronavirus patients. Whether that happened or not, I was certainly on the right track. Just two weeks later? All elective surgeries were canceled at Mayo.

While I was in the hospital in Minnesota, back in our apartment in D.C. John started feeling sick. He was more tired than usual and had a slight temperature. He didn't have much knowledge about the virus's symptoms except for what he had gleaned from TV stories and newspaper reports—but he knew the disease was starting to spread, and he knew enough to know he didn't feel well.

Yet despite waking up with his mind in a haze the day he started feeling sick, he made some extraordinarily good decisions. First, he didn't attend and speak at my weekly "Minnesota Morning" breakfast in my office in the Dirksen Building, with fifty-plus visiting Minnesotans. He had originally planned to fill in for me when I was at Mayo so my constituents would be greeted by a friendly face. Also, as a professor at the University of Baltimore School of Law, he decided not to take the train from D.C. to join what he didn't know then would be the last in-person faculty meeting for over a year. That decision saved multiple fellow faculty members—not to mention his fellow train passengers—from being exposed.

He then didn't get on a crowded Delta flight from D.C. to Minneapolis late that afternoon as we had planned. He didn't walk into the Mayo Clinic that evening to pick me up and drive me home from the hip surgery. You see, all of that had been the plan. And hardly anyone was wearing masks. As we now know, with his symptoms and the timing, he would have been contagious to the max. But instead of just blowing it off as a cold and going on with his day and keeping his promised commitments (which he is always wont to do), he decided to stay home "just in case," thus saving hundreds and hundreds of people from a potential deathly exposure.

These are among the many reasons I love my husband.

Back in Minnesota, I kept calling John in D.C. He seemed to be maintaining his spirits despite a headache and fever. COVID tests were extremely hard to come by, so he thought he would just quarantine himself and power through. Friends gave me a ride home from Mayo and brought me food. My recovery in Minnesota was quite short-lived, however. Only three days after leaving the hospital, I had to return to D.C. on crutches and still in pain to start voting on what would become our first major COVID relief bill. The voting went on for days.

Meanwhile John was getting sicker and sicker. I had my phone permanently fixed to "speaker" mode and kept toggling back and forth between taking calls from constituents about the coronavirus legislation—everyone from neighbors to small and big businesses to medical associations to hospitals and retail stores—to calling John for reports on his symptoms. For a while, he seemed to be staying the same, or even improving. But after a week his temperature was going up and not down. He was coughing more and more. I kept asking him if he was drinking enough. He just kept sleeping. Friends dropped 7UP outside his door.

I remember repeatedly researching whether, if he had COVID, it was better for him to take Tylenol or Advil. Could Advil make it worse? Answer? No. At some point he went into a clinic and got a COVID test. They told him it would take up to two weeks to get the results. Offering no additional tests, they sent him home to wait.

As the days went on, John was getting stranger and stranger on the phone—not remembering if I had just called him and not tracking his temperature or if he had even taken it. After he started coughing up blood, I implored him to go to a hospital. At some point I threatened to call the ambulance myself. I then called—and made him call—Dr. John Symington, a good friend of ours and the husband of my college roommate, Meg. John is an excellent infectious disease doctor in the Fairfax, Virginia, system. He was out of town, but thought the quickest way to get some tests would be at a smaller hospital in the Fairfax system—Mount Vernon.

With my husband knowing that he couldn't expose a cabdriver to the potential virus, he drove his own car and met a hospital staff member—donning protective gear to the hilt—in the ER parking lot. They brought him in and did a bunch of tests, including a chest X-ray. He was clearly having trouble breathing and his oxygen saturation level was dangerously low—dropping into the sixties. They immediately checked him into the hospital. They determined that he had pneumonia and consistently low oxygen levels, and they put him on oxygen but not a ventilator. The earlier COVID test he had taken had still not come back, but the ER staff was fairly certain he had the virus.

Ironically, the positive test would not come through until ten days after he'd taken it and five days after he checked into the hospital. At that point they were so certain that he had COVID that they told me if it came back negative it would have been a "false negative."

For days he was on full-time oxygen and the virus temporarily messed with his mind. He was convinced he should leave the hospital and kept telling me his oxygen level was really in the high nineties. When I called the doctors they told me, "No, that's where it is with oxygen! Without the oxygen it's in the sixties." He wanted his laptop to teach his classes remotely, even though every time he talked his breath hitched.

When John left for Mount Vernon Hospital that first day, he had no idea he would be checking into the hospital and staying for a week. All he had with him was his phone. For days he asked for his laptop, but the hospital wouldn't let anyone drop anything off because of the uncertainty of the viral surface issue. At the time they just didn't know if sanitizing the outside of the laptop was good enough to kill the virus.

On the morning of March 23, 2020, when the test came back and we all knew that he definitely had COVID, I made a public announcement. I noted that I loved my husband so very much "and not being able to be there at the hospital by his side is one of the hardest things about this disease."

Lots of people texted and emailed John their well-wishes. I tried to cheer him up with all kinds of good tidbits: President Obama had called, as did Joe Biden. Jane Sanders, Bernie's wife, was one of the first I had spoken to about it, and she broke into tears, she was so worried about him. Ted Cruz's entire church was praying for him. And my friend and former fellow Senator Al Franken got through to John to cheer him up with multiple jokes.

I spoke with my husband on the phone every day. I talked to the doctors and nurses, and we waited. Over three weeks of isolation (first at home and then in the hospital) was taking its toll. Our daughter Abigail tried getting her dad to play online games on his phone, and the day he finally relented and agreed to play Battleship was the day we knew things were slightly improving. Doctor friends wrote that I should "break him out" of the small hospital and send him to a bigger medical center, but once again—just as I would later do with my dad—I thought the best plan for John was to keep him where he was. At the same time, even during the week John was there, the numbers of pandemic patients at Mount Vernon—along with other hospitals across the country—were exponentially increasing. Soon Mount Vernon Hospital would house several COVID patients on ventilators. People were starting to die in droves throughout the country.

John finally got slightly better and the doctors made the decision—which they admitted was a difficult one—to send him home. He was still really sick and gulping in air with every other breath.

My wonderful colleague and friend Minnesota Senator Tina Smith gave me sanctuary in her apartment in D.C. while John had COVID as well as when he was recovering.

When I moved into Tina's place and she went back to Minnesota, I vowed to leave it just as I found it. But despite my best efforts to leave the place untouched, like many who were stranded during the pandemic I learned that semi-quarantining makes for desperate circumstances. Even the best-laid plans get turned upside down as the isolated days turn into weeks and months. In this case, within only four days of moving in I realized I had charged three movies to her streaming accounts, worn her mittens and scarves, tried on her shoes, and cleared out her refrigerator of every food item that hadn't passed its expiration date. In one particularly low moment, I ate her last frozen burrito. And the final indignity? I had to explain to her that I accidentally broke one of her vintage kitchen chairs while standing on it to open a cupboard drawer.

For some untold reason, Tina chose to stay back in Minnesota the entire time while the Senate worked remotely until John got safely out of quarantine and I got out of her apartment. As she later said, that's what friends are for.

And yes, I did buy her replacement burritos.

In the end, John got better, with no actual long-haul symptoms despite living through the loneliness of more than a month of isolation. He ended up working with me to lead an early public effort to encourage people who had recovered from the virus to give plasma, something he did at the Mayo Clinic four times himself. My hip healed with few in the Senate noticing I was on crutches. We passed the first major coronavirus bill. Our family returned to Minnesota where—like so many other Americans—we went on to deal with the long slog of the pandemic.

For me, there are still three enduring memories from that time period. One is the kindness of the doctors and nurses at the hospital in Mount Vernon who saved my husband's life, as well as the friends like Tina who helped me. One friend in Minnesota literally brought over chicken noodle soup as I recovered from the surgery. The second is that my husband thought he was perfectly safe to meet a friend at a bar as long as the surfaces of the table and beer glasses had been cleaned off. I will never forget what I didn't know then but I know now: Donald Trump personally knew early on that that wasn't true—he knew the virus transmittal was mainly airborne—but he just forgot to tell the rest of us.

The third and final memory is how close I came to losing my husband. That's why, nearly one year later, I found the "Field of Flags"—the 191,500 American flags planted in rows across ten full blocks of the National Mall during the Biden inauguration—to be one of the most evocative and haunting tributes to those who couldn't attend. The flags memorialized Americans who couldn't be there, but also constituted a "call to action" going forward. As noted by President Biden, so many people at the time were sitting at their dining room tables looking across to an empty chair.

If not for the decision my husband made to go to the hospital and get the oxygen and the medical help—as well as the fact that he was one of the lucky ones who recovered—one of those empty chairs would have been for him.

## Action

When the first people died in China and the initial cases were reported in the U.S., we were still in the midst of the presidential primaries. President Trump was completely downplaying the virus at the time, noting in January that "we have it totally under control . . . It's one person coming in from China." The issue came up in my very last primary debate in South Carolina, and I criticized the President for not formally addressing the nation on something so consequential to the country. I also asked all Americans to follow CDC guidance. That was on February 26. While Trump participated in press conferences and did interviews downplaying the virus, he didn't formally address the nation from the Oval Office about COVID-19 until March 11, over forty days after the secretary of Health and Human Services declared the virus a public health emergency.

About two weeks later, on March 24, despite having declared COVID-19 a national emergency, President Trump predicted that upcoming Easter church services would be "packed" and that it would be a "beautiful time." Throughout 2020 he undermined the CDC and the advice of medical experts—from his comments on mask wearing to his proposing wild-eyed, nonsensical treatment options to his handling of his own illness at the debate shortly before the election. At the presidential debate—during which we now know he knew he had COVID—he endangered the lives of political opponent Joe Biden and debate moderator Chris Wallace. The final affront to public health? When he got seriously sick from COVID, he chose to go on a public joyride straight from his hospital bed at Walter Reed, where doctors had advised him to do no such thing. In fact, Dr. James Phillips, then a Walter Reed emergency room physician, called Trump's irresponsibility "astonishing" and said it was "insanity" for him to expose his Secret Service detail to the virus.

But despite all that (and it was a lot), there were people within the Trump administration and on Capitol Hill who acted responsibly to lead our country through the crisis. The administration's and Congress's decision to fund major research, immediate human trials, and the production of vaccines on an expedited time line made a major difference. The world's scientists' decision to share research data and what they knew about the makeup of the virus paved the way for a worldwide race for a vaccine, with multiple companies in multiple countries testing vaccines and collaboratively sharing research.

All of that led to one of the fastest developments of vaccines in world history.

Back in the nation's capital my staff and I focused on two things: (1) crafting and supporting legislation that responded to the trio of interrelated economic, personal, and medical crises Americans faced by funding testing, vaccine research, hospitals, direct help, and programs for struggling or shut-down businesses; and (2) directly assisting our constituents, from advising people who were calling in who were homebound, sick, or in bad straits economically, to helping employers who were closing their doors at a rapid pace.

In addition to the economic and medical/research legislation we were all part of, I introduced a bevy of bipartisan bills on rural broadband (access to high-speed internet became increasingly important as the pandemic went on), mental illness, domestic violence, child care, senior fraud, help for music and theater venues, and many other subjects. Several of my bills were included in legislation that was later signed into law.

On March 25, 2020, by a 96–0 unanimous vote, the Senate passed the CARES Act, a sweeping $2 trillion economic stimulus package. The legislation included provisions to bolster just about every facet of American life: loans to help small businesses stay afloat; expanded unemployment insurance for the millions of Americans who lost their jobs amid the turmoil; funding to make sure state and local governments could continue to provide crucial services; resources for hospitals; up to $1,200 in stimulus checks for individual Americans making less than $75,000 per year and lesser amounts for people at certain higher incomes, with allowances for more help for Americans with children. Like any bill passed in the early days of an unfolding crisis, it had its flaws, but for millions and millions of people, it made all the difference. The day after the Senate acted, the House immediately passed the bill by a voice vote, and President Trump signed it into law on March 27.

The following month—with so many businesses closed—a major part of the CARES Act began landing in the states. It was called the Paycheck Protection Program (better known as "PPP"), and it helped many businesses keep employees on the payroll and/or keep their doors open. It was a major financing effort involving nearly all banks across the country, with many difficult private and public sector implementation issues. While the PPP was far from perfect, this bipartisan program was a game changer for many employers—and employees. It bolstered the economy during its darkest days.

The year 2020 was a long and eventful one for all of us, but while much had changed by year-end, some things were unfortunately very much the same. We knew a lot more about the virus, but so many families and businesses still weren't sure how they were going to get by. That's why even after Donald Trump lost in November—but before Joe Biden was installed in the White House—we knew we had to act again. A number of programs we'd funded through the earlier CARES Act had run out of resources, and there were still many major areas of the economy that had never gotten relief in the first place.

Most significantly, the pandemic had not gotten better, as some—including Trump—had predicted. While the vaccines were incredibly promising, they had just started being distributed, and the predictions—because of logistics and manufacturing—were for a slower rollout than anybody wanted. COVID deaths were on the rise, and the virus was still around. My days were marked by multiple consoling phone calls with constituents about their lost loved ones and sick relatives, dreams and hopes dashed. As usual, our Minnesota state team rose to the occasion, helping so many people during that difficult time.

That time period between the November election and the January swearing-in had all the makings for gridlock, but the nation demanded action. This end-of-year "lame duck"[28] effort to pass an appropriations bill with special funding for enhanced unemployment benefits, additional resources for small business loans, rental assistance, and funding for coronavirus vaccine distribution and testing was truly admirable. Every member of the Senate and House was involved in some way, and—per usual—a number of members formed one of our infamous "gangs" to find common agreement. People involved in that effort initially included Senators Susan Collins, Joe Manchin, Mark Warner, Bill Cassidy, Jeanne Shaheen, Lisa Murkowski, Angus King, Mitt Romney, and Maggie Hassan, and Representatives Josh Gottheimer, Tom Reed, Anthony Gonzalez, Dusty Johnson, Dean Phillips, Abigail Spanberger, and Fred Upton. Later, several others joined on both the Senate and House sides.

It would have been very easy—with an angry President who had lost his election stewing and ranting and raving day after day in the White House—to do nothing. Somehow—despite the fact that the insurrection was fomenting and the very control of the Senate depended on two hotly contested

---

28. In this context, "lame duck" refers to the closing days of a Congress between an election and the arrival of a new Congress.

Georgia Senate races that were set for a runoff on January 5—we grinded through the partisanship and for the good of the nation got our act together and passed a $900 billion bill on a 92–6 Senate vote, even after the President threatened multiple times to veto it. Still fuming over his election loss, President Trump spent a week coming up with reasons not to sign the bill—including that he didn't like the bipartisan foreign aid agreement and that he wanted MORE for individual stimulus checks than $600. But on December 28, 2020, he caved.

On a personal note, the bill included the Save Our Stages Act, the $15 billion grant program based on my bipartisan bill with Texas Senator John Cornyn to save music venues, theaters, and museums across the country. These venues were the first to close when the virus hit, and we all knew they would be the last to open. You simply can't stand in a mosh pit—or an orchestra pit, for that matter—in the middle of a pandemic. The outside-the-Beltway effort to pass the bill was led by the extraordinary Dayna Frank, the head of Minneapolis's iconic First Avenue, the incredibly cool music venue where Prince both got his start and performed impromptu concerts throughout his storied career.

My involvement with Dayna and the bill started on a Saturday night in April of 2020, when she called and told me she needed help not only for First Avenue, but for all the music and theater venues across the country. Since she headed up the national association of independent venues, Dayna and I talked for a long time that night. I told her the only way for us to get a too-often arts-adverse Congress to act and to appreciate the dire straits of the venues was to do this on a strictly bipartisan basis and to make it positive. The group set out and harnessed all its resources—which in this case wasn't money for ads or major lobbying, but instead the creative spirit of its venues. Its musicians, theater actors and actresses, and yes, fans were all part of a national positive effort. Texas—with its many arts venues—was a significant part of the association. And from the beginning Senator Cornyn (thank God for Texas country western bands) and I worked together to get the bill passed.

Shortly after I spoke with Dayna, the Save Our Stages effort was launched, and John Cornyn and I—along with varied arts organizations, from small theaters in Fargo, North Dakota, and Lanesboro, Minnesota, to New York's Broadway, to musical venues from Tennessee to Oregon—kept our coalition and our funding formula together. At first, leadership on my side of the aisle was skeptical, telling me that another broader bill (which I was also cosponsoring) was a better alternative. I told them that while I liked the other bill, if we wanted to get something done now while Donald Trump was President— and go for something bigger later—this bill had the street creds and the members to get it done. Because of Kentucky bluegrass music, we even had Mitch McConnell as a cosponsor. At one point I remember being told at a leadership meeting, "Good luck with it, but the other bill is the one with legs."

But soon nearly everyone was cosponsoring Save Our Stages.

Democrats weren't the only converts. The rapper Pitbull helped us out with Marco Rubio. Senator Kevin Cramer of North Dakota got on the bill after hearing from the Fargo Theatre.

In any case, we passed the bill as part of the year-end package. It ended up including other venues like museums and zoos and was in fact the biggest investment our country has ever made in the arts. Chuck Schumer, Mitch McConnell, and Roy Blunt were helpful to the end, adding funding to include the additional venues and making sure they got covered. As a result, Chuck got mentioned at the Tony Awards. But I got the best thing of all—a coveted star on the outdoor wall of First Avenue, right next to Alice Cooper and six stars away from Prince. They tried to get it done right after we passed the bill, but a severe snowstorm set in and the paint froze in the middle of the star painting. For months, until they could fix it in the spring, the star said only "Amy."

Despite a few glitches, the Save Our Stages program was a smashing success. During the pandemic, so many people realized how much music and art were a part of the fabric of life of this country. They watched haunting videos of violinists playing alone on their front steps; orchestras combining Zoom screens and still making music; plays performed virtually. Not only did this get people through many a day and night, it also made them miss the live performances, the young artists appearing for the first time, the street musicians, the joy of sharing art and music and performances with other human beings.

When people asked us how our bill got to the front of the line, I answered like this: It was arts that got many of us through this pandemic, and a whole lot of people realized they didn't want to let the music (or theater or movies or museums, for that matter) die.[29]

29. "The day the music died" is a line in Don McLean's 1971 song "American Pie." It refers to the day in 1959 when, after performing at the Surf Ballroom in Clear Lake, Iowa (a place I have visited many times), Buddy Holly, Richie Valens, and J. P. Richardson—"The Big Bopper"—together with pilot

While the economic work—including the implementation of Save Our Stages—continued, the arrival of the Biden administration was marked by a serious effort, headed up in the White House by Jeff Zients, to take on the logistics of vaccine distribution[30] and more available and affordable testing, as well as a major education campaign to convince people to take the vaccines. Republican and Democratic leaders publicly got the shot and—before it all broke down into a weird right-wing attack on the vaccine—it felt in the early days like vaccines were going to be one source of nationwide agreement. After all, the vaccine had been developed during the Trump administration, and both President Trump and Vice President Mike Pence were publicly supportive of the vaccines and got the shots themselves. It might have helped if Donald Trump—like Joe Biden and Mike Pence—had allowed himself to be photographed while getting the vaccine, but that didn't happen.

More COVID legislation was also passed in 2021 under President Biden's leadership. With the Senate split between Democrats and Republicans 50/50, it only happened because of Vice President Harris's ability to cast a tie-breaking vote. Called the American Rescue Plan, the bill was a landmark piece of legislation that paid for the national vaccination program, lowered health-care costs for millions of Americans,

---

Roger Peterson, were killed in a plane crash near Clear Lake. The plane was bound for a concert in Moorhead, Minnesota.

30. While there were many creative outreach attempts on social media, I particularly enjoyed Dolly Parton's personal video, in which she promoted the vaccine with a song. She converted the words of her famous "Jolene" to "Vaccine," cajoled her fans with the reminder "Please don't hesitate," and ended the video with a smiling statement: "I want to say to all of you cowards out there, don't be such a chicken squat, go out there and get your shot."

put money in the pockets of families with children, extended unemployment benefits, saved many restaurants (in addition to the stages we had rescued the year before), gave state and local governments funding to retain teachers, firefighters, and police officers, and funded another—and a final—round of stimulus checks.

Once the Rescue Plan was passed and implemented, the virus and the pandemic didn't end, of course. In the fall of 2021 we were confronted by the Delta variant, and then, after that, the many stages of Omicron. Omicron was much less deadly for people with vaccinations, but it continued to hospitalize and take the lives of seniors, people with certain preexisting conditions, and unvaccinated people at alarming rates.

Much of what our nation's elected officials—particularly our governors—were doing at the beginning of the pandemic was very popular. Their "tough love" approach was welcomed by many. But as time wore on, the political headwinds got stronger. People resented the masks. They were tired of being cooped up at home. My governor, Tim Walz, like so many of the nation's governors, stepped into the breach and governed with competence and courage. A year later, Tim summed it all up for me at a time when politicians were confronted with both decreasing favorability ratings and the 2022 political dilemma of how to talk about all the good work that had been done: "When you save someone from drowning, they are forever grateful," he said, "they just don't want to hear you talk about it all the time."

Regardless of the challenges of the pandemic politics, like everyone else I found it helpful to have some self-awareness and a dose of good humor to make it through the "stay-at-home" era. In fact, I still have two giant quart-sized containers of pumpkin yogurt in my freezer as a frozen testament to my COVID online grocery ordering days. Of course I have long lost any interest in eating those gigantic containers of yogurt, and I am more than well aware that I should have thrown them away a long time ago. Yet they remain, greeting me every time I open the freezer, two frozen monuments to my having made it through the pandemic.

I was new to online grocery ordering when the pandemic started. I always seemed to *almost* order the right things. Sometimes the errors were mine, and sometimes they were the stores' slipups. The mega-potatoes that replaced normal ones—chalk that one up to Target. The weird automatic replacement items like large bouquets of wilted tulips and weirdly spiced granola, we'll put on Amazon. But by the fall of 2020 I thought I had it down, and my online ordering mishaps had gone down to a minimum. Feeling like I had reached a new level of competence when it came to online ordering, I truly rejoiced in October when I finally found online the pumpkin-spice-flavored yogurts I used to buy—and cherish—at our local Minneapolis grocery store. Having searched for weeks on multiple sites, I amazingly found an entry marked "Specialty item: pumpkin-spice yogurt." Stunned by my find, I exuberantly and quickly clicked to order four of them. The next day they arrived in all their glory. That's when I learned that I'd checked not four *five-ounce* containers, but four *quarts* of the yogurt. Yes, four QUARTS of specialty pumpkin yogurt.

It didn't end there. John and I were happy to take in our twenty-five-year-old daughter AND one of her friends (not to mention their extra laundry) for the summer of 2020. For the most part we welcomed the company and loved hanging out. But like many families who were reunited once again, there were many interesting "discussions" about WiFi and who had to go outside to use the internet while I was doing my Zooms with other senators or using the network for live national interviews. At one point I actually uttered these sentences: "Yes, I know you guys want to do the weekly online 'game night' with your friends, but I am going on Stephen Colbert with Mayor Pete and I can't risk your game-playing over-loading the WiFi. You have to go outside and find a public network."

Bandannas turned to pretty cloth masks to medical-grade blue ones to N95s. Even though my husband claimed his only long-haul symptom was an adverse reaction to cleaning out the basement, I continued to go down there and—as the pandemic refused to abate—waded through tons of old papers and baby clothes. I ordered sizable closet organizers (which John and Abigail constructed), and labeled an endless string of boxes. My husband and I explored Minnesota hiking trails we didn't even know existed, getting lost in swamps and on horse trails and seeing incredible river and lake views we never thought possible.

In the end, despite the silver linings of the completion of long-delayed projects, the beautiful walks, family pods, rejuvenated relationships, and time to reflect on one's true purpose, it is fair to say that so much of that time was pro-foundly sad for a lot of people, including the loneliness and the stories of those we lost and those whose lives were forever changed. So many tears were shed over missed weddings and funerals and canceled graduations and proms. That's why it is so easy—with so much of it now in the rearview mirror—to want to put it permanently out of our heads and simply look beyond it. Politically there is more than enough reason to do that as we all move on to the mounting challenges of today and tomorrow.

But for so many moral and human reasons, we must never forget.

## The Remains of the Day

As I write this, America has lost more than one million people to the virus. People are still dying of COVID in our country, albeit at a much slower rate. And in the world? Pandemic deaths are well over six and a half million and counting, with many countries still struggling with vaccine distribution and vaccination rates. Some of the loss just can't be measured (how can you put a price on never being able to call your mom again?), but some of it can be documented by hard numbers. Kids missed a lot of school, and many of them experienced learning losses that will be difficult, if not impossible, to regain. We had too many job openings before the pandemic, and now our workforce is further eroded by the tragic loss of hundreds of thousands of workers who died from COVID, even as others are dealing with long-haul symptoms and many more are experiencing a difficult adjustment to back-to-work life. Mental health problems are way up. There are worldwide supply chain issues and inflation. And the list goes on.

But what sometimes gets lost in all of this is the damage the pandemic—as well as the politicization of the federal, state, and local governments' response to it—has done to our collective sense of well-being and trust. In short, losing a million people makes you lose faith that we can get it right. This has all been exacerbated in the U.S. by a variety of factors, including our divided politics, Donald Trump and the January 6th, 2021, insurrection, disinformation on social media, economic and racial disparities, and a rise in crime. Many of these challenges were with us before COVID even landed on our shores, but the virus laid bare our country's political, economic, and cultural divides. It is on all of us to make it better.

The pandemic gave us some time to step back and think. It would be ironic indeed if we just closed our eyes and moved on. It's tempting to do that. But looking back at all of it gives us much greater insight into how we respond to its repercussions and how it changed us and the way we interact with each other both in the short and the long term. What follows are the "remains of the day." What matters is how we deal with it. In other words, we can't screw this up.

## 1. The economic hit and solutions

No country's economy emerged from this nearly three-year pandemic unscathed. There are supply chain issues and workforce problems. Some people sadly profited off of others' misfortunes (Exhibit A: the international shipping conglomerates charging four times the pre-pandemic amount for containers while making sevenfold the profit off the backs of American manufacturers, farmers, and, ultimately, consumers). And aside from the gut-wrenching heartache of it all, the large-scale loss of life, the long-haul symptoms and lifestyle disruptions, COVID has had major impacts on the world's workforce. Caused by a variety of factors, supply chain disruptions, millions of unfilled jobs, and inflation are all contributing to Americans' economic woes.

We also know that the virus wasn't evenhanded in its wrath.

The virus wasn't fair, not by a long shot. It hurt an inordinate number of seniors, people of color, frontline workers, and those working in health care. All of that should create an impetus for long-term political change within the health-care arena and out- side of it—from more and better housing and public transpor- tation to more available and affordable preschool and child care and elder care so people can return to work. Tax changes—like reversing the Trump tax cuts for the wealthy and dialing up the corporate tax rate to, say, 25 percent—could pay for it. While placing a minimum 15 percent tax on major corporations that weren't paying taxes was passed as part of the Inflation Reduc- tion Act in the summer of 2022, bringing up the corporate rate and reversing the extreme portions of the Trump tax cuts would raise much-needed revenue, with part of it designated for debt reduction.

Immigration reform to allow more workers to legally join our workforce and incentives to encourage students and existing workers to enter fields where we need the help would also be a positive for our economy. Taking on monopolies and corporate consolidation, which has exacerbated our consumer price and supply chain issues, is a big undertaking but would yield many long-term benefits. Improving our country's infrastructure and transitioning to clean energy must happen. The bipartisan in- frastructure bill and the Inflation Reduction Act that we passed were good; now we need to both implement them and build on them.

For the sake of our economic future and our social fabric, we also have to get the right balance between remote and in-person work. During the pandemic, so many people worked from their homes and apartments. We had parents trying to balance their laptops on their desks and their toddlers on their laps. We had first graders at home learning how to use the "mute" button (which I still maintain they do a lot better than U.S. senators).

At the same time there were millions of people in our country, across a range of jobs, who kept working as usual throughout the pandemic, at hospitals and nursing homes and construction sites, on farms and ranches and in food processing plants, in fire departments and police precincts, at warehouses, ports, and supermarkets. They went to work every day. And they still do.

For so many reasons, we have to acknowledge the change in the concept of work for certain employees and industries—and similarly understand that, at the same time, for a great number of workers, things have pretty much remained the same. The good news? Some people now have much more flexibility with work-from-home schedules. The challenges and opportunities? Post-pandemic, how will we continue to maintain this flexibility for parents and workers whose jobs allow it? How will the expansion of online class offerings change post-secondary education? Without some equilibrium between working in person and at home, what if coworkers never—or very rarely—see each other in person? What will it mean for urban—and even midsized and small-town—ecosystems, from cafes to theaters to retail establishments? What about the new employees who need to understand a workplace culture or have a mentor or be trained hands-on? What about honest personnel discussions and friendships and making sure things don't fall through the cracks? What about the effect on those frontline workers who are required to go physically into work every day? Will we need more incentives to keep them in those jobs, and if we don't provide them, will they leave their frontline work and choose instead to work at home from a perpetual Zoom screen?

We will eventually sort all of this out, but as a country we must acknowledge the broader societal implications of remote vs. in-person vs. hybrid work and craft both private and public sector policies that work for everyone.

## 2. Being prepared for the next one

As all the COVID variants have shown us—as well as the last decade with Ebola, Zika, and mpox—this isn't just going away. One of the things Washington, D.C. does not do well is tackle tough issues BEFORE they become urgent. When it comes to a future pandemic response, that means putting more resources into disease monitoring and vaccine research—even and especially when we aren't in the middle of an outbreak.

We've seen the benefits of investing in science. There is a direct line between the decades of research into the potential of mRNA vaccines and the unprecedented speed at which the scientific community developed effective vaccines that greatly reduce the severity and the mortality rate of the coronavirus. Thanks to my colleagues Senator Patty Murray and former Senator Richard Burr, provisions from their 2022 legislation, the PREVENT Act, will go a long way toward preventing the next pandemic. Continuing to make these kinds of investments will put us in a much better place going forward.

As we saw throughout the pandemic, a continual U.S. presence in international coordination and planning not only gains our country goodwill, but saves lives at home. The more we can work with governments and scientists in other countries on mutual health issues, the better off we will be. By its nature, so much of this building-block work must be done in the "off years," before a new virus strikes. And sadly, as we know from scientists like Minnesota's own Dr. Michael Osterholm, it's most likely only a matter of time before a new health crisis hits.

The coronavirus also revealed some serious gaps in our public health infrastructure, including lack of personnel (as noted repeatedly by Bill Gates, who—along with Melinda Gates—was way ahead of so many leaders on this) and, in some cases, protocols. Michael Lewis's book *The Premonition* is a worthwhile, quick read about the consequences of good—and bad—planning, as well as the importance of not only a better-functioning Centers for Disease Control and Prevention, but workable health infrastructure and plans, all the way down the line to the local level. Continual investment in and the use of telehealth is also critical. For many people telehealth made it possible to get medical care without straining hospital capacity during the pandemic or increasing their risk of disease exposure. We also saw the huge potential telehealth has to help people access both routine and specialized medical care outside the context of a pandemic. Telehealth has already proven to be hugely beneficial for rural America, and we need to continue building on this progress.

Then there is the issue of well-stocked emergency supplies and immediate implementable plans when we do need supplies. We don't want to be a country where our doctors and nurses are left to fight novel diseases in antiquated surgical masks and gloves. The federal government must invest in the Strategic National Stockpile so we can adequately safeguard our health-care professionals, as well as the people they serve. One way to ensure that the stockpiled items do not expire is to create a public-private stockpile partnership so that the private sector keeps rotating the medical ventilators, masks, drugs, and other supplies and selling and replacing them at regular intervals. As noted by experts, including Dr. Gianrico Farrugia, the head of the Mayo Clinic, this partnership would be a smart way to make sure that the national stockpile will always have the latest technology and nonexpired items. In addition, we must make sure that our supply chain for medical equipment is resilient enough to deliver through a global pandemic. That means building relationships with allies while manufacturing our own supplies here at home.

Finally, as discussed in greater detail below, this pandemic put a magnifying glass on the stark reality that disinformation is a public health issue. Viral social media content raised skepticism about the effectiveness of masks at a time when they were people's best defense against the coronavirus. And to this day, there are people refusing lifesaving vaccines because of lies they read or see on digital platforms like Twitter, Facebook, and YouTube. Combating disinformation must be a key part of any future pandemic response plan.

## 3. Frustration, anger, depression, and how to restore trust

During the pandemic, the countless contagion-related decisions people had to make every day and the ever-looming possibility of making the wrong one grated on their sense of control. Those everyday, seemingly minuscule but hard-to-answer questions, as well as the loneliness and disconnect so many experienced at the time, wore on all of us.

Like many, I was constantly questioning what the best decision was for me and my family. It was like I went through a grocery list of personal health decisions each and every day, many best suited for a medical professional:

> *Since the rules just changed for the eighth time and I don't remember what they are, mask or unmask?*
> *Eat outside or inside?*
> *Hug, handshake, or elbow bump?*
> *Moderna or Pfizer?*
> *Test or no test?*
> *Did I do the test right?*

*Should I try to move my seat on the plane instead of sitting next to that coughing guy?*

*Should we go see my dad or just do FaceTime?*

*Can we send him presents?*

*Should we wear a face shield at his assisted living place?*

*How do we get a face shield?*

*Should our daughter risk coming home for Christmas?*

*Can we bear it if she doesn't?*

*Is my husband going to make it?*

*Is my dad going to make it?*

*Did I pick the right doctor?*

*Did we pick the right hospital?*

*Should I have a work meeting in person or do it by Zoom?*

*Should I fly?*

*Should I take an Uber?*

*Should I go into the Senate chamber when Rand Paul isn't wearing a mask?*

*Is Ted Cruz contagious?*

*What would Dr. Fauci do?*

The answers to these questions varied with time. And as I knew from my own experience, one wrong decision (like the drink my husband had with a friend) could potentially cost you your life. The psychological helplessness of all of that got into people's heads. Losing our most vulnerable—the elders who raised us, the grandmas and grandpas to our kids—also unmoored us. Coming to grips with not even being there to say goodbye to a mom or dad or grandma or grandpa makes you feel guilty even if it happened only because of the pandemic and the hospital rules.

It was also incredibly hard on so many parents with children at home as they struggled to do multiple jobs: doing their paid work from home or away, raising their kids with little or no child care and limited school access, helping their relatives. The sheer disconnection between some people working way too hard in dangerous conditions and some people working from the comfort of home also created a lot of resentment. The loneliness was omnipresent. Suicides and drug overdoses spiked, and so many young people became depressed. While there is no denying the long-term impact the pandemic had on our economy and lifestyles, our psyches also suffered.

That's why I wasn't surprised that when we emerged from the worst of it, there was a lot of pent-up anger. It was just festering as the months went on, creeping into people's thoughts, and then, once those ready-to-blow-up people got out there with other people, it was too late to rewind. Maybe that wouldn't have happened if the pandemic had lasted only six weeks, or even six months. But after about a year, things changed.

In all my years in politics, I have never had so many people just randomly yell at me on the street, for many different reasons. I heard the same thing from my colleagues. The anger wasn't necessarily coming from one political point of view or another. People were just mad and recognized someone to yell at, but I'm pretty sure that they also yelled at perfect strangers for nonpolitical reasons, like waiting too long in line at a store or getting cut off in a turn lane. Anything could set certain people off. At one point a seemingly normal-looking person in the Minneapolis-St. Paul airport started yelling at me down the gateway, "Blood on your hands, Senator, blood on your hands!"

Another guy chased down Senator Ossoff and me in a restaurant and claimed we were having dinner with a lobbyist. "We aren't doing that, man," we said with some amusement. "We are alone at a table . . . There are only two of us."

"Yes, you two are sitting with a lobbyist," he said insistently, flipping his phone out to record his voice and then repeating the absolutely untrue assertion: "You two are sitting with a lobbyist."

From everyday frustrations in checkout lines and parking lots to serious threats against—and attacks on—local officials, emerging from the pandemic was certainly not the sweet rosy embrace we hoped it would be. I am not arguing here that the cause of all of that violence was the pandemic. Far from it. Nor am I saying that all of the anger manifested itself in physically harmful activity. Most of it didn't. I am simply saying that all the pandemic-related isolation made it more difficult to catch people with problems, and that meant their anger fermented and got scarier and scarier. People spent days on their own on the internet without any human contact. And many of them—when they came out of their solo pods—just started saying and doing things that they either read about or posted online themselves. In other words, when the real world finally intervened in their previously anonymous online world, all hell broke loose.

The answers to all of it? In addition to the obvious solution of getting people the help they need for their mental health issues and addictions (the bipartisan gun safety bill we passed in 2022 included over $8 billion for mental health, which should be very helpful), we must also build faith and trust that we can fix things for people again. That means federal, state, and local governments that can function and respond to their needs. That means some honesty about what we can do and what we can't do.

We also need to start operating off a shared set of facts and take on the issue of people's exposure to disinformation. To recapture people's trust in our institutions we should make it easier, not harder, to vote. We should work toward transparency and stop the spread of untruths about our elections. We must put rules in place to limit disinformation and hate online and hold those who profit off it accountable. We must change the U.S. Senate rules so we can pass laws that track the challenges of our time and more quickly confirm a president's team, radical idea that it is. We must respond to the needs of our constituents without fear or favor.

But it isn't only government's responsibility. All of our institutions, big and small—from businesses to religious institutions to nonprofits—must do all they can to bring people together again. That means asking them to actually, physically, join in—from parades to sporting and civic events to guest speakers at work to pancake breakfasts. That means seeing each other again in person. It means looking up at each other instead of down at our phones.

All of it matters.

Politics in a democracy is part purpose, part advocacy, but what overlays all of it is a belief in the collective good. Chat rooms and Zoom screens and social media platforms can be great, but they are not a complete substitute for civic engagement. Civic engagement means learning something new from someone you usually wouldn't talk to unless you were in the company break room; going to a parade to see your kid in the band and meeting your local legislator who you thought was a jerk but turns out to be okay; seeing your mayor at a soccer game and being able to talk to her about the need for a stop sign on the corner; and seeing your U.S. senator at her state fair booth (that would be me). For people who are the most involved and have the time, civic participation also means door knocking and volunteering and attending meetings and forums. That's still a core part of a functioning democracy.

The question becomes whether we are resilient enough as a country to move out of our too often joyless politics to a new elevation on the mountaintop. We can't easily go back to the old plateaus, as comfortable as they were, but we can commit ourselves to shared facts and better respect for each other. A lot of this has to do with how we emerge from this pandemic. Can we venture out of our comfort zones and escape our pods and see each other again? Can we look up from our phones and see each other? Can we check some of the anger, stop some of the snark, and clamp down on the cynicism? As *Washington Post* conservative columnist Kirsten Powers noted in her recent book, *Saving Grace*, we need to speak our truth, "stay centered," and "learn to coexist with people who drive you nuts."

**4. Protecting the truth (and holding up the truth-sayers)**
One last time from Camus's *The Plague*:

> "Here but again and again there comes a time in history when the man who dares to say that two and two make four is punished with death. The schoolteacher is aware of this. And the question is not one of knowing what punishment or reward attends the making of this calculation. The question is one of knowing whether two and two do make four."

"Punished with death" for telling the truth? Lest you think I have gotten too melodramatic, oh yes, it still happens today. The haunting audio recording of the grisly murder of

*Washington Post* journalist Jamal Khashoggi in the Saudi consulate in Turkey; dissidents imprisoned and killed in China; journalists who are victims of car bombs and shot down around the world; the foes of Vladimir Putin poisoned and eliminated or, like two major opposition leaders/dissidents—Alexei Navalny and Vladimir Kara-Murza—sent to rot in prisons away from public view with post-poisoning indeterminate sentences. The death of Mahsa Amini in the hands of Iran's "morality police" for breaking hijab rules.

Then there is the American political version of castigating the truth teller: political death by a thousand cuts (or more aptly tweets, censures, and denouncements). So many of my colleagues—like Arizona Republican Senator Jeff Flake and Nebraska Senator Ben Sasse—are no longer able to run for re-election in today's Republican Party simply because they felt the moral compunction to directly criticize Donald Trump or they had the audacity to find common ground on the issues of our day. Liz Cheney and Mitt Romney were censured by their own parties for denouncing an insurrection, with Cheney losing her primary. Chris Krebs—the former head of Trump's Homeland Security division with jurisdiction over election protection—declared the 2020 election the safest in American history and was then promptly fired from his job. From U.S. ambassador to Ukraine Marie Yovanovitch to Lieutenant Colonel Alexander Vindman, there are multiple examples of American diplomats and military leaders being publicly humiliated and forced out of their positions simply because they spoke truth to power.

During the pandemic, people were repeatedly exposed to false information and anti-vaccine rhetoric online. Doctors told me that patients would sit in their offices spouting fanciful horror stories about the vaccine that they had read on the internet instead of listening to their longtime physician's medical advice. While the social media companies made an effort to take down falsehoods and untrue accounts (much of it at my and others' urging), to say the damage was done already is a gross understatement. In fact, in the first crucial months after the vaccines came out, a news story implying that the COVID vaccine was somehow involved in the death of a doctor was the most viewed link on Facebook in the first quarter of 2021 (information that was contained in a report that Facebook shelved for months). According to a report the company later released, the questionable post about the doctor was viewed by a whopping fifty-four million U.S. users. In addition, in March of 2021 National Public Radio found that on almost half the days in the first few months of 2021, a story about someone dying after receiving a vaccine was among the most popular vaccine-related articles on social media.

Taking on misleading information or downright falsehoods—especially when those allowing the falsities to spread are big established interests—has its costs, but we must meet the moment. The last few decades have been filled with stories of whistleblowers and mavericks standing up to power and telling the truth: from former Brown & Williamson tobacco executive Jeffrey Wigand's blowing the whistle on the tobacco industry for hiding the undeniable fact that cigarettes were in fact addictive to lawyer Rob Bilott's case against the DuPont chemical company for hiding the knowledge that its chemicals were poisoning people to former Facebook employee Frances Haugen's chilling testimony about how Facebook's algorithms knowingly subject young people to all kinds of really bad stuff, including exposing teenagers to content that glorifies eating disorders.

While all of these David vs. Goliath stories make for great TV and movies, most of them don't come with fairy-tale endings.

For elected officials daring to do something brave and take on the special interests, the water is even murkier. When my friends Democratic Senator Mark Warner and former Republican Senator Bob Corker stood up together to set some new rules of the road for a segment of the financial industry, they—along with other members of the bipartisan coalition backing their legislation—were relentlessly attacked by special interest groups that criticized them in the press and on the airwaves. Elizabeth Warren has been attacked repeatedly for doing the same.

And for those of us willing to take on Big Tech when not one piece of competition legislation has passed since the advent of the internet to rein in these all-powerful companies? That's one of the hardest arenas of them all.[31] Believe me, I know. The Big Tech companies employ and contract out with thousands and thousands of lawyers and lobbyists. Several of these companies also have the ability to use their own monopoly platforms to stage attacks.

---

31. At one point Facebook actually hired a Republican consulting firm called Definers Public Affairs to take on senators from both sides of the aisle who served on the Senate Intelligence Committee for taking political contributions from—gasp, get this—their very own company. Why? They were trying to get the general public to question the elected officials' credibility before they held a hearing that the company didn't like. Surely the senators were hypocrites if they had taken a $2,500 PAC check from Facebook and then questioned the company in any critical manner. At least that was the logic.

And then there are the ads. In 2022, four of the Big Tech monopolies (Amazon, Apple, Facebook, and Google) spent well over $150 million in negative ads against my bipartisan tech competition bill. By the third quarter of 2022 they had exceeded any other industry's spending on lobbying ads! That even beat pharma's endless national spending on negative ads against my provision to allow Medicare to negotiate better prices for prescription drugs. As my husband said to my daughter one day when she was visiting us in Minnesota, "Be nice to your mom this weekend. She has the biggest companies the world has ever known going after her and she was just banned from Russia."

The policy answers? There are many, but they include limits on monopoly power; more transparency on the algorithms; federal privacy legislation; liability for knowingly amplifying false information (with a standard that fits the tech ecosystem and full or partial removal of the immunity provisions under what's known as Section 230 of federal law); lifting up unbiased fact sources; and making sure we literally don't lose the news (another tech-related problem related to local news outlet closures and ad revenue).

But it isn't only policy changes that matter. Holding up the truth tellers and finding the heroes who rise above the muck has never been more important. That's why Facebook whistleblower Frances Haugen was heralded by both Democrats and Republicans. That's why Liz Cheney captured the nation's attention with her willingness to meticulously make the case that the insurrection wasn't just a family picnic in the park or a group of tourists at the Capitol but instead a violent assault on our democracy. That's why President Volodymyr Zelenskyy caught a cynical world by surprise when he defiantly stood in the streets of Kyiv and spoke out against the inhuman barbarism of Vladimir Putin with the simple words, "We are here."

And that's why, in the context of the pandemic, Dr. Anthony Fauci emerged as an unexpected folk hero, his work having spanned multiple administrations from Ronald Reagan to Joe Biden. With his concrete COVID medical advice, Dr. Fauci was so clear in his mission that he was literally unflappable (save for a few clap backs at congressional hearings; to my mind, battling Rand Paul would drive anyone temporarily off the deep end).

Dr. Fauci stood calmly before the nation—despite the threats on his life and the "Fire Fauci" Trump rally chants—and simply said, to paraphrase Camus, two plus two DOES equal four. Wear a mask. Get a vaccine. Get a booster. It can save your life.

Yet in the pre-vaccine year of 2020, as the public grew more desperate and Election Day came closer, Donald Trump repeatedly undermined Dr. Fauci's and other experts' public health recommendations, desperately peddling all kinds of dangerous and despicable lies—from drinking bleach to using ultraviolet rays as a treatment. At one point in June 2020, during a rally in Tulsa, then-President Trump even publicly refuted the total number of COVID cases by stating: "If we didn't do testing, we'd have no cases."

Yet Dr. Fauci, the indefatigable (and yes, even merry)[32] wise man, served as the truth-sayer, the explainer-in-chief. Maybe it was his background and résumé. He is the son of a pharmacist. He attended Regis High in Brooklyn and captained

---

32. Dr. Fauci is still the only guy who at the ripe old age of eighty got to be played by Brad Pitt on *Saturday Night Live*.

the high school basketball team despite being only five-foot-seven. He went to Holy Cross for college and Cornell for medical school. He joined the National Institutes of Health (NIH), where he conducted research on the immune system and rare diseases. He is an AIDS expert and became one of the main architects of George W. Bush's President's Emergency Plan for AIDS Relief (PEPFAR). An author of well over a thousand journal articles and an adviser to six U.S. presidents, he was a public health leader during the SARS, Zika, and Ebola outbreaks.

Yet at a time of deep national discontent, Dr. Fauci stood tall for science. He was far more than a heavily résuméd expert. He was a savior. A teacher. And at times simply a calming presence. The answers Dr. Fauci once gave to *The New York Times* sum it all up for anyone that's in a tough job but knows they have a duty to stay there:

QUESTION: Did you ever think about quitting?
ANSWER: Never. Never. Nope.
QUESTION: Were you concerned that you would be blamed for the failures if you didn't resign?
ANSWER: When people just see you standing up there, they sometimes think you're being complicit in the directions emanating from the stage. But I felt that if I stepped down, that would leave a void.

Dr. Fauci saw his purpose, even in the darkest days with Donald Trump. He rose to the occasion. He was resilient and centered in the middle of one of the worst crises our nation and the world have ever faced. He emanated confidence and actually seemed to like his work.

Resiliency—with Dr. Fauci as its medical standard-bearer—is truly one of the major lessons to be learned from the pandemic. Thanks to science and good medicine and, yes, some fearless frontline workers, to borrow from President Zelenskyy, we are still here.

## 4

# The Reckoning

Life Lesson: *"In every life, there comes a day of reckoning—a time when unsettled scores demand retribution, and our own lies and transgressions are finally laid bare."*

—EMILY THORNE, FICTIONAL CHARACTER
ON THE ABC TV SERIES *REVENGE*

I wasn't an avid fan of the 2011–2015 series *Revenge*.[33] In fact, I was completely unaware of its existence until one of those pandemic "What else am I going to watch at midnight and my husband has gone to bed and he would really hate this show?" moments. Nor, despite my profession, do I like—or am I very good at—ACTUAL revenge, or its prerequisite: holding a grudge.

But reckonings? I like those. I am always up for a tanta-

---

33. Just in case you haven't caught the show *Revenge*, it's about a young woman obsessed with settling scores with those who destroyed her family after they sent her hedge fund manager dad to prison based on false accusations that he channeled money to a terrorist organization that downed a jetliner. The story is allegedly based on the Alexandre Dumas novel *The Count of Monte Cristo*, written in 1844, when they didn't have hedge fund managers—or jetliners.

lizing laying bare of "lies and transgressions" and its accompanying "retribution" for "unsettled scores."[34]

And while I may not have been a *Revenge* fan, I love the "reckoning" quote. It succinctly sums up the "what comes around, goes around" life lesson of "reckonings." Its sheer Mafia-like verbiage truly describes the "reckoning" Donald Trump faced with eighty-one-million-plus American voters on November 3, 2020, as well as his continued reckoning two years later when Chair Bennie Thompson gaveled to order the United States House Select Committee to Investigate the January 6th Attack on the U.S. Capitol just as a series of civil and criminal state and federal investigations into Trump's conduct heated up in New York City, Washington, D.C., and Atlanta. And then there was the voters' rejection of so many of his election-denying endorsed candidates in the 2022 midterms, from the U.S. Senate to secretary of state races across the country. The voters simply said, "No thank you."

The other appealing thing about the *Revenge* quote? I figure we can't neglect an entire modern medium when it comes to life lessons. We can't rely only on Nobel Prize winners for guidance. They don't come around too often. TV series, on the other hand? There are a lot of them. And, as if you need another reminder, you start where you are, whether your head's in a book or your eyes are on a screen.

Like many Americans, during those endless homebound pandemic late nights, I binge-read books and binge-watched

---

34. See House of Representatives summer of 2022, January 6th hearings. Thanks, Bennie Thompson. Thanks, Liz Cheney and the rest of the January 6th Select Committee.

both miniseries and—for lack of a better description—maxi-series. I started with *Ted Lasso* and *Mare of Easttown* and the new *Perry Mason*. They were really good. I happily watched *The Queen's Gambit* (wondering how my life would have been different if I played chess or had red hair), *The Plot Against America* (yes, it could happen here), and *The Gilded Age*. I re-watched season one of *True Detective* for the sole reason that I very much like Matthew McConaughey and Woody Harrel-son since I already knew how it ended (and it wasn't pretty).

But then my "Matthew Rhys was so good in *Perry Mason*" obsession led me down some rabbit holes that I would NEVER have gone down during a nonviral time. I watched Rhys in *The Americans*—an addictive Cold War drama in which two Russian sleeper cell spies go undercover as a married couple in Northern Virginia (and yes, in the end, Matthew Rhys and Keri Russell really got married, both in the series and in real life).

After that, completely unleashed and still following the trajectory of murder and mayhem, my long-standing admiration for the Minnesota-born Coen brothers—and their movies—naturally (at this point) led me to check out what other films or series actor Steve Buscemi had starred in. That seemingly minor googling episode set me on a long trek involving lots of graphic violence warnings, as in the Al Capone–era series *Boardwalk Empire*. In fact, I liked the show's lead-in and music so much—and, in particular, the sand from the beach in gang-ster "Nucky" Thompson's two-toned wing-tip shoes—that I never once skipped through the opening credits.

On the political end of the reckoning spectrum, after catching up on the remaining episodes of *Madam Secretary* (my favorite) and Shonda Rhimes's ultimate reckoning show

*Scandal* (what can I say?), I took a turn. After *Billions* and *The Crown* and *Yellowstone* and its prequel miniseries *1883* (a lengthy foray that was triggered when an old lady in the Atlanta airport mistook me for the actress who plays the Montana governor in *Yellowstone* . . . I WISH), I had no choice but to turn to the Danish miniseries *Borgen*, which I watched in dubbed-in English. I would highly recommend it to anyone who likes Nordic light fixtures and wants to know what it is really like to balance political office, family, and hot flashes (see season 4, Greenland episodes; see chapter 1 of this book).

Branching off into some delicious but suitably dark Nicole Kidman series felt like a low point. Not because of her—hair, makeup, voice, clothes, serenity . . . she is the real deal—and not actually because of the content, which keeps you interested. It was just that the plot lines were so diabolical that they didn't really feel like an escape from my day job. And the titles were also just too close to the truth: *Big Little Lies* (HELLO Washington!); *The Undoing* (HELLO Washington again!); and *Nine Perfect Strangers* (okay, that could be a Supreme Court analogy . . . as in nine—correction: six—perfect strangers decide what you can do with your body).

But for non–miniseries constituents who are now truly concerned about my grounding as their U.S. senator and how I spend my leisure time, please note: (1) I have never gotten much sleep and am just one of those people who enjoys being awake; (2) the male leaders spend much more time watching sporting events, trust me on that; (3) I still work really hard at my job; (4) watching that stuff during the pandemic made me MORE grounded (at least that's what I told myself); and (5) my now-concluded pandemic-era obsession with the likes of *Little Fires Everywhere* and *The White Lotus* also featured the viewing of extraordinary documentaries/nonfiction shows like Barack Obama's *Our Great National Parks*; David Letterman's *My Next Guest Needs No Introduction* interviews; and Ken Burns's *Benjamin Franklin, Hemingway, The Central Park Five,* and *Lewis & Clark*. And yes, I rewatched *John Adams* (even though it was admittedly a little jarring to watch Paul Giamatti switch from playing U.S. Attorney Chuck Rhoades in *Billions* to portraying a founding father).

But I digress. Back to the matter at hand.

"In every life, there comes a day of reckoning—a time when unsettled scores demand retribution, and our own lies and transgressions are finally laid bare."

The American 2020 reckoning meant a lot of different things to different people. There is the obvious: the reckoning for Donald Trump, his sins and transgressions laid bare for all to see—the blatant lies, the corruption and self-dealing, the crazy meandering rants, the House impeachment. And, despite Trump's ultimate impeachment acquittals by the Senate both in 2020 and in January of 2021, the clear revulsion directed his way from a majority of Americans across the land was a direct affront, laid bare courtesy of the 2020 election. A record number of citizens voted that year in the middle of the biggest public health crisis in our lifetimes. And Donald Trump? He lost the election by seven million votes, including in several states he had won only four years before, as in Wisconsin, Pennsylvania, Michigan, Arizona, and Georgia.

While the voters had many reasons to throw out Trump in 2020, the true nature of his sins—and the punctuation mark on his reckoning—were not actually laid bare until nearly two years later. Then, just when everyone thought they'd lost interest, the House of Representatives' Committee hearings dramatically made the case that democracy and telling the truth actually do matter, followed by the 2022 midterms where election-deniers lost across the country.

Liz Cheney's tenacity and courage in prosecuting the case against Donald Trump and her perfectly scripted odes to our democracy, as well as the jaw-dropping revelations from former White House aide Cassidy Hutchinson and other Republican witnesses, reinforced what so many Americans already knew by the time they voted in 2020: Donald Trump is a bad guy. He's not just some bombastic reality TV star with shady business deals in his past. He's a really bad guy. He's flouted the law, lied to the American people, and incited an insurrection, thereby endangering the Capitol police officers and food service workers and janitors who work day in and day out on behalf of the American people.

But Donald Trump wasn't the only one with "transgressions laid bare" in 2020. As covered in the last chapter, there was also the ongoing reckoning of the pandemic, where years of underinvestment in public health and international epidemiology as well as our country's ongoing political chasms contributed to a much more deadly—and an ultimately more economically damaging—bout with the virus.

And of course—front and center—was the reckoning triggered by the murder of George Floyd in my state. After Floyd's murder in Minneapolis at the hands of police officers, protests swept across the nation—and indeed, the world—as people expressed outrage not only in response to George Floyd's murder, but also about the many other police-related shootings and deaths in multiple states. People wanted the racism to end. They wanted accountability. And they protested across the world to demand it.

Many other political and policy challenges confronted the nation, all bearing a big "IOU" sign when it came to federal action. The Trump-era deliberate backsliding on climate change is one example. A reckoning on climate is here, right before our eyes, with rising temperatures, melting icebergs, raging forest fires, and devastating floods. Severe weather events are in fact the predictable product of global warming. As someone once told me, it's like every time the newscasters call a hurricane, flood, or storm a "once in 100 years" weather phenomenon, Mother Nature looks down, shakes her head, and says, "Hold my beer."

The widening income disparities in the U.S. and other countries have also created predictable reckonings within our political systems, with rent and homeownership and savings becoming more and more out of reach for so many people. And while wages have gone up post-pandemic, long-festering cost-of-living issues—including the price of pharmaceuticals—as well as the lack of serious legislative response to monopoly power and corporate consolidation have furthered people's frustrations and economic woes.

Then, finally, there is the ongoing reckoning of years of a full-out methodical Republican master plan to stack the U.S. Supreme Court with extremely conservative and out-of-the-mainstream justices. This strategy was hatched among the Federalist Society, Leonard Leo, and Republican politicians long before Donald Trump, but his election victory was the key to its ultimate success. The hubris of this plan—including its brazen, bare-knuckles politics—has resulted in a Court hell-bent on reversing long-standing precedent on abortion, gun policy, and voting rights.

Thus we face challenges on multiple fronts, and in a number of places around the globe the world is literally on fire.

Other than that, everything is fine.

## "When Someone Shows You Who They Are, Believe Them the First Time."[35]

On January 20, 2017, Donald Trump was inaugurated as President of the United States. I sat between John McCain and Bernie Sanders on the inaugural stage. I had returned from a trip with John and Lindsey Graham to Ukraine and four other Baltic states only a few weeks before. This trip wasn't a coincidence. McCain was well aware of Trump's ties to Russia, and he planned the trip right after Trump won and in advance of his inauguration to make the point to our allies that America stands with these proud Eastern European countries and their democracies against the tyranny of Vladimir Putin. The countries that bordered Russia—as events later revealed—had every reason to be concerned about further Russian expansion.

That trip I took with Senator McCain is forever etched in my memory, not only for its obvious political symbolism, but because it was among McCain's final trips after decades of leadership on the world stage. One and one-half years later, we lost him to a brain tumor.

The irony of sitting between John and Bernie—two

---

35. The poet Maya Angelou said this in an interview with Oprah Winfrey in 1997. Winfrey has said it was her most important life lesson.

unique friends of mine from completely different sides of the political spectrum—was not lost on me or on either of them. Both had run unsuccessfully for president. They couldn't have been more different in so many ways, but they had one thing in common: they loved our country and disdained Donald Trump. They both knew that what they did for the one hour of that inauguration mattered. They both knew that inaugural tradition required that they respectfully listen to the new President. In America, our national elected officials (save for one in 2020 who did all he could to cling to his power) stand by our government's peaceful transition of power, a tenet of our democracy that has been followed ever since George Washington turned over the reins of his office to the second United States President, John Adams.

There were many luminaries on the 2017 inaugural stage, including Hillary Clinton, who was there with her husband, former President Bill Clinton. Like John McCain, Hillary knew her role on that stage, one so much different than she had ever imagined when she started running for president two years before. It was especially tough because she had actually won the popular vote in 2016. Yet, just like Al Gore several elections before, she had lost the Electoral College vote—which is the vote total that matters for winning the presidency under our Constitution.

I like and respect Hillary very much and consider her a friend and mentor. She would have made a great president. So many things went wrong that election year, but once again, there she was, doing the right thing for all the right reasons. It was something straight out of a Shakespearean drama.

As we waited for the ceremony to begin, the clouds got grayer, the rain threatened, and Bernie was grumpy. If ever there was a day to be grumpy, this was it. John, on the other hand, was always up for some dark humor.

I remember him turning to me and saying with that impish smile as the guests filed onto the platform, "This Trump inauguration has already set one important record."

"What's that?" I asked.

"Most money ever spent on plastic surgery on an inaugural stage," he quipped.

I took a selfie of the three of us to commemorate the moment, never knowing that just a few years later we would lose John and that Bernie and I would be running against each other for president. It was a great photo, until a news organization took a picture of me taking the selfie and then posted it with the following caption: "A woman takes a selfie with Sen. John McCain (R-AZ) and Sen. Bernie Sanders (D-VT) on the West Front of the U.S. Capitol on January 20, 2017 in Washington D.C."

The photo and the post went viral, particularly during the Women's March the next day. Loads of people quote-tweeted the picture and the news organization's caption with comments like, "It was the 'senators-only' area, come on."

Or "Don't believe that sexism in politics is still a thing? That unidentifiable woman is SENATOR AMY KLOBU-CHAR with same title as Sanders/McCain."

And multiple times: "This is why we march."

Those amusing memories aside, what most sticks in my mind from that day was how horrified—speechless, really—the three of us were by Trump's dark rhetoric. It is all so vivid now: helping McCain put on his poncho[36] as the dark clouds unleashed rain onto the stage; Bernie looking down, so troubled by what we were hearing. As it went on all three of us acknowledged through gritted teeth that the speech, and most particularly certain phrases in the speech, were worse than we ever thought they would be. (Although my guess is that Bernie had predicted it would be just that bad.) The fact that Trump never even mentioned his opponent Hillary Clinton in his remarks—as she sat stoically right behind him there on stage—was a bad beginning. This was not a bury-the-hatchet, let's-work-together-to-unify-the-country moment. There was no salve, no attempt to put past grudges behind. It was just very, very dark.

The thing about America is that we believe in promise. We believe in hope. As ardently as the three of us didn't believe Donald Trump should be standing in front of that podium, as much as we abhorred his conduct during the campaign—from the "reach-outs" to Vladimir Putin, to grotesquely mocking a reporter with disabilities, to the sexist comments, to the xenophobic and hateful rhetoric, to the in-your-face lies, lies, and more lies at his rallies and on the debate stage—we wanted him to be so much better. Yet that day he was at best a coarsening force in our politics. And by

---

36. Because of John's POW injuries—inflicted at the hands of his torturers during his five-plus years of captivity in Vietnam—he couldn't raise his arm to comb his hair or pull on a non-buttoned-up raincoat. Needing help to put on a simple rain poncho due to war injuries was just one more piece of irony as John McCain sat there seething, listening to Donald Trump, who'd viciously attacked him the year before, claiming McCain was "not a war hero" because he'd been captured and held as a POW, even noting once "I like people that weren't captured."

the end of his term—and as history has shown us, by the end of that speech—he was corruption and demagoguery personified. He would do anything to anybody to get ahead.

With each and every word of the speech, John McCain—always the historian—started whispering to me under his breath the specific dates and places of speeches given by dictators and demagogues during the past century. Trump's phrases and words—"American carnage," "glorious destiny," "tombstones," and "Only America first; America first"—triggered it. Do I wish I had written McCain's words down the minute I left that platform? I do. But I didn't. I do remember this: John mentioned Mussolini. He mentioned Huey Long. He mentioned places and dates of speeches. He groaned and grimaced under his rain poncho.

John McCain knew more about what was about to happen to our country than any other person on that stage. He knew the evil that lurked behind the printed page from which Donald Trump read. He knew what we were in for.

And so many times over the next four years, I would recall McCain's virulent reaction. I felt like I lived a lifetime of vindicating his predictions: the heartless rhetoric, the corruption, the evisceration of opponents in the President's own party in addition to mine, the disrespect—the utter contempt—for our democracy. And I would add: the reckless economic policies that benefited the billionaires and multimillionaires at the expense of everyone else, the many attempts to strike down the Affordable Care Act, the Putin worship, the appointments of extreme Supreme Court justices, the never-ending lies.

To paraphrase Maya Angelou, when someone shows you who they are the first time, believe them.

When the speech ended, the three of us got up and walked out together. We all had a congressional lunch to go to with the new President and, as incoming ranking member of the Senate Rules Committee, I would be seated right next to the President's brother (who, for what it's worth, spent a good amount of time at that lunch asking my husband and me about our astrological signs).

As John, Bernie, and I walked down the corridor to the lunch, we ran into a couple of reporters. I remember we all had gone into the speech thinking that whatever happened, we would calibrate our responses in light of the moment. This was, after all, historically a day when party differences are put aside, when members of Congress try their best to put on brave faces and smile and pledge to work with a new administration. While later all three of us would comment on the speech, at that moment we didn't say much. We just kept walking.

But Donald Trump, he didn't lose any time. As women gathered in record numbers the day after the inauguration to march for their rights from Washington, D.C. to Denver to Seattle, Trump got to work. He visited the CIA in an effort to improve relations with agents after maligning their work during the campaign. His unfortunate choice—as the Women's March appeared on the TV split screen—was to hold a press conference in front of the sacred CIA memorial, the wall of anonymous stars for each agent lost in service to our country. Yes, Trump chose to go there. Standing directly in front of the memorial, he attacked the media for their estimate of his inaugural crowd size the day before. (As someone who was there, I can attest: Trump's crowd wasn't even half the size of Barack Obama's first inaugural . . . I had a front row seat to both.) Not stopping there, at his CIA press conference Trump even lied about the inauguration's weather, saying it stopped raining during his address. Again, I was there. It *started* raining during his address.

The CIA visit and the embarrassing tirade in front of the agency's hallowed wall may have gotten lost in the history of the Trump presidency. But not for me. I remember it in Technicolor. I remember watching it with my husband John right after I had come inside from the Women's March. Our President looked unhinged as he talked bitterly about crowd size in front of a wall of stars for heroes who had died in the line of duty. Any last vestige of hope I had that things might not be as bad as I thought they would be got smaller and smaller with each and every word coming out of his mouth. By the end, there was nothing left.

This was just wrong.

From there President Trump began putting the words and promises of his campaign rallies and inaugural speech into action. He immediately doubled down on his presidential campaign's obsessive grudge-holding. In his first meeting with Democratic and Republican leaders he made a point of continuing his false claims about illegal votes cast during the election. He dispatched Kellyanne Conway, his counselor, and Sean Spicer, his press secretary, to go on TV shows to claim that the media was wrong about his inaugural crowd size. It was on *Meet the Press* that Kellyanne memorably told Chuck Todd that there was such a thing as "alternative facts."

Of much more import, the President signed numerous harmful and irresponsible executive orders in just the first few weeks, including the reinstatement of the global "gag rule" prohibiting international organizations from getting federal funding if they provided or even spoke with patients about abortion services.

By the end of his first week in office he signed the mother of all executive orders: he blocked all travelers from entering the U.S.—including those preparing to come to our country as refugees—from seven majority-Muslim countries: Iraq, Iran, Syria, Yemen, Sudan, Libya, and Somalia. Protests ensued at airports across the country, including at airports that didn't even host international flights.

Constituent calls poured into my office from both international refugee organizations and individual families who were in the midst of adopting kids from these countries. The two cases I remember the most? One involved a mom, a Somali woman living in Minnesota. Before she came to my state, she was with her kids in a refugee camp in Kenya. That's where she had gained permission to come to my state as a refugee. The hitch? She had permission to bring only two kids, and she was pregnant with a third.

The mom had to decide between rejecting the refugee status offer for the family and staying in the camp with her two, and soon to be three, kids—for what would most likely be the rest of their lives—or leaving her newly born baby behind. In the end, she made the difficult choice to come to the U.S. with her two children after the baby was born and place the child she didn't have permission to bring to the U.S. with friends at the refugee camp. But the minute she landed on our soil, she started to work with Minnesota's Lutheran Social Services (now there's a radical group) to bring her third child to the U.S.

It had taken years, but in 2016 she had finally been granted permission. It was in the works, and the child was ready to get on a plane in January of 2017 with an escort to join the rest of her family in Minnesota. Then Trump issued the refugee ban. I remember calling General John Kelly (then Trump's new appointee to head up Homeland Security) to plead for help on the case. My fellow Minnesota Senator Al Franken, did the same. In the end—in just a few weeks—we got the child exempted from the Trump ban. The little girl boarded the plane bound for America, where my constituent services head, Clara Haycraft—who had worked extensively on the case—stood with the family in the airport as the child arrived. There were tears of joy all around.

The other case? It was another adoption, this time out of Lebanon. A family from Mankato, Minnesota, had been in Lebanon for months trying to cut through the red tape to get an orphan out of a Lebanese camp and bring him home as their adopted child. While Lebanon wasn't on Trump's list, Syria was, and this child was Syrian. On this delicate problem I called our ambassador in Lebanon and pled the case, and against all odds she found a way to place the child on a flight with his new family. I still remember the mom telling me that she put the baby in an American flag–themed, red-white-and-blue sweater for his long journey, just in case he got stopped at customs because of the ban.

But those two success stories were the rare ones, to be sure. So many other constituents and Muslim families across our nation lived through heart-wrenching experiences of families separated and dreams dashed due to Trump's Muslim ban. In the end, courts would dramatically delay and alter that order, as well as some of the other mean-spirited Trump immigration and refugee policies. Sometimes the President's people would change them themselves.

But unfortunately, the President was just getting warmed up. By September he had his attorney general, Jeff Sessions, announce that they were ending protections for DREAMers, reversing the Obama program that shielded from deportation undocumented immigrants who had come to America as children, many of whom had lived in our nation for years. The President also instituted a new policy of separating undocumented kids from their parents at the border, which created such chaos and heartbreaking stories that he later backed down.

On the national security front, Trump appointed his controversial right-wing message guru Steve Bannon to be a permanent member of the National Security Council, the key advisory group on all matters related to U.S. security. Traditionally this group includes the director of national intelligence, the secretary of state, secretary of defense, secretary of energy, and the chairman of the Joint Chiefs of Staff, among others. It doesn't include people who have no particular national security expertise, title, or role. Bannon's title was "White House chief strategist," whatever that meant. I still remember telling former Senator and Secretary of State John Kerry about the Bannon appointment at an event after the Washington, D.C. Alfalfa Club dinner, which that year included both Ivanka Trump and Jared Kushner among its guests. I had read the breaking news about Bannon online. Kerry just didn't believe me, left, and then came back a few minutes later. "You were right," he said.

Another campaign promise? President Trump took America out of the Obama-European-negotiated Iran nuclear agreement, which I, along with many Democrats, had supported. Given that one of our nation's most significant foreign policy goals is to keep nuclear weapons out of the hands of Iran, and despite the fact that the agreement wasn't perfect, I don't think we have ended up in a better position with Trump's decision. We are now in a far worse place.

As for Russia? This is what Donald Trump said at the July 2018 summit in Helsinki, Finland on his own intelligence community's assessment that Vladimir Putin had attempted to interfere in our nation's 2020 elections: "I have great confidence in my intelligence people, but I will tell you that President Putin was extremely strong and powerful in his denial today." Then later: "He [Putin] just said it's not Russia. I will say this: I don't see any reason why it would be."

That was truly an unbelievable moment among many startling and disturbing Trump transgressions. Despite the seemingly meaningless add-on that he had "confidence" in his intel community, the damage was done. As the world watched, an American president sided with Vladimir Putin over his own country's intelligence leaders.

And it continued. Instead of using his perch in a Nixon-goes-to-China manner[37] to move our country reasonably ahead (understanding he would far from embrace Democratic orthodoxy on these subjects), he doubled down on his campaign rhetoric. He rejected the scientific evidence on climate change and reversed key environmental rules. On June 1, 2017, he announced America's withdrawal from the Paris

---

37. This is a reference to then-President Nixon's decision to open up talks with China and ultimately visit the country after years of his own anticommunist and anti-China rhetoric.

Climate Accords (a pact America would later rejoin under President Biden). In a speech from the Rose Garden, Trump said: "I was elected to represent the citizens of Pittsburgh, not Paris." What he neglected to mention? As of today, the only other countries not in the agreement are Iran, Eritrea, Libya, and Yemen. And, what's more, the people of Pittsburgh have every right to be as concerned about the climate crisis as the people of Paris.

On the economic front, President Trump precipitated the longest government shutdown in the history of America and exacerbated income disparity by pressing for and passing enormous tax cuts for the wealthy. The corporations knew after his election that their tax rate was going down, but the common understanding back then—even among major companies— was that the Republican/Trump proposed cuts would end up at around 25 percent.

In the end, Donald Trump insisted on taking the rate down to 21 percent. Every percentage point below 25 percent cost $100 billion over ten years, money that could have been used to finance child care or health care or even a payback on the debt.

Trump was also a whirling dervish of chaos and corruption when it came to the rule of law. He unceremoniously fired acting Attorney General Sally Yates after she stood up to him and refused to legally defend his executive order that quickly became known as the "Muslim ban." In a similarly caustic manner, he fired FBI director (and my former law school classmate) Jim Comey on May 9 of the first year of his presidency a few months after Trump had requested a number of one-on-one meetings with Comey in the White House. Comey, who took scrupulous notes, reported that at one meeting on February 14, 2017, Trump asked him to shut down the investigation into Michael Flynn—the President's former national security adviser who had resigned the day before—with the words, "I hope you can let this go." Months later, Trump fired Comey, and years later—on November 25, 2020—the President pardoned Flynn after Flynn had pled guilty to making false statements to the FBI about communications he had with Russian officials prior to Trump's assuming office.

Trump's pardons didn't end with Michael Flynn. His flaunting of and disrespect for the law is well illustrated by his series of pardons and commutations designed to provide impunity for his political cronies. During the arc of his presidency, he granted most of his pardons and commutations to people with whom he had personal or political connections, like former Arizona sheriff Joe Arpaio; former media mogul Conrad Black; disgraced former Republican congressmen Duncan Hunter, "Duke" Cunningham, and Rick Renzi; four Blackwater private security contractors who killed Iraqi civilians; and former Trump campaign advisers Roger Stone, Steve Bannon, and Paul Manafort.

Yes, in the past a number of presidents from both parties have pardoned people to whom they were connected, but Trump? Strictly by the numbers and the percentages and the substance, he took it to a whole new level.

Yet by far Donald Trump's most historically significant judiciary/legal-related act was when he—with Mitch McConnell at his side—pushed through three extremely conservative Supreme Court justices: Neil Gorsuch, Brett Kavanaugh, and Amy Coney Barrett. The decision to go bare-knuckles on the Senate's Supreme Court confirmation process—as well as the decision to choose these three particular judges—will reverberate throughout our country for years. The *Dobbs v. Jackson Women's Health Organization* majority opinion, in which the three Trump-appointed justices—along with three others—decided to reverse nearly fifty years of *Roe v. Wade* precedent, is just one example of his judges' hubris. With Donald Trump egging them on from the sidelines after appointing them to the bench, these justices directly told the young women of this country that they will have fewer rights than their moms and grandmas did. This decision, of course, was one of the many reasons the Democrats held the Senate and did so much better than expected in the 2022 midterm elections. Reversing *Roe v. Wade*—a position supported by the vast majority of Republican candidates—was just plain out of touch with the views of so many Americans.

During the course of the Trump presidency, as both a senator and a presidential candidate, I had called out the Trump administration's seemingly never-ending list of bad policies, abuses of power, and inappropriate appointments. And, as a member of the Senate Judiciary Committee, I intensely questioned his three Supreme Court nominees about their views and judicial philosophies during their confirmation processes. I knew where they stood. The public needed to know it too.

During the Amy Coney Barrett hearing, I specifically questioned the nominee about whether or not she felt *Roe v. Wade* was a "super-precedent"[38] like *Brown v. Board of Educa-*

---

38. Super-precedents have been defined by one key constitutional law expert—Michael J. Gerhardt—as "those constitutional decisions in which public institutions have heavily invested, repeatedly relied, and consistently supported over a significant period of time. Super precedents are deeply embedded into our law and lives through the subsequent activities of the other branches. Super precedents seep into the public consciousness, and become

*tion*. In a telling moment of things to come in the later *Dobbs* decision in which she joined the opinion to overturn *Roe*, she said it was not.

In another line of questioning pertaining to voting rights, I asked the nominee if she considered voter intimidation to be a crime. While she wouldn't answer yes or no, I was able to point to the federal statute that firmly stated it was. Upon conclusion of my questioning, I immediately received a text from Al Franken, my former seatmate on the Senate Judiciary Committee and someone I've been friends with before, during, and after his time in the Senate. "Those were good questions," he said, "but I have an idea for you tomorrow, since she wouldn't answer the question about whether voter intimidation is a crime."

"What's your proposal?" I asked.

"On your next round of questions start out like this: 'I know you wouldn't answer the question about whether voter intimidation is a crime, but could I ask you this. . . . Do you consider grand theft auto a crime?'"

Much to Al's chagrin, I didn't ask his question. I asked about antitrust instead.

My most notable exchange with a nominee was during the second phase of the nomination hearing of Brett Kavanaugh, which involved the allegations of sexual assault made against him by Christine Blasey Ford. I asked a fairly calm and straightforward line of questioning about whether the judge's memory of the night in question might have been impaired by his drinking. Kavanaugh had said that while he had drunk more than he should've in the past, he had never consumed so

---

a fixture of the legal framework." Michael J. Gerhardt, "Super Precedent," *Minnesota Law Review* 90 (2006): 1205.

much alcohol that his memory was impaired; but others, including a college roommate, had basically said that wasn't true.

I acknowledged that many people struggle with both alcoholism and binge drinking and noted that my own dad had struggled with alcoholism throughout his life and had "got in trouble for it" and was now sober and still attending AA meetings at age ninety.

I then asked Judge Kavanaugh if he had ever drunk so much that "he didn't remember what happened the night before or part of what happened."

Rather than answering, he shot back combatively, "You're asking about [a] blackout. I don't know, have you?"

"Could you answer the question, Judge?" I responded with surprise. "That's not happened? Is that your answer?"

"Yeah, and I'm curious if you have," he shot back again.

"I have no drinking problem, Judge."

"Nor do I."

After that surprising exchange, Chairman Grassley immediately gaveled a break, and ten minutes later Judge Kavanaugh returned to the hearing room and publicly apologized to me—a first during the hearing.

"I started my last colloquy with Senator Klobuchar saying how much I respect her . . . and she asked me a question at the end and I responded by asking her a question and I'm sorry I did that," he said. "This is a tough process. I'm sorry about that."

"I appreciate that," I said. "I'd like to add when you have a parent that is an alcoholic, you're pretty careful about drinking." I also noted my intent: "I was truly just trying to get to the bottom of the facts and the evidence . . ." I called again for a reopening of Kavanaugh's FBI background check.

The hearings for many of the Trump judicial nominees were very difficult since I knew full well what their confirmations would mean in the long term. But there was another constant challenge I shared with so many other members of Congress, governors, and leaders both in and out of government. That is the challenge of maintaining your intense opposition to a leader's actions—and, for that matter, your own credibility with the people you represent—while also holding up the citizens' end of the bargain, which means not letting our government completely collapse and the people go unserved, particularly during a crisis.

The government—regardless of who holds the reins of power at the top—has to keep working. People need help—often urgently. That was part of the reason I voted for at least some of Donald Trump's cabinet members. While they certainly wouldn't have been my choice, I strongly believed that you needed to have someone—as in a sane person—between Donald Trump and the frontline agency workers for the good of the public.

For these same reasons, I also worked with the administration on particular issues on which we had common ground. Those included the First Step Act, which reformed federal sentencing laws; human trafficking—which I had long been involved in combating; and workforce training. I also supported the Abraham Accords between Israel, the United Arab Emirates, and Bahrain and the United States-Mexico-Canada Agreement ("USMCA") on trade, and I was the first to say I supported the USMCA on the Democratic presidential primary debate stage. And during the pandemic, I worked with Trump's former White House legislative affairs director, Marc Short, who had changed positions to become Vice President

Mike Pence's chief of staff on pandemic-related issues and approvals for vaccines and testing. (Then-Vice President Pence chaired the White House Coronavirus Task Force, set up in early 2020 to deal with COVID-19 issues.)

Reaching agreement across the ideological divide is something our democracy has traditionally thrived on. Yet, looking back years later, one of the most difficult "remains of the day" when it came to governing during the Trump presidency was that while it had become increasingly hard to work across the aisle in Washington, Donald Trump made it exponentially worse. As noted by journalist Maggie Haberman in her much heralded and insightful book *Confidence Man: The Making of Donald Trump and the Breaking of America*, Trump capitalized on already present deep-seated resentments within our country and found his moment by "fueling and benefiting from the collapse of cultural and political identities . . . as the country cleaved along the lines of whom you hate, or who hates you back."[39] Thus, Trump made it hard on Republicans who tried to be close to reasonable; he would call them out as "RINOs" (Republicans in Name Only) and oppose them in their prima-

---

39. Maggie Haberman, *Confidence Man: The Making of Donald Trump and the Breaking of America* (New York: Penguin Press, 2022), p. 4. There are also a number of other detailed and insightful books on the Trump presidency. See, for example, Carol Leonnig and Philip Rucker, *I Alone Can Fix It: Donald J. Trump's Catastrophic Final Year* (New York: Penguin Press, 2021); Jonathan Karl, *Betrayal: The Final Act of the Trump Show* (New York: Dutton, 2021); Jonathan Martin and Alexander Burns, *This Will Not Pass: Trump, Biden, and the Battle for America's Future* (New York: Simon & Schuster, 2022); Peter Baker and Susan Glasser, *The Divider: Trump in the White House, 2017–2021* (New York: Doubleday, 2022); and Bob Woodward, *Rage* (New York: Simon & Schuster, 2020).

ries whenever they would even mildly criticize him or try to work out an agreement with Democrats, particularly if it was on subjects like immigration or hot-button social issues.

But he would also make it acutely uncomfortable for Democrats. Attempts to work across the aisle or with his administration directly could so easily be labeled as selling out or, worse yet, evidence that you were in bed with him and his policies. Thus, whether you were a Democrat or Republican, even when you were acting in good faith to do the right thing for all the right reasons, the chances were high that Trump would find a way—almost any way—to undermine you.

I could spend this entire chapter tracing how a number of our nation's current difficulties are based in part on decisions made—or work delayed—during the Trump administration. That being said, there is plenty of blame to go around Washington for a longtime neglect of difficult policy issues, which in many cases pre-dated the Trump administration. But the hardening of the loss of faith in our politics and the coarsening of the rhetoric and the complete breakdown of civility? That's on Trump. And while history will be focused on his role leading up to and during and after the January 6th insurrection, it is a mistake to neglect the fact that Donald Trump ushered in four years of reversals and inaction on so many key policy issues. On some fronts, we are now playing catch-up, but on others, like the composition of the Supreme Court, which is now tilted completely out of whack, our country will be living with the upheaval caused by the Trump presidency for many years to come.

My point here is this: the reckoning that Trump got handed from the voters on November 3, 2020, wasn't the end. Unless the public shows the willingness to rise above the petty, angry politics of Donald Trump and vote for (or shall I say hire) representatives who are willing to work collectively for the best interests of our country and tackle the major challenges of our time, the reckoning will simply continue, but the challenges will only get worse.

Of course, we saw voters push back against Donald Trump in the 2022 midterms when they rejected his candidates in multiple states. As we head into the future, the public's anger may be and should be directed against additional obsequious elected officials in Trump's own party who wake up every morning to trumpet the cause—or cult—of the former President. Yet unfortunately for America, so many other leaders who didn't toe the line have ended up as roadkill. That has included Republicans who have had the courage to stand up to him and the corrosive effects of Trumpism, but it also includes Democrats caught up in the public anger over the perceived lack of action.

Some of that inaction can be blamed on my own party for blocking or opting not to take more immediate action on major problems before us, such as Big Tech monopoly and privacy issues and pharmaceutical prices (although it was a welcome change when Democrats—and only Democrats—finally passed part of my prescription drug Medicare negotiation bill in 2022, something I had championed for years). But Republicans have more than taken the prize for blocking solutions when it comes to workforce issues (yes, we need major immigration reform); climate (yes, it is that bad); gun safety (the recent limited bipartisan agreement was a start, but just that); child and elder care (zero) and health-care costs (repeatedly refusing to take on Big Pharma and making their cause célèbre for years the defeat of the Affordable Care Act). On the latter score, they have repeatedly called for a "repeal and replace," but they've never offered any kind of concrete replacement package that would actually control skyrocketing prescription drug prices and help Americans be able to afford health care.

So unless my Republican congressional colleagues truly want to live out their lives on a perpetual hamster wheel of reckonings, maybe, just maybe, they should choose to reject Trump's divisiveness and work together for the good of the country. But as attested to by the 2023 House speaker vote drama, the path appears rocky.

## Nine Minutes and Twenty-Nine Seconds

In 2020 the country was confronted with another reckoning that was long in the making: accountability for systemic racism and police-related brutality and shootings. While unquestionably precipitated by the May 25, 2020, nine-minute, twenty-nine-second, knee-to-the-neck murder of George Floyd by former Minneapolis police officer Derek Chauvin, as well as a series of gut-wrenching police-related shootings in states across the country, the impetus for criminal justice reform didn't just happen overnight. The cry for racial justice—from civil rights to economic participation—more than predated the Trump presidency.

In truth, the roots of racism in America are gnarled beneath our nation's history. They can be traced way back to the Native Americans, who were both killed and systematically excluded from their lands. And, in the case of African Americans, as far back as 1619—more than four hundred years ago—when the first enslaved Africans were brought to the English colony of Virginia. In colonial and early America, the enslaved were governed by separate legal codes and they were regularly hanged, lashed, and subjected to other horrific punishments merely for seeking their freedom.

Over 150 years later, our country's Declaration of Independence loftily proclaimed that "all men are created equal" and "that they are endowed by their Creator with certain unalienable Rights." Yet neither minorities nor women were included in the nation's social compact at the time—and it would take the Civil War and the women's suffrage movement before minorities and women would even be enfranchised and allowed to vote.

And, as notorious U.S. Supreme Court decisions—including the 1857 *Dred Scott* case holding that persons of African descent were not citizens of the United States and the 1896 case of *Plessy v. Ferguson* establishing the "separate but equal" doctrine—make clear, for decades our laws were repeatedly used as tools of overt racial prejudice. It was not, in fact, until the U.S. Supreme Court's 1954 decision in *Brown v. Board of Education* that the "separate but equal" doctrine was declared unconstitutional. And even then, it took the Civil Rights Movement—with the leadership of Martin Luther King Jr., former Congressman John Lewis, and many others—another decade before Congress passed the Civil Rights Act of 1964, the Voting Rights Act of 1965, and the Fair Housing Act of 1968.

American history thus shows us that our laws—and people's views of our laws—rarely changed overnight. But sometimes all it took was one outrage—or one larger-than-life hero—to bring us one big step up the mountain to justice. From the Underground Railroad of the 1800s to the Freedom Riders and civil rights crusaders of the 1950s and 1960s to the justice reformers of today, in every generation there have been Americans willing to hold up Harriet Tubman's lantern and directly confront slavery, racism, and unequal treatment under the law.

On May 25, 2020, in my home city of Minneapolis, that lantern transformed itself into a cell phone, a modern-day video camera in the hands of a seventeen-year-old girl, Darnella Frazier. Darnella was out walking to the corner grocery store in her neighborhood in south Minneapolis that fateful evening to get snacks with her nine-year-old cousin. That's when she saw a Black man—who we now know was George Floyd—pinned to the pavement by Minneapolis police officers. One of the men—Derek Chauvin—had his knee firmly on George Floyd's neck. As seventeen-year-old Darnella watched, Floyd repeatedly told the officers that he couldn't breathe.

In broad daylight, Darnella took out her phone and started filming the murder in front of Cup Foods. She later publicly released the video. The day after Floyd's murder, Darnella said, "The world needed to see what I was seeing. Stuff like this happens in silence too many times."

Darnella's video showed then-Minneapolis Police Officer and now-convicted murderer Derek Chauvin—as well as three other former officers, all of whom have now been criminally convicted of civil rights violations—callously killing George Floyd. The video—which has been watched by millions and millions of people—captures the last moments of Floyd's life. In nine minutes and twenty-nine seconds, a human life was coldly and brutally extinguished before our eyes.

While the film documents the end of George Floyd's life, we also now know what happened in the moments leading up to his death. Minutes before he was pinned to the pavement,

George Floyd was taken into custody by Minneapolis police officers after Christopher Martin—a nineteen-year-old clerk at the Cup Foods convenience store—was handed a $20 bill by Floyd for a pack of cigarettes. The clerk suspected the $20 bill might be counterfeit, and after discussing the matter with a store supervisor, called 911, and the police were called to the scene.

Later the clerk said he felt "disbelief and guilt" that his actions had somehow led to George Floyd's murder. On surveillance video, Martin could be seen clasping his hands raised above his head as he looked on helplessly from the sidewalk while Floyd's life was taken.

During his videotaped encounter with the Minneapolis police officers, George Floyd—a father and former college athlete, originally from Houston, Texas—said the words "I can't breathe" twenty-seven times. In spite of his pleas, neither Derek Chauvin nor any of the three other officers changed their conduct or stopped the murder in progress. Derek Chauvin's knee—bearing down on the back of George Floyd's neck—literally cut off Floyd's ability to inhale and exhale.

"I can't breathe" had, by the day of Floyd's murder, already become the rallying cry of protest for the Black Lives Matter movement. In fact, those three simple words—"I can't breathe"—were the last words uttered by Eric Garner, another unarmed Black man, who'd been put in a chokehold by a New York City police officer in 2014. Garner said "I can't breathe" eleven times before he lost consciousness and died during his deadly run-in with police on Staten Island on suspicion of another petty offense—selling cigarettes from packs without tax stamps.

In *His Name Is George Floyd*, a book detailing Floyd's life, his murder, and the aftermath, *Washington Post* reporters Robert Samuels and Tolu Olorunnipa follow George Floyd's life down a trail of poverty and angst through the lens of a difficult and often racist system. The authors take readers on Floyd's journey from the Houston housing projects through the Texas criminal justice system to a new start of work and friendships in the Twin Cities, to the disruption of the pandemic, and finally to his murder at the hands of Minneapolis police.

But without Darnella's cell phone video—without her lantern of righteousness—George Floyd's murder, which shocked and outraged the world, might have been lost and covered up forever.

Despite her heroic actions, Darnella testified at the Derek Chauvin murder trial that she, like others at the scene, continues to be haunted by what happened that evening. "When I look at George Floyd, I look at my dad, my brothers, my cousins, my uncles, because they are all Black," she said. "I look at how that could have been one of them," she testified on the stand. She added that she still stays up at night "apologizing to George Floyd for not doing more and not physically interacting, not saving his life."

Darnella Frazier, of course, has nothing to apologize for. It was her actions that directly led to the conviction of George Floyd's murderer. As noted by many—from the Pulitzer Prize committee that awarded her a Special Citation to director Spike Lee, who introduced her when she received the PEN America Courage Award—her video changed the world.

The morning after the murder, I watched the video. Like everyone else who saw it, I was outraged. That afternoon on a weekly telephone call with Democratic senators, I urged my colleagues to watch it immediately. That same day I contacted

George Floyd's family, and later spoke with his family members, including his brother Philonise. I also attended George Floyd's Minneapolis memorial, where the Reverend Al Sharpton and the family's lawyer, Ben Crump, gave beautiful and powerful eulogies.

I pledged three things to the Floyd family that day: First, I would do all I could legally do to ensure that the case was appropriately prosecuted. Second, I would call upon the U.S. Justice Department to immediately conduct what is called a "pattern and practice investigation" of the Minneapolis Police Department. Third, I would work with my colleagues at the state and federal levels to pass police reform.

Meanwhile, more and more people were watching Darnella's video. They were horrified. Pressure had already been mounting across the country demanding accountability for police-related shootings and deaths. George Floyd's death at the hands of the police followed Eric Garner's, Philando Castile's, Breonna Taylor's, and so many others. But it was George Floyd's murder—and the fact that the excruciating horror was captured by Darnella's video—that sparked worldwide protests on a scale never seen before.

In the anger and frustration that immediately followed George Floyd's killing, the vast majority of the protests and marches for racial justice were peaceful, including in Minnesota. But in the Twin Cities, senseless criminal rioting and looting and arson broke out, escalating over the course of several nights. These criminal acts ultimately led to the damage and destruction of more than 150 commercial buildings in Minneapolis and St. Paul, including the burning of the Minneapolis Third Police Precinct on May 28, 2020, three days after George Floyd's murder.

During that highly charged and emotional time, I felt it was important to be clear in differentiating between what I believed was unquestionably a criminal act (the murder of George Floyd while in the custody of four Minneapolis police officers) and the ongoing work of police and the National Guard who were there to protect our community. I also felt it was imperative that we differentiate the righteous marches of multitudes of peaceful protesters making the case against racism and police brutality from the criminal behavior of rioters—a number of whom were not even from my state—who came to destroy property, burn buildings, and hurt people.

I called for (1) the immediate investigation into and prosecution of the Floyd murder case; (2) changes in Minneapolis police policies and in state and federal laws, including introducing a bill with my colleague Senator Tina Smith to ban chokeholds; (3) the encouragement of peaceful protests; and (4) the condemnation of the criminal rioting. As I promised George Floyd's family I would do, I led a letter with Senator Smith and several members of our congressional delegation calling on the United States Justice Department to immediately conduct a pattern and practice investigation that could ultimately allow the Justice Department to assert supervisory authority over the Minneapolis Police Department. The investigation was opened on April 21, 2021, by Attorney General Merrick Garland.

In addition to the brutal murder of George Floyd, the May 28 rioting and damage and destruction also shook our state. The day after the burning of the Third Precinct, it was actually unclear to many citizens if local law enforcement could get the violence under control. The governor called in the National Guard and police departments across the metropolitan area for assistance. Religious leaders—as well as those of us in political leadership—bluntly called on people to stay home after a nighttime curfew went into effect. Expressing our support for peaceful protesters who had every right to march and demand change, we begged them not to be used by those who wished to wreak damage and destruction on our communities. People listened. The cities operated under the curfew for days. By the day after the precinct burned, the rioting and burning had been greatly minimized. The National Guard was a big help. Prosecutions of those who committed crimes would follow.

Yet for a community already mourning the loss of George Floyd, the destruction of inner-city businesses—so many of them minority-owned—made things even harder for people already traumatized and reeling from months of the pandemic. At the time I visited multiple pop-up outdoor community service centers, where volunteers distributed meals and personal items. So many Minnesotans rose to the occasion. Grief counselors and medical staff were on the scene. My state has always been known for its volunteerism, and volunteers were everywhere, bringing food and water and clothing and supplies to the communities in the vicinity of the murder, as well as to areas that were suffering from the destruction of their grocery stores, pharmacies, and other local neighborhood businesses.

While there have been many stops on the Twin Cities' long and ongoing road to recovery—from changes to police practices, to private and public investment in the communities and rebuilding damaged and destroyed buildings, to continued work on a memorial honoring George Floyd—it was clear from the beginning that there would be no redemption for the murder without the successful prosecution of the criminal and civil rights cases against those responsible for killing him.

With federal cases pending, the state prosecution of Derek Chauvin was the first major trial. That case was led—with help from prosecutors from the Hennepin County Attorney's Office—by the Minnesota Attorney General's Office and my friend Attorney General Keith Ellison. Keith and I had gotten to know each other during my days as a prosecutor, when he was a defense attorney. When the U.S. Senate seat opened up in 2005, he urged me to run and was the first one to contribute to my campaign. As it turned out he also ran that year—for the United States Congress—becoming the first Muslim ever to serve as a U.S. representative. In 2018 he ran for attorney general, becoming Minnesota's first Black statewide officeholder.

From the very beginning, Keith decided to put a trial team together that would make George Floyd and our community the focus of the case, not the lawyers. The state district court judge assigned to the case—Pete Cahill—was my former chief deputy of six years in the County Attorney's Office. Judge Cahill ran a tight courtroom and made the right decision that the case should be televised. The public needed to see the justice system in operation.

For days the public watched the heartbreaking testimony of the community members who witnessed the crime, and their tearful statements that they wished they could have prevented the death. It was clear they would bear an undue and unfair burden from their experience that day for the rest of their lives. The police officers who testified—including

Medaria Arradondo, then Minneapolis's chief of police—forcefully gave witness to the fact that nothing that happened that evening was acceptable officer conduct. It was a murder.

Keith rightfully made the case about the community instead of about himself or his lawyers. He assembled a first-rate team that worked together seamlessly, with a focus not on legal grandstanding but on doing the right thing and securing a conviction in the case. Among the prosecution team members he chose: Jerry Blackwell, a prominent Minnesota attorney whom President Biden—on my and my colleague Tina Smith's recommendation—nominated to serve as a federal judge. Jerry was confirmed by the Senate in 2022.

Keith also kept the morale of the team strong and refused to be sidetracked by all the national attention. They wouldn't allow justice for George Floyd's family to be turned into a crass spectacle, no matter how much attention the case was getting. And while a few national doubters questioned why Keith had left the case in the hands of what were mostly a group of local attorneys—highly respected in Minnesota's legal community but not well known nationally—Keith knew that his team was the right one for the job.[40]

From beginning to end, Keith understood that what mattered was putting together a team of excellent lawyers—from Blackwell to Assistant Attorney Generals Erin Eldridge and Matthew Frank and former federal prosecutor

---

40. I later learned an astounding fact from Jerry's aunt at her nephew's judicial confirmation hearing: in his thirty-five years as a lawyer, he never lost a case. He attributed it to good fortune, but his aunt quickly corrected him. "That doesn't just happen."

Steve Schleicher to former Assistant Attorney General Lola Velazquez-Aguilu—all of whom understood our state and our community. In addition, Neal Katyal, a national appellate expert who I had recommended to Keith, was also part of the team. All of the assigned lawyers had the experience to handle the pressure in the high-stakes trial, to check their egos, and to work together to present a complex case. Keith would not let the public pressure on the team get in the way of their quest for justice.

The jury selection for the case began on March 9, 2021, and ended two weeks later on March 23. The trial ran from March 29 to April 19. On April 19, the jury started deliberating following the closing arguments. On April 20, after ten hours of deliberation, the jury announced it had reached a verdict.

I will never forget the day the jury came back. I was in Washington, but I talked to Keith on his way into the courtroom and after the verdict. Like many, I thought it was a good sign that the jury made its decision in just ten hours. It just seemed impossible that all members of the jury could decide that quickly to acquit Derek Chauvin. What had always been most concerning was that the jury would somehow come back hung because one or two members didn't want to convict. The relatively quick time period from the moment the jury went into deliberations to its reaching a verdict meant, of course, that no juror was holding out. Keith, an experienced lawyer, felt similarly positive. But in the end, you never know until the verdict is read.

Then came the verdict—on TV for the world to see. There was the Floyd family. There was Keith. There was my former deputy Pete Cahill, the presiding judge. Millions and millions of people were watching for the verdict. I held my breath.

Judge Cahill announced the jury's verdict.

"Guilty" . . . "Guilty" . . . And "Guilty."

Guilty of second-degree unintentional murder. Guilty of third-degree murder. Guilty of second-degree manslaughter.

Tears and hugs broke out in the courtroom and outside on the lawn in front of the Hennepin County Government Center. People were relieved, and actually quite stunned that it had all happened so fast.

Two months later, Judge Cahill sentenced Derek Chauvin to twenty-two and a half years in prison for second-degree murder. That sentence—delivered on June 25, 2021—was a justified upward departure from Minnesota's sentencing guidelines. In July of 2022, Chauvin would plead guilty in federal court to violating George Floyd's civil rights, for which he was sentenced to simultaneously serve twenty-one years in prison. And on February 24 of that same year, the three other former Minneapolis officers—Thomas Lane, J. Alexander Kueng, and Tou Thao—were also criminally convicted by a jury in federal court of violating George Floyd's civil rights by not giving him medical aid and failing to intervene to stop Chauvin. They all were given prison sentences—albeit much shorter ones. Their state prosecutions also ultimately resulted in similar findings of guilt.

The courts, the prosecutors, the investigating officers—and the community, as represented by the jurors—did their jobs. And most of all, the people who testified did an extraordinary thing by standing up for justice, carrying a burden they should have never had to shoulder in the first place. Yes, there was accountability and redemption. There was justice. But it wasn't complete justice.

Complete justice will only be found when there is a true shared understanding of how a fair and effective criminal justice system should work. Strong law enforcement leadership, as well as good practices and rules—on the local, state, and federal levels—will provide accountability while respecting the difficult work of officers. Justice will be found in passing funding for mental health and sensible gun safety legislation (something we finally got a start at on the federal level in 2022 with the passage of bipartisan gun safety legislation) and police reform (which my friend and colleague Cory Booker has spent years trying to get done but has been sadly stopped by Republican resistance). Justice means changes to certain police procedures—such as requiring body cameras (something I've long advocated for) and eliminating dangerous police practices, such as chokeholds. It means an acknowledgment and response to racism and a more diverse police force. It means increased funding for police officers and training and recruiting at a time when we need dearly to fill vacant police jobs. It also means a community that understands that there are so many hardworking police officers who put their lives on the line for our safety every day.

I know firsthand the challenges we face as well as the opportunities we have to improve our criminal justice system. Before coming to the Senate, I was the chief prosecutor for Hennepin County, an area that included Minneapolis and forty-four metropolitan suburbs. My number one responsibility was to keep our communities safe—and that meant working with many good police officers to fight crime in the county. But public safety also means a system that holds officers accountable when they don't follow the law. One example? While I had long supported outside investigators being assigned to review police-related deaths, at the time I was county attorney, grand juries—in my jurisdiction and elsewhere—would routinely make decisions about culpability in police-related cases. My office—like others throughout the nation—would present each and every police-related death case to a grand jury and allow the grand jury to decide whether or not charges should be brought. I now believe there is more accountability if the district attorneys themselves—or in the case of Minnesota, county attorneys—take the responsibility for making charging decisions in police-related cases. This is now happening in many jurisdictions, as it did in the Derek Chauvin murder case. And, in addition to changes to how charging decisions are made, post-conviction reviews—including the use of conviction integrity boards and DNA reviews—are also good and necessary reforms that further the cause of justice.

One thing we have learned from all of this: without continued vigilance, injustice will breed more injustice. The work for justice in my state—and in the country—certainly didn't end when that jury verdict was read in Minnesota. Americans must continue to confront racism and injustice wherever and whenever we see it.

## Get Off Our Lawn!

Given the nation's history of discrimination, it wasn't a surprise to anyone that when Joe Biden announced his candidacy for President over a year before George Floyd's death, he led with a call for racial justice. He criticized then-President Trump's reaction to what had happened during a protest in Charlottesville, Virginia, when a white supremacist, James Alex Fields Jr., deliberately ran his car into a group of innocent protesters, killing one and injuring thirty-five. While the horrific cold-blooded murder of civil rights activist Heather Heyer in Charlottesville at the 2017 Unite the Right rally predated the Floyd murder, Trump's reaction—that there were "two sides" to the story—outraged many Americans and became a rallying cry for Joe Biden and a number of us running for president.

Our country's struggle with racism long predated Donald Trump. But to come full circle to the political reckoning of 2020—the defeat of Donald Trump—it is important to remember that throughout his presidency, Trump poured fuel on the fire of brewing white supremacism with his racist comments and actions, which included: inciting an insurrection on January 6th, 2021; declaring that there were "two sides" to the murder in Charlottesville; racist comments that offended Native Americans, Asian Americans, Hispanics ("Who do you like more? The country or Hispanics?"), and all immigrants (describing immigrants from Haiti and African nations as coming from "shithole" countries); repeatedly invoking the now-indicted Proud Boys in seemingly complimentary ways during speeches; and having peaceful protesters forcibly removed and tear-gassed in front of the White House so he could get a photo op holding a Bible in front of Washington, D.C.'s historic St. John's Episcopal Church during the height of the Black Lives Matter protests.

As the Episcopal bishop of Washington, D.C. stated after the President's Bible photo: "I was not given even a courtesy call that they would be clearing with tear gas so they could use one of our churches as a prop, holding a Bible, one that declares that God is love and when everything [Trump] has said and done is to inflame violence."

Set against the backdrop of nationwide racial protests and in the middle of a public health crisis, the 2020 presidential general election campaign will go down as one of the most virulent and polarizing presidential contests in our nation's history. Of course, there is an obvious reason: Donald Trump was one of the candidates. And in the opposite corner of the ring? Joe Biden, a true believer that government can be a tool of good, and a man who has made comity and civility one of the hallmarks of his long career. And Joe Biden's vice presidential running mate—Kamala Harris—set to make history as both the first Black and first Asian American woman ever to be nominated for the post. Her opponent? Mike Pence, a staunch conservative.

In addition to all that, the pandemic created an incredibly limiting—and strange—political environment. Biden's campaign staff tried their best to follow the COVID rules, including novel, if weird, car rallies where participants were required to stay in their vehicles during their candidate's speech, honking whenever they liked something he said; socially distanced photos with masks; smaller outdoor rallies with big circles six feet apart to mark where participants could stand; no handshaking or hugging; severe testing requirements for every event; and an entirely remote nominating convention.

Trump, on the other hand, did everything he could do to flaunt and mock his own administration's CDC rules:

maskless crowded rallies; the candidate appearing at a debate while refusing to take a COVID test, then sources later revealing (big surprise) that the President actually knew he had had COVID; a Fourth of July rally at a national park with fireworks amidst the ponderosa pines; a super-spreader Supreme Court appointment announcement; a joyride from Walter Reed Hospital while he was still hospitalized with COVID.

But it was the White House lawn setting of the final night of the RNC convention that I full-stop predict will never be repeated again in American history. After greatly reducing the plans for his convention in Charlotte, North Carolina due to COVID, Trump's campaign canceled the convention's last main event—the President's acceptance of the nomination before a planned stadium-style rally. Instead—after apparently searching for the most flagrant use of government property for a political purpose that could be found—Trump topped even his own use of Mount Rushmore for his Fourth of July–themed July 3 shindig by deciding to hold his convention's final evening on the White House lawn, a clear violation of the Hatch Act, the purpose of which is to ensure that taxpayer dollars are used to run the government, and not to subsidize one political party or candidate.

But it was so easy to get to!

There was, of course, a lot going on in the days leading up to that final night. Kim Guilfoyle, the girlfriend of the President's son Donald Jr., and best known for later being paid $60,000 for a two-minute introduction of Don. Jr. at the January 6th "Stop the Steal" rally, spoke during the RNC's first night. She basically screamed out her entire convention speech, including the memorable closing: "THE BEST. IS YET. TO COME." Okay, that just scared a lot of people. But that speech, it turns out, was just a warm-up.

The closing night spectacle at the White House—where, as described by ABC News, "a giant political rally" was "held at the most famous residence in the United States"—was unmatched. Humongous brightly lit "TRUMP-PENCE" signs were displayed on either side of the presidential residence as Donald Trump and the First Lady walked out of the White House onto a red-carpet runway. And, as also described by ABC News, there was a certain cognitive dissonance occurring on stage as speaker after speaker focused in on the theme of "American rot and violence," while the public was exhorted to reelect the very man who was in charge of it all.

Watching it at home with my husband, I just couldn't get over the ethical and moral affront of holding the convention at the White House. I was all ready for a typical radioactive Trump speech. I truly was. I just wasn't ready for the hubris of holding a political convention in the place where every president since John Adams has lived, where heads of state and kings and queens and popes have visited, where Abraham Lincoln signed the Emancipation Proclamation, where Franklin Roosevelt and his cabinet managed our country through a world war and the Great Depression, and where Ronald Reagan addressed the nation after the explosion of the Space Shuttle *Challenger*. The White House is a symbol of our shared national history. As Jacqueline Kennedy once said, "The White House belongs to the American people."

So I typed out on my phone a tweet that quickly went viral. I think it captured what a lot of people were thinking that night. It was simple:

GET OFF OUR LAWN.

That example aside, not everything I did—or really anything anyone else but Donald Trump did—got a lot of attention during that 2020 campaign. Far from it. It was an unusual time to be a surrogate for a presidential candidate, that's for sure.

When my own presidential campaign ended, I had decided to devote myself to my work in the Senate and to electing Joe Biden to the White House. In normal times that would have meant headlining rallies across the country and campaigning in states where I could be helpful. When we exited the race, Mayor Pete and I had even tentatively agreed to do some rallies together. But then COVID struck. And while COVID made for an unorthodox campaign to be sure, like so many other volunteers for the cause—from phone callers to door knockers to sign holders—I had one mantra: do everything they ask.

So, as I returned to the Senate—both remotely and in person—to tackle all the work that needed to get done as the virus surged, I also hit the campaign trail, but this time for Joe. My only actual "rally" happened at the very beginning, just before the campaign realized that all these types of events would need to be canceled or greatly curtailed because of the virus. You simply can't have people wall-to-wall in a high school gym or a major stadium in the middle of a pandemic. Donald Trump tried that and people died.

I never would have predicted that the public rally–style event I did for Joe Biden in Grand Rapids, Michigan, on Saturday, March 7, 2020—only five days after I'd gotten out of the race and endorsed him for President—would have been one of my last during the 2020 election cycle. The speech went well, but in a foreboding moment, a reporter fainted in a room that wasn't one bit hot. People do faint at campaign events, but usually not reporters. The speech wasn't long, and I often look back at the moment and wonder if the reporter had COVID or was worried she was going to get it. In any case, it felt like a sign.

From there I joined Vice President Biden at his virtual events. It was at the very beginning of online fundraising and organizing. Back then (for one brief moment that quickly passed) people actually thought it was cool to show up in a Zoom box and see elected officials in another one.

I spoke to Joe Biden a number of times during that time period, including once when he called to tell me I had done well on TV. It reminded me of another time he had called me late in the evening. I was new to the Senate and he was right off his presidential run in 2008, but it was well before he was chosen to be Barack Obama's running mate. I had just finished a speech to an empty Senate chamber. I had tried to garner all the passion I could for the judiciary-related topic, but literally no one was there except the clerks, the pages, and the presiding officer—a senator who kept looking at his watch to figure out when he could go home.

As I left the Senate chamber, my cell immediately buzzed. I thought maybe it was my mom, who had been watching the speech on C-SPAN, but I immediately dismissed that idea, figuring that not even my mom was watching that late at night. I answered the phone. It was Joe Biden. "Great speech, kid," he said, "great speech. I watched the whole thing."

That's Joe. And it was the same Joe—then the vice president—who answered when I called to thank him for coming out to Minnesota for me in my 2012 re-election campaign. During that call I shared with him that the husband of one of my best friends who had helped with the event had suddenly died. The vice president immediately offered to call my friend to give her his condolences and advice. "No," I said, "a note is fine . . . You have too much going on."

"No," he said, "give me her number."

I did.

A few days later my friend Kathleen was driving home from her first day back to work since her husband had died. It was a really hard day. She had three teenage daughters and was suddenly a widow. The cell phone rang. She answered. It was Vice President Joe Biden. "Kathleen," he said, "I heard what happened to your husband and I'm so sorry."

She started to cry. He told her how hard it was when he suddenly lost his wife, at an even younger age than her husband John had died. He gave her all kinds of advice, including to disregard awkward things people say when your spouse dies. They are just trying to be nice, he said. He told her that for a year after his wife died, he had written a number on each day of a calendar to summarize how he felt. For months he never got beyond lower numbers.

Then he said, "Kathleen, I want to check in with you again and I want you to write down my cell number so you can call me whenever you want."

Crying, she said, "I can't, Mr. Vice President, I'm driving."

He said, "Pull over, I'll wait."

She pulled over and wrote his number on her hand. She never did call him, but when she visited Washington for my Senate swearing-in in January of 2013 and he stopped by the party, he pulled her aside and they spoke again. He remembered everything she had told him.

She wasn't famous. She wasn't a big donor. She was just a person who had experienced an unbelievable tragedy. And he helped her.

Given all that, I didn't really feel like I needed to know more about Joe Biden when I—along with many great candidates—was asked to interview that spring to be his vice president. I knew he was a good man. But nevertheless—always wanting to be prepared—I decided to order his autobiographies online.

My being a big fan of bookstores (which were then mostly closed due to the pandemic), when I placed my order for the Biden books, it was one of my first online book orders. When the link popped up to order Michelle Obama's book *Becoming*, I also decided to order it since I hadn't been able to read it while on the campaign trail. I remember that Michelle Obama's book arrived the next day. It took ten more days to get the future President's. I finally ended up listening to it on audio. In any case, I smartly decided against reciting minute details gleaned from Biden's autobiographies during the vice presidential interviews, but I did remember something Jimmy Carter once told me about Walter Mondale: he knew how to say Rosalynn's name. Some of the other vice presidential candidates who came to Plains to interview mispronounced it badly, he told me. The Carters noticed.

My interviews with Biden's top people in the vice presidential sweepstakes were solely by Zoom and phone. The interviews seemed to go well, though that soon became irrelevant.

While I both wanted the job and thought I would have been good at it, sometimes in politics—and in life—the timing just isn't right. In the wake of the George Floyd murder and so many other ever-widening racial chasms in our country, I came to believe that the vice president should pick a woman of color. On June 19, 2021, I took myself out of the running. As I said on *The Last Word with Lawrence O'Donnell*, "This is a historic moment, and America must seize on this moment."

"There are many incredibly qualified women," I told Vice President Biden when I called him the night before I made the public announcement, "but if you want to heal this nation right now, this is sure a hell of a way to do it."

It was obviously a jolting change to give it all up after having run for president for over a year and then being considered in the top tier for vice president for the months since. And the plain truth was that while it wasn't easy to adjust, my work, and the enormous needs of my constituents around me—as well as the discovery the same day that my ninety-two-year-old dad had COVID—kept me going. There was just too much to do to dwell on what could have been.

In the weeks following my announcement, I had work to do both in Minnesota and in the Senate related to the pandemic. The many repercussions of the Floyd murder were also obviously ongoing, with judiciary hearings in Washington on police reform as well as meetings and discussions at home on rebuilding our community. But after my dad was out of the woods with COVID, John and I took the two weeks off for our trip out west, and I finished up a book I'd been working on for years before the presidential campaign—okay, a tome—on antitrust, something I had long felt was a neglected area of public policy.

On August 12, Joe Biden chose Kamala Harris as his running mate. The day before he made the announcement I was in a car near Hinckley, Minnesota, headed up north for a family weekend, with plans to get outdoors and hike before what I knew would be a busy week of helping the Biden camp during the convention. En route, President Biden's longtime friend and adviser Anita Dunn called me. She told me they were announcing Kamala Harris as the candidate for VP the next day and asked if I would do *Good Morning America* and appear on various other news outlets on Kamala and Joe's behalf. I said of course I'd be happy to help and turned around in a gas station parking lot and drove back.

Kamala and I had worked together on the Senate Judiciary Committee and had run against each other for president, and I had a lot of respect for her. I was honored to support the ticket. My husband also did interviews about Kamala's husband, Doug.

Five days after Kamala was announced as the vice presidential candidate our Democratic National Committee virtual convention began. I spoke to a number of the state caucuses from across the country by Zoom and met virtually with various groups who were part of the convention. Along with Saint Paul Mayor Melvin Carter, I taped Minnesota's announcement of our delegates (the fifty states', territories', and District of Columbia's delegate announcements were one of my favorite parts of the remote convention, including the guy from Rhode Island holding a plate of calamari in one hand and the delegate sign in another). I also—at the invitation of the campaign—gave a live, prime-time speech from the Minnesota History Center with the State Capitol as a backdrop (although nothing quite compared to Bernie's woodpile).

At some point during the two-week period leading up to and during the convention, I remember noticing that I had developed this weird rash on my leg that was almost exactly in the shape of a stop sign. I had heard of COVID toe, but not COVID leg, and after a test, to my relief, COVID was ruled out.

I finally went to a doctor.

"Yep, wow, I've never seen anything quite like this. This rash is in the shape of a . . ."

"A stop sign," I said.

"Yep," the doctor said. "It is really amazing how much it looks like a big red stop sign."

"Yep," I said, "I know."

"Maybe it is a sign you are doing too much," she said.

"Don't go there," I said.

It was diagnosed as shingles. I got some medication and it went away. But one of my friends still maintained that maybe I had given just one too many speeches and attended one too many virtual gatherings and my body finally said, "STOP. ENOUGH."

But the stakes were too high. Just because a chicken pox virus that had been lying dormant in my body from the last time I got shingles nearly forty years before had decided to make a command appearance in the shape of a stop sign on my leg, I wasn't going to take the bait. I kept going.

Meanwhile, back at the Biden campaign virtual headquarters, they were trying to spice things up, since everyone's Zoom events were getting pretty mundane. They needed to generate more . . . well, online excitement! They decided to pair elected officials with celebrities. I got some great pairings, doing a half-hour Instagram live with Broadway star Billy Porter (lots of hearts emanated from Instagram for that one, and fairly quickly I figured out they weren't for my answer on expanding the child tax credit). I paired up online with Jamie Lee Curtis (with whom I'd had a blast campaigning for Hillary in Iowa back in 2016, including an event at a shopping mall where Jamie Lee had to tell the crowd not to be concerned about the people at the back of the room who were holding daggers . . . they were simply fans of her *Halloween* movies and they came to events with daggers for her to sign. That happened). The great *SNL* star Rachel Dratch (who played me and my bangs on the show and who even dressed like me for the virtual event) and I did a Halloween-themed Zoom (no daggers) event together. And the most memorable of all? The cast of *Supernatural* (Misha Collins, Jensen Ackles, and Jared Padalecki) and I paired up as a group and had a great time, although I've still never met them in person, which makes sense, I guess, given the subject matter of their show.

I did tons of things in-state (Minnesota had always been on the Biden campaign's radar, since Trump had done better than expected there in 2016 and the President—and Mike Pence—came to campaign in our state multiple times). And, within the COVID restrictions, I did public events for Biden in New Hampshire (we won there), and Florida and Iowa (where we didn't). I also spent a lot of time in what we will call "battleground state number one": Wisconsin. Going into the fall, the Biden campaign wasn't at all certain they could win Georgia or Arizona (those were very possible, but stretches), but they had to win Wisconsin, a state that was lost to Trump in 2016.

Since there's a whole swatch of Wisconsin that gets Minnesota TV and my mom was from there, I was happy to help. I Zoomed in on Wisconsin TV across the state and called in for radio interviews. I did a big farm/rural event near La Crosse. It was all set up beautifully for broadcast, with haystacks and cows in the background, but a killer wind almost brought an entire stack of hay on top of my head.

My most high-wire Wisconsin event had little to do with politics. On November 1, 2020, the Vikings were playing the Packers at Lambeau Field. The Biden Wisconsin crew decided it would be really cool if my friend Wisconsin Senator Tammy Baldwin and I did a Biden campaign event together in Green Bay all decked out in our teams' colors (green for Tammy; purple for me) right before the game and less than a week before the election.

Knowing that some of these kids who thought this was such a great idea were not exactly steeped in the true nature of the deep fan rivalry between the Vikings and the Packers, I called a week before with some questions:

ME: Are we going to be anywhere near Lambeau Field with me in that purple outfit and Vikings horns?

CAMPAIGN GUY: You don't have to wear the horns.

ME: Okay, good answer, but still, are we going to be at Lambeau Field or near a bunch of Packers fans when I'm holding the Biden sign in my purple outfit? It really could backfire on you guys.

CAMPAIGN GUY: No, we're doing it outside of the Democratic Party headquarters.

ME: Great. Then are we going to make sure Tammy and I are together in every shot so you don't just have TV footage of me alone in all that Vikings gear in front of the

Biden sign? I mean, what if the Vikings win? It really won't help with the fans up there.

CAMPAIGN GUY: Don't worry about it. The Vikings aren't going to win. The Packers are way ahead in the polls. I mean the odds. The Vikings are 1–5 and the Packers are 5–1 and they're playing at home.

ME: But what if they DO win?

CAMPAIGN GUY: They won't.

ME: What's the weather supposed to be like?

CAMPAIGN GUY: Really good.

That Sunday it was in the low 30s with sleet and 30 mile-per-hour winds. It was bone-chilling cold.

The Vikings won 28–22. The headline on PACKERS-WIRE (an online publication that features a chunk of cheese as its logo) read "Minnesota stuns Green Bay at Lambeau Field."

The next morning I got a text from former Hillary Clinton communications director Jen Palmieri, who was covering the national Biden/Trump race for the Showtime political series *The Circus*.

JEN: Good morning from Green Bay where your Lambeau Field event led the morning news!

ME: (texting back hopefully) Did the purple Vikings outfit even show up behind the podium with the wind and sleet and all?

JEN: Oh yes, it looked so great.

ME: (again hopefully) Okay, but could you see Tammy in the green?

JEN: No, I just saw you in the purple.

In any case, a few days later the people of Wisconsin looked beyond the purple to the greater good (or I should say the greater green). To this day I don't carry the forever burden of losing Wisconsin for the Biden campaign. The Biden/Harris ticket ended up winning Wisconsin by about 21,000 votes, including—yes—a victory in Green Bay: Joe Biden won the Packers' hometown 25,036 to 21,123, flipping five voting wards that Trump had won in 2016.

But who's counting?

## Election Night(s)

In the end, there was a lot of counting. They counted and they counted and they counted. In fact, by virtue of multiple Trump campaign lawsuits, they counted—and recounted—over and over again. The truth is that when November 3, 2020, arrived, the vast majority of Americans had already voted—either by mail, early in-person, or by drop-off box—since by then they had clearly gotten the message about the pandemic risks. Nevertheless, our nation's courageous local election officials—Democrats, Republicans, and everyone in between—staffed the polling places, from town halls to schools and from community centers to senior centers.

And Americans—knowing the stakes—voted in droves. In fact, well over 159 million people cast their votes in the 2020 election. In the middle of a public health crisis, they voted like they had never voted before. It was, in the end, the highest turnout in over 120 years and the largest vote total ever. According to the U.S. census, nearly 70 percent of voters either cast their vote by mail or voted early in-person. That's compared with 40 percent in 2016.

No matter how cynical one might be about American politics, the sheer fact that this many Americans cared about their democracy enough to go to the polls and vote—in some cases risking their lives to do so—should give everyone some solace about the state of our democracy going forward. In person and in masks, by drop-off boxes in Michigan and mailboxes in Utah, they voted. Despite endless lawsuits and disinformation campaigns and ever-changing election rules, they voted.

On election night, the early results were incredibly positive for Joe Biden. He was surging ahead—or expected to surge ahead—in a whole bunch of states Trump had won in the last election. With the exception of what I'll call the stretch states of Florida and North Carolina, he had a strong chance of winning (and later did in fact win) five key states Trump had won in 2016: Wisconsin, Michigan, Pennsylvania, Arizona, and Georgia.[41]

By the next day it was clear that the mail-in ballots that still were being counted were trending Biden. One by one the states got called for Biden, with Fox News correctly calling Biden's win in Arizona before anyone else did. Finally, four days after Election Day, with CNN calling it fifteen minutes before the networks, the election was called for Joe Biden, based mostly on the fact that his lead in Pennsylvania—which reached 34,000 votes on Saturday morning—was simply insurmountable.

Yes, Joe Biden won the national election. He won it by about seven million votes.

---

41. And as we now know, several years later, these five states continued to be key swing states for governor, U.S. Senate, and U.S. House races in the 2022 midterm election.

A few hours later, a happy Joe Biden gave his victory speech in Wilmington, Delaware, after being introduced by Vice President–Elect Harris (which was a historic moment all on its own).

In his speech from Delaware, the President-elect reached out across America to the supporters of Donald Trump with these words:

> For all those of you who voted for President Trump, I understand the disappointment tonight. I've lost a couple of times myself. But now, let's give each other a chance.
>
> It's time to put away the harsh rhetoric, lower the temperature, see each other again. Listen to each other again. And to make progress, we have to stop treating our opponents as our enemies. They are not our enemies. They are Americans. They're Americans.
>
> The Bible tells us to everything there is a season, a time to build, a time to reap, and a time to sow. And a time to heal. This is the time to heal in America.

Joe Biden rightfully declared victory that night. The people had voted. Yes, it was a reckoning on Donald Trump's four years as President. But what President-elect Biden was trying to capture that night was that it was also a reckoning on the ugliness that had dominated our politics and the attacks on our democracy. A reckoning on the paralysis in Washington. People wanted change. They voted for something different.

But did anyone really think Donald Trump would let it end there?

# 5

# Insurrection and Resurrection

Life Lesson: *"I do solemnly swear that I will support and defend the Constitution of the United States against all enemies, foreign and domestic; that I will bear true faith and allegiance to the same; that I take this obligation freely, without any mental reservation or purpose of evasion; and that I will well and faithfully discharge the duties of the office on which I am about to enter: So help me God."*

—OATH OF OFFICE, UNITED STATES CONGRESS

## Stoking the Fire

Donald Trump had just gotten started.

By the early morning hours after the election, every network maintained that Trump was either behind or projected to fall behind in several key states. Yet at 2:30 A.M., Trump chose to hold an unhinged press conference where he infamously said, "We were getting ready to win this election. Frankly, we did win this election."

And, a few days later, after every network—including Fox—had declared Joe Biden the victor in the 2020 election,

Trump still lied and claimed he won. After Biden's gracious victory speech in Wilmington in which he specifically reached out to Republicans, Trump said he won. And after nearly every world leader had congratulated the new President-elect—including the heads of state of Russia and China—Donald Trump still would not concede.

Trump was out there spreading lies and trolling for fake votes and fake electors wherever he could find them. He did it through his lawyers—bringing over sixty lawsuits in multiple states. And he did it directly, by calling Michigan Republican canvassing officials and lawmakers and inviting them to the White House. He pressured top Republican officials in Arizona, Pennsylvania, and Wisconsin to overturn votes.

And in the most troublesome and infamous call of all, he demanded to speak with the Georgia Secretary of State, Brad Raffensperger, just days before the insurrection. On a January 2, 2021, hour-long recorded conversation, the President of the United States told Raffensperger and other Georgia officials to "find 11,780 votes" (which just happened to be only one more vote than the margin of Joe Biden's victory in the state). President Trump even made a not-so-veiled threat to the secretary of state and his attorney: "[Y]ou know what they did and you're not reporting it. That's a criminal—that's a criminal offense. And you can't let that happen. That's a big risk to you and to Ryan, your lawyer."

As Steve Bannon—one of Trump's closest advisers—said to a group of his associates on October 31, 2020, exactly three days before Election Day: "What Trump's gonna do is just declare victory. Right? He's gonna declare victory. But that doesn't mean he's a winner. He's just gonna *say* he's a winner."

You see, that had been Donald Trump's plan all along. The

evidence was there for months, hiding—as they say—in plain sight. In the months leading into the election, the President attacked vote-by-mail, something that had long been a point of voting pride not only in Democratic-leaning blue states, but also in a number of independent purple and Republican-leaning red states, including Utah, where for years 75 percent of the state's electorate had voted by mail.

The reasons for Trump's vigorous 2020 attack on vote-by-mail? Yes, he wanted to sow confusion to suppress turnout among Biden voters as mail-in balloting was more prevalent on the Democratic and Independent side than among Republican voters. But there was another even more insidious reason: Trump was simply laying the groundwork in the pre-election months so that he could later falsely allege fraud and cast doubt on the ultimate outcome in the event Biden won (which was becoming more and more likely as the election season went on).

Donald Trump knew what we knew: millions of mail-in ballots would *not* be counted by Election Day, because certain state laws mandated that the counting not start until either that day or the next. He would then use those perfectly LEGAL state requirements—in place in both blue states and red—to declare the election illegal. He would do it by casting doubt on the validity of the later-counted ballots. Since some states didn't even start counting their early (and mostly mail-in) ballots until later, the immediate results would seem skewed in favor of Trump. He could then manipulatively use that fact to fraudulently claim corruption and declare himself the victor.

The Trump attacks on the mail-in ballots, the underfunding of the post office and the removal of mail collection boxes, the chaos caused by multiple Trump campaign pre-election lawsuits challenging everything from ballot deadlines to ballot signatures—it was all part of the same plan. That's why it wasn't hard to predict that Trump's undermining of our democracy would continue on Election Day and beyond.

It was clear Donald Trump would use any delay—including legally mandated ballot-counting requirements—to cast doubt on the entire election. That's why I felt it was very important to build public trust in the election system by calling him and his allies out on voter suppression and false election claims whenever and wherever they happened. People needed to understand what was going on, because in several instances Republican lawsuits resulted in changes to the way people could vote, with several court orders issued just weeks before the general election. That happened in multiple states, including my own, when a last-minute court ruling based on a GOP legal challenge created uncertainty about the deadline for submitting mail-in ballots. When the notoriously conservative Eighth Circuit came out with its decision on October 29, 2020—less than a week before the election—I drove from local TV station to local TV station late one night to do interviews. I wanted to make sure everyone in my state—regardless of who they supported—knew the new deadline and didn't delay in sending in their ballots.

I also felt it was really important to educate the public—and the media—on a national basis about the individual state counting rules and the delays they could expect to encounter in getting results in certain states on election night.

Since I also thought there was a strong possibility that Trump would never concede if he lost, I felt it was my job as the Democratic leader of the Senate Rules Committee—which has jurisdiction over federal elections—to prepare the public by providing important information about the differing state election rules. People needed to anticipate why we would know the results right away in some states, but not know them in others. They needed to know that was normal and to be expected so Trump couldn't exploit it.

Others shared this concern with me, including Senate Majority Leader Chuck Schumer and Senators Bernie Sanders, Tammy Duckworth, Martin Heinrich, and Chris Murphy. Our group started working together well before the election to inform the public and the media about the state-by-state rules and how they could be falsely exploited to cast doubt on the election. My major focus was putting together and publishing a report that detailed each state's ballot-counting rules and timing. We used the public report to explain the situation to anyone who would listen, including the public, elected officials, and numerous media outlets, editorial boards, and reporters.

In the report we divided the states into four categories:

1. Twenty-three states that required mail-in ballots to be received on or before Election Day and allowed early processing of ballots so that vote totals on election night would include most of the mail-in ballots. This category included both Arizona and Georgia (although both those states still encountered some delays in counting because of unexpectedly high turnout).

2. Seventeen states and the District of Columbia that allowed ballots to be received by mail after Election Day so long as they were postmarked by Election Day. Those states still counted what they had beforehand and included it in their

totals, although some ballots would not be added to the total until after the election. This category included Nevada and North Carolina.

3. Five states that required ballots to be received on or before Election Day and had little or no advanced processing, although vote totals on election night included some absentee ballots. This group included Michigan and Wisconsin.

4. Five states that allowed properly postmarked ballots to be received after Election Day with little or no advanced processing, and vote totals on election night would include few, if any, absentee or mail-in ballots. This category included— significantly—Pennsylvania.

With the report and a map in hand, we explained each key state's vote-counting rules and warned that in some states election night vote totals wouldn't give us a complete picture. We noted the expected breakdown of the percentage of Democrats voting by mail as compared with Republicans. We ended our presentations by explaining how the immediate election night results could change in certain states the next day (or days) when all the ballots were counted.

We specifically warned the country that "President Trump's rhetoric indicates he may exploit [the states' different voting and counting patterns] to claim victory for himself, then falsely claim that there is 'massive fraud' in mail-in ballots that have not yet been counted or reported."

We warned Americans that they should be "prepared to reject misinformation" and "be patient about results in places where counting ballots may take longer."

Despite our prescient warnings, I still don't think anyone would have imagined how far Donald Trump would take this.

After decisively losing the 2020 election, Trump—as was thoroughly documented in the House Select Committee hearings—deployed a multipronged strategy to overturn the election results. In addition to the early assault on vote-by-mail, one of his most visible tactics was post-election litigation centered on swing states where he had come up short, including Arizona, Georgia, Michigan, Pennsylvania, and Wisconsin. Craven as these efforts were, they were not successful. His campaign and his allies filed and lost more than sixty lawsuits— several of which were subject to blistering rejections by judges Trump himself appointed.

But the losing didn't stop there. As it became clear that judges would play no role in overturning the election, Trump turned his sights on state and local election officials. He hoped to pressure them into refusing to certify the results, but they stood their ground and did their jobs, oftentimes at great personal costs to themselves and their families. I still recall the haunting story the former Republican city commissioner of Philadelphia, Al Schmidt, told at a Rules Committee hearing Senator Blunt and I held on threats against local election officials. Commissioner Schmidt reported that he had received ominous phone messages surrounding the election, including one where the caller noted that there is "a reason why we have the Second Amendment." When Schmidt appeared on TV to defend the integrity of the ballot counting in Philadelphia shortly after the election, Donald Trump and his staff called him out by name. Stalkers tracked down Schmidt and a staff member, who is Jewish, leading to anti-Semitic attacks.

After the election, Schmidt and his family received numerous threats by text and email, including one calling for his kids to be "fatally shot" and stating that the "treasonous Schmidts" should have their "heads on spikes." One text message said: "You lied. You a traitor. perhaps 75cuts and 20bullets will soon arrive."

Schmidt's wife and his three children had to leave their house, as their home address was placed on the internet.

Schmidt was not alone. The heartbreaking House Select Committee testimony of the former Georgia poll workers Ruby Freeman and her daughter Shaye Moss vividly captured what it was like to be singled out by the President of the United States and falsely accused of election fraud. After receiving numerous threats after Trump's false accusations against them, Shaye said she went into hiding and gained sixty pounds.

The saddest part of their story, the one that sticks with me? When Ruby talked about how she used to proudly wear shirts with her nickname—"Lady Ruby"—emblazoned on the front. "Now," she testified, "I won't even introduce myself by my name anymore."

In her words, "Do you know how it feels to have the President of the United States target you? The President of the United States is supposed to represent every American. Not to target one. But he targeted me, Lady Ruby, a small business owner, a mother, a proud American citizen, who stood up to help Fulton County run an election in the middle of the pandemic."

As we learned during my October 26, 2021, Senate hearing on election threats, Lady Ruby's, Shaye's, and Al Schmidt's stories were replicated over and over again across the nation, in towns large and small, with many local—and even volunteer—election officials receiving security protection. But sadly, as we also learned at our hearing, some of the jurisdictions were just too small to provide security, despite multiple verifiable threats.

When the threats against local election officials weren't bearing fruit, Trump and his attorneys turned to yet another scheme: they tried to create fraudulent alternate slates of electors in states Biden won—hoping that Trump could convince Congress to declare him the victor in the midst of a constitutional crisis. Once again, Trump failed.

Following increasingly desperate attempts to push the fraudulent slates as well as identify false cases of voter fraud—including contemplating the seizure of election equipment—Trump looked to Attorney General William Barr and later acting Attorney General Jeffrey Rosen and the United States Department of Justice to carry his fraudulent fight forward. They all refused.

Trump then went after his very own vice president, Mike Pence, and repeatedly called on him to refuse to certify the election for Biden. After consulting with his own team of advisers, Pence explained he had no such authority—it would be illegal—and he refused to do it.

In the end, Trump's only viable option to unlawfully continue as President was to leverage his most ardent supporters, many of whom were more than ready to take up arms on his behalf after being stoked for months by his false and inflammatory rhetoric, tweets, and actions. He had methodically spent years sowing mistrust in the electoral process. As the former Trump Deputy Press Secretary Sarah Matthews (who quit her job on January 6th) testified before the Select Committee, Trump's supporters "truly latch on to [his] every word

Our family loves hiking in Wyoming's Grand Teton National Park. This is the day in 2020 I almost made it up to Lake Solitude . . . and learned some lessons along the trail.

On the presidential campaign stage with John and Abigail. They were there for me every step of the way. (Associated Press)

Campaigning has always been a family affair: my dad on his lawn chair in the snow; my mom and the sign she held up in parades during my campaign for Hennepin County Attorney; Abigail as a middle-schooler down in Austin, Minnesota, with "Sir Can-A-Lot," a mascot for Hormel's SPAM. (Top photo: Terry Gydesen)

My teacher Miss Kalionen's note on my fourth-grade report card: "Speak up and out! Louder!!" After I got elected to the Senate, she sent me a note in the same handwriting: "You really learned how to talk louder."

My first elected office and one of my first committee meetings! Ridgemount Junior High, Plymouth, Minnesota, circa mid-seventies.

Announcing my first campaign for U.S. Senate in my mom's driveway.

Walter Mondale was my mentor from college on. Here we are with Keith Ellison (then a congressman and now Minnesota attorney general) at the 2016 Democratic Convention in Philadelphia.

This photo of me taking a selfie at the 2017 Trump inauguration went viral when a news organization described it as: "woman takes selfie with John McCain and Bernie Sanders." It was quote-tweeted at the Women's March the next day with the words: "This is why we march."

Walking back from the Women's March in Washington, D.C., the day after the Trump inauguration, I met this little girl. She was so proud of her sign.

Joy in the snow with Abigail. After my presidential campaign announcement speech, I went with the Minnesota stocking hat! (Getty Images)

Laying out my rural America plan at a farm in Iowa.

New Hampshire, Fourth of July. I love a parade. (Associated Press)

Calling for contributions at
campaign headquarters.

Bringing our signature hotdish to Thanksgiving
dinner with staff at our campaign chair And
McGuire's house in Des Moines.

Our green bus!

A typical scene
on the campaign
trail. Our national
press secretary,
Carlie Waibel, is
trying her best to
get us through the
crowd!

One of my favorite photos from the Los Angeles presidential debate. Bernie and I had a lot of fun at those debates. (Getty Images)

oe Biden and Tom teyer in a major rgument in South arolina. I couldn't tep away because would have fallen ff my one-inch ox. (Reuters)

Elizabeth and me in our matching outfits on the debate stage in Detroit with Pete and Bernie. (Associated Press)

Laughs with Cory on the campaign trail (and who knows what it was about, but it was good).

Kamala and me with our husbands at t California State Democratic Conventi in San Francisco. Doug and John got be friends and sometimes teamed with Elizabeth's husband, Bruce, a Pete's husband, Chasten.

Our increasing momentum and our third-place finish in New Hampshire was the surprise of the night! (Reuters)

A joyful endorsement of Joe Biden in Dallas. Both Jill and John were there!

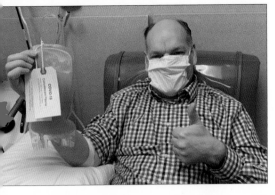

After a serious case of COVID, John helped others by donating plasma at the Mayo Clinic.

When John was sick, my friend and colleague Senator Tina Smith let me stay in her apartment in D.C. Here we are at an airport hangar in Thief River Falls, Minnesota. Photobomber in background? County Commissioner Darryl Tveitbakk.

My live prime-time 2020 Democratic National Convention speech. Since it was virtual and filmed in Minnesota, I didn't even need to wear my shoes.

Five days before the election, Wisconsin Senator Tammy Baldwin and I campaigned for Joe Biden in Green Bay, Wisconsin, right before the Vikings/Packers game at Lambeau Field.

Insurrectionists climbing up on the inaugural platform outside the U.S. Capitol, January 6th, 2021. They nearly took down the media tower nearby. (Julian Leshay)

With COVID cases up, the incoming Biden administration decided to blanket the National Mall with inaugural flags in honor of those who couldn't be there because of the pandemic. It was a moving sight. (Architect of the Capitol photo by Thomas Hatzenbuhler.)

(*Left*) Giving remarks at the 2021 inauguration. It was important to remind everyone that this was a true celebration of our democracy. (Official U.S. House of Representatives Creative Studio photo by Kristie Baxter.) (*Right*) I was the first person to introduce the new President of the United States, Joe Biden. (Architect of the Capitol photo by Sean Greene.)

My cryptic notes on a Post-it when I received the call giving me the test results that showed I had breast cancer.

Within a few minutes of learning about my cancer diagnosis, I was back on the Senate floor for votes. (C-SPAN)

Advocating for mammograms and encouraging people to get their tests and checkups.

Leading a breast cancer march out of U.S. Bank Stadium in Minneapolis.

The women senators have always been a source of strength for me. Here we are in 2015 bowling at the White House. Thanks to former North Dakota Senator Heidi Heitkamp for the bowling shirts!

Former Republican Senator Roy Blunt of Missouri and I chaired the Senate Rules Committee for years and led the inauguration of Joe Biden. We are good friends and got a lot done together. (Official U.S. Senate photo by Rebecca Hammel.)

The summer of 2022 was a very productive time in the Congress. We passed multiple bills including the PACT Act for veterans. Amie Muller (pictured here) was a brave vet and a young mom when she died from pancreatic cancer after being stationed next to one of the most notorious burn pits in Iraq. I worked with her husband, Brian, to pass legislation to get better treatment for vets. (Courtesy of Brian Muller)

The president signing a bill Roy Blunt and I passed to honor our police officers killed in the line of duty. I led a January 6th security investigation, which resulted in security changes at the Capitol and more resources for police.

Dayna Frank heads up Minneapolis's iconic First Avenue, where Prince played multiple times. She and I teamed up with Senator John Cornyn of Texas to lead a national effort to save our music and theater stages during the pandemic. That's my star next to Alice Cooper's!

Speaking at a Planned Parenthood rally in St. Paul, Minnesota, after the *Dobbs* decision overturned *Roe v. Wade.*

Marching with Representative Jim Clyburn and many others over the Edmund Pettus Bridge in Selma, Alabama, to advocate for voting rights.

On the National Mall with the courageous Gabby Giffords, standing up for victims of gun violence.

Campaigning in Arizona during the 2022 midterm election with Senator Mark Kelly, husband of Gabby Giffords. If you need to hitch a ride, always a good idea to do it with an astronaut.

I went all over the country in 2022 to help my colleagues. Here I am in New Hampshire where Senator Maggie Hassan and I just had to stop for this little one!

Receiving the Order of Merit, First Class from President Zelenskyy on a trip to Ukraine with then-Ohio Republican Senator Rob Portman in August of 2022.

Always more work to do in the Capitol! I like how this photo captured me walking past the many male statues to the Senate floor! (Getty Images)

Always more peaks to climb. Here we are at the top of Pincushion Mountain on Lake Superior in northern Minnesota, October 2022.

and tweet." In short, Trump had long groomed his supporters for a confrontation on his behalf, and they were ready to roll.

In the weeks leading up to January 6th, Trump promoted his "Stop the Steal" rally in Washington, timed to take place just as Congress formally began counting the electoral votes. He ominously tweeted, "Be there, will be wild!"

For years, the day designated for the congressional counting of the Electoral College votes had not even been close to being called "wild." Mundane? Yes. On C-SPAN? Certainly. A few objections here and there? Yes. But "wild"? Never.

Four years before, as the then-incoming ranking member of the Rules Committee, I was one of the elected officials who actually presided over the counting of Trump's 2017 Electoral College win. There were a few objections that were ruled out of order by then-Vice President Biden because there wasn't a senator who joined in making an objection. The entire process was conducted in less than two hours.

But this time—in 2021—there were multiple red flags marking trouble. And it wasn't just because of Trump's actions. A number of my own colleagues—including Ted Cruz and Josh Hawley—declared that they were going to object or join objections to the Electoral College count in certain states. They made it clear that they would do all they could to deny the certification of the Electoral College vote to Joe Biden.

In the days leading up to January 6th, I called multiple Republican senators to gauge their support for upholding the election results. I especially made it a focus after December 30, 2020, when Hawley became the first senator to announce he would be joining House Republicans in objecting to the Electoral College certification. Cruz soon followed, and that's when the dam broke. By January 5—the day before the vote and what would become the insurrection—about a dozen GOP senators all said they would object to one state or another, despite Republican Leader Mitch McConnell's publicly stated view that the results were correct and should be upheld.

Josh Hawley's decision was significant, because under the archaic Electoral Count Act of 1887 (think President Rutherford B. Hayes), just one senator could wreak havoc on the process. That's because under the original law (the reform of which was the subject of a major bipartisan bill that I—along with Senators Susan Collins, Joe Manchin, and Roy Blunt—passed in 2022) if any one of the senators objected, the House members' objections would be cloaked with enough "legitimacy" to gum up the process for hours, days, or longer.

Within a few days of calling my Republican colleagues, I knew that while we had publicly lost ten to twelve Republicans, I had commitments—or got commitments through others—to easily put us up over the majority requirement. Even Republican senators who had remained quiet about how they would vote recognized their constitutional duty and planned to uphold the Electoral College state-by-state results. Some of the senators were keeping their decisions private, but in the end no one who had said they wouldn't object changed their minds. I figured we had somewhere between eighty-eight and ninety-two Senate votes to uphold the Electoral College results in each of the key states for which there would be objections.

Senator Roy Blunt and I conferred multiple times in the weeks leading up to January 6th. We knew that Republican senators' public pledges to object to multiple states meant that we were going to face at least twenty-four hours of a proceeding (based on planned objections from both houses that at the very least could include Arizona, Georgia, Wisconsin, Nevada, Pennsylvania, and Michigan).

Under the 1887 Electoral Count Act, it is not just the *actual* objection to a state's certified electoral results that prompts the delay. That just takes a few minutes. It is what happens after the objection that takes so long. In fact, the total time for each objection—which includes the objection being made, the debate in each chamber, the actual votes on each objection in both houses, and the process for the senators leaving and returning to the House chamber—can take upward of three to four hours per state.

In addition, the ceremonial procedure Roy and I were entrusted with overseeing—while important for historical purposes—was not exactly efficient. The pomp and circumstance (if it could be called that) is designed as the last step before Inauguration Day to carry out the peaceful transition of power. The leaders of the Rules Committee traditionally gather in the Senate and walk with the vice president to the House to "call the roll of the states." With us on our journey are several members of the Secretary of the Senate's and parliamentarian's staff, as well as three pairs of Senate pages or aides, each carrying a historic mahogany box filled with the states' certified electoral ballots.

Once we arrive at the House of Representatives, we join the two House Rules Administration Committee leaders on the dais. Starting with Alabama, the four of us—officially designated as "election tellers"—take turns reading off the winning ticket in each state and the number of electoral votes awarded. If there is an objection it is heard, but, as explained above, under the original act it only creates a mandatory vote in each chamber if at least one senator and one House member object. If that happens, the senators walk back to the Senate, the House members stay in the House, and each chamber embarks on a lengthy debate on the objection, to be followed by separate Senate and House votes.

If the objection is overruled by a vote of a simple majority of either house, then we start the whole process over again and walk back to the House with the mahogany boxes filled with the ballots to announce the results and call the next state. The role of the vice president in all of this is, of course, purely ceremonial, although Donald Trump and his supporters liked to pretend it was much more.

Again, while the 2020 outcome was clear, Roy and I estimated that the entire process could take in the range of twenty-four hours, depending on the moods of the objectors. The day before January 6th I warned our caucus members of the day looming before us and the importance of being there for each and every vote (which, mind you, was during one of the worst times of the pandemic, and there was no remote voting in the Senate). I told them to figure out where they would sleep for one to two hours in between the votes while a few of us went back and forth to the House to hear the objections. I told them that while the process would start midday, it would go through the night and most likely well into the next afternoon.

In the week leading up to January 6th, in consultation with Leader Schumer, I set up a speaking schedule—starting with Arizona—for each of the six states for which we anticipated objections. I divided up the six states so nearly every Democratic senator who wanted to would be able to give a speech. I called all the members and explained their roles. My role was to directly follow Ted Cruz near the beginning and rebut, something I'd gotten used to doing on the Senate Judiciary Committee.

Given how vitriolic Trump and his supporters had been—and especially after we found out that the President was holding a "Stop the Steal" rally in front of the White House—a number of us started raising security concerns with the Capitol Police. The then-Capitol Police chief directly and repeatedly assured my Rules Committee staff and me that they had a good plan in place, as they assured many other senators. As we later learned, while the chief may have had a plan, it was far from adequate.

All of this was going on smack dab in the middle of countless other important events, crises, and intrigues. The Georgia Senate runoff election—which would determine the control of the U.S. Senate (then in the hands of Mitch McConnell) was on January 5—just one day before the Electoral College count. We had a seething Donald Trump in the White House, ranting and raving and repeatedly challenging the election outcome with both legal action and words. COVID was on the rise, and despite repeated veto threats by the President, we debated and passed a bipartisan COVID relief package during the weeks leading into January 6th. As the country was confronted by the worsening pandemic—and continuing high hospitalization and death rates—the vaccines were finally out. But there were problems with vaccine distribution, and the operations supporting it straddled both the outgoing and incoming administrations. Finally, there were new and critical Biden cabinet appointments being announced and debated, as well as the filling of White House jobs that is part and parcel of any White House transition. The last point alone more than captured the attention and gossip of the inside-the-Beltway crowd.

With all this going on, I still figured that I had one major job that went to the top of the heap: despite all the noise and horror stories coming from the Trump White House, I was the senator responsible—along with Roy Blunt—for making sure that Joe Biden got his rightful Electoral College vote. He had, after all, won the election.

## It's a Republic If We Can Keep It[42]

On the night of January 5, I stayed up late with my staff going over the plans for the Senate speakers and the Electoral College process in the Senate and House. I also prepared my remarks for the next day. All through the night I had one eye on my prep papers and the other on cable TV, where they were reporting on what would end up being an astounding election evening in the state of Georgia. Both Georgia Senate seats were on the line in two long-awaited runoffs. By the early morning hours of January 6, it became apparent—as borne out by the results later in the day—that both incumbent Republican senators were going to be defeated by two young and exciting Democratic leaders. In one night Georgia had given the nation two historic firsts: the state elected its first Black United States Senator Reverend Raphael Warnock—and its first Jewish United States Senator Jon Ossoff.

The most common response I heard to the question of

---

42. A grand quote loosely attributed to Ben Franklin, with some historical intrigue. See Gillian Brockell, "'A Republic, If You Can Keep It': Did Ben Franklin Really Say Impeachment Day's Favorite Quote?" *Washington Post*, December 18, 2019.

whether anyone ever truly predicted that control of the U.S. Senate would flip based on two Democrats beating two incumbent Republican senators in Georgia on the same night?

"I didn't see that coming!"

But many of us had believed in Raphael and Jon from the start. Stacey Abrams—the incredible leader from Georgia—while not on the ballot that year, had repeatedly told me she thought they could win. Her voter turnout model—focused on increasing the numbers of new voters, and particularly voters of color, including Black, Asian American, and Hispanic voters—was right on in 2020, and the major and deciding factor in the surprising double election win.

I got to speak with both Raphael and Jon late on the evening of January 5. I woke up on the morning of January 6th realizing that not only did we have a big day ahead certifying the Electoral College results, but that I would soon become the chair of the Senate Rules Committee. Victory in both Georgia races meant that the Senate would go 50/50. But because our party controlled the White House, Democrats would take over the committee chairs.

I got to the Capitol mid-morning. It was about an hour before we were to walk over to the House to start the roll call of the states, the timing of which not coincidentally co-incided with Trump's scheduled "Stop the Steal" rally on the other end of the Mall. Our time had been set forever. He had scheduled his rally for maximum chaos and disruption.

While we were promised increased security on the perimeter of the Capitol, all I could see as I drove in was a bigger officer presence and some additional areas of fencing, in addition to rows of bike racks erected as makeshift fences. There was a group of pro-Trump protesters gathered by the Capitol. I later learned that they were harassing Republican senators, like Senator Todd Young of Indiana, who had pledged to follow the law and uphold the state Electoral College votes. This was the same group that Senator Josh Hawley saluted with a jab of his clenched fist on his way into the Capitol. While it was a sizable and angry group, there was no sign of the mayhem yet to come. They had not, of course, yet been joined by the belligerent mob that, after being fed still more lies, was about to march down the National Mall at Donald Trump's direction.

I made some last-minute changes to the Democratic-side speaking order after getting the names of the speakers from the Republicans. I warned some of my colleagues to keep their speeches within the time limits. Our goal was to make our points of rebuttal but not to add time to the agenda, which was already predicted to take at least twenty-four hours because of the series of expected objections. In retrospect it seems ironic indeed that I was focused on speaking order and time allocations, but that's the thing about government ceremonies. They are supposed to be formal and dignified. Details matter.

Several of my staff members were there with me because of my leadership role on the Rules Committee. They were either in the Senate chamber or in a room right below the chamber that we designated as the Rules Committee "war room" because of the predicted objections to the Electoral College votes in at least six states. I would be making remarks throughout the evening and the next day, organizing the responses of others, and coordinating with Senator Blunt.

Despite our differing views and political parties, Roy and I are very good friends. We passed multiple bills together, and before Roy left the Senate in early January 2023, we co-chaired both the Senate Adoption Caucus and the Senate Travel and Tourism Caucus. Together, we also handled many difficult and delicate issues as chair and ranking member of the Rules Committee, including updating the Senate sexual harassment rules, planning the inauguration, and dealing with all kinds of thorny issues—from what senators can wear in the Senate chamber to the oversight of the Smithsonian museums on the Mall. But the most important for our nation? On January 6th—on the issue of the Electoral College certification—there was no daylight between us. We both firmly believed that under the law the state certifications should be approved. Our democracy depended on it.

On schedule at 1:00 P.M., Vice President Pence, Senator Blunt, and I led the Senate procession to the House of Representatives, along with both leaders and many members of the Senate. When we got to the House, I remember seeing a number of Trump-aligned House members who I knew planned to object; all told there were dozens and dozens of them. I remember seeing Ted Cruz. I knew then that his plan was to join Republican House member Paul Gosar in objecting to Arizona's certification. I remember seeing Liz Cheney, who was then number three in the House leadership, and who most definitely was not going to object. I remember seeing Representative Jamie Raskin, whose beloved son Tommy—a second-year student at Harvard Law School—had died by suicide less than a week before. Yet Jamie was still sitting there near the aisle in the House chamber fulfilling his constitutional duty. And I remember the House clerk's booming voice as we entered: "Madam Speaker, the Vice President of the United States, and the United States Senate."

We entered to applause in the House, as always happens for formal proceedings.

The first to enter the House were the three pairs of young Senate staff assistants, each pair carrying a large mahogany box full of state ballots. The use of the mahogany boxes—which combined contained the Electoral College ballots for all fifty states and the District of Columbia—has been a Senate tradition since 1877.

Next came the vice president. Then Leader McConnell. Then Senator Blunt and me.

Speaker Pelosi invited us up to the rostrum.

As we waited for everyone to sit down, the speaker and the vice president spoke for a while, both unaware that they soon would be taken into protective custody. Unbeknownst to them—as they stood on the House rostrum preparing to do their jobs—a group of insurrectionists had other ideas. Only a few hours later, rioters would enter the House speaker's offices, calling out "Where are you, Nancy?" in ominous, mocking tones. Multiple insurrectionists would call for the hanging of Mike Pence.

I greeted the vice president and the speaker and took my place on the rostrum next to Senator Blunt.

It all seemed so normal.

Members kept filing in. Because of COVID and House rules, the House Chamber was about half full.

Speaker Pelosi noted that it was an important, historic meeting.

Vice President Pence stood up and stated, "Pursuant to the Constitution and the laws of the United States, the House and the Senate are meeting in joint session to verify the certificates" of the presidential election.

After Republican House members made a few objections about COVID policies and the number of members allowed in the House chamber, the clerk started the roll call of the states. We began with Alabama. Senator Blunt took to the rostrum and stated that the state's certificate was authentic and that Donald Trump and Mike Pence had won Alabama and received its nine Electoral College votes.

No objections.

Next was Alaska. House Committee on Rules and Administration Chair Zoe Lofgren read those results. She announced the three Electoral College votes from Alaska for Trump and Pence.

No objections.

Next up was me. It was my job to read the certified results from Arizona. I announced that the certificate was "regular in form and authentic" and that Joe Biden and Kamala Harris had received the eleven Electoral College votes from Arizona.

This time?

An immediate objection.

Paul Gosar, the Trump-aligned representative from Arizona, jumped up and objected on behalf of himself and sixty of his colleagues, including Senator Cruz, who had also signed the objection. Applause broke out, with a standing ovation from the objectors' ranks.

I would have loved to debate Gosar, but in my procedural capacity all I could do was sit down.

Vice President Pence then announced that the Senate would return to its chamber and that the Senate and the House would separately debate the objection as provided for by the rules.

We went back to the Senate. It was 1:14 P.M. Trump had

already addressed his assembled supporters at the Ellipse adjacent to the National Mall. His crowd was beginning their march to the Capitol. We had no idea what was coming.

The juxtaposition of an angry Trump-incited mob gathering on one end of the Mall with what we now know were flagpoles, riot shields, and bear spray while the nation's leaders took part in this seemingly ministerial procedure to count the votes that had already been counted is not lost on me. But it was our duty and the Constitution demanded it.

And while the Cruz/Gosar sixty-member objection—with more to come—may have seemed like normal partisan fighting, it actually wasn't.

There were only two other times in history when joint House/Senate objections had been lodged under the 1877 Electoral Count Act, and they previously involved just one state. The first time was in 1969, when Democrats were making what could be called a "friendly" objection to one state's results. Senator Ed Muskie of Maine and Representative James O'Hara of Michigan objected because a North Carolina elector—known as a "faithless elector" for his actions—broke from Richard Nixon and supported segregationist George Wallace. The senator and the representative hoped to dissuade future faithless electors and highlight what they saw as a flaw in the democratic process. The votes weren't close in either chamber, and, as noted, only involved one state. Even that election's presidential victor—Richard Nixon—later responded by saying that he agreed that the Electoral College should be reformed.

The second time there were actually votes on objections under the Electoral Count Act was in 2005, when the race between George Bush and John Kerry came down to one state: Ohio. Based on accounts of Black disenfranchisement and long lines in Black precincts, Representative Stephanie Tubbs Jones, Democrat of Ohio, objected. She was joined by Senator Barbara Boxer, Democrat of California, but the objection failed 1–74 in the Senate and 31–267 in the House.

Our "situation" in 2021 was very different. Objectors had pledged to challenge at least six states, and the vast majority of those objecting had made it clear that they wanted the election overturned and were publicly aligned with a President who had not conceded and was challenging the results.

When we got back to the Senate chamber to begin the debate after the objection was filed on Arizona, it was around 1:30 P.M. Unbeknownst to most of us, the mob had already broken through police barricades. Majority Leader McConnell began the proceedings, followed by Minority Leader Schumer (who we all knew at that point would soon be the majority leader, given the Georgia results). Senator Cruz would speak next in his capacity as the objector, then me, then Senator Pat Toomey, followed by Senator Kyrsten Sinema (since the first state that prompted an objection was Arizona), Senator James Lankford, and several others.

Leader McConnell began his remarks by expressing his disdain for what had just happened in the House: "We are debating a step that has never been taken in American history: whether Congress should overrule the voters and overturn a presidential election." He noted that in his thirty-six years in Congress, it would be the most important vote he ever cast.

McConnell added: "The voters, the courts, and the states have all spoken. They have all spoken. If we overrule them, it would damage our Republic forever." He further noted that the election was not even unusually close and that the elections in 1976, 2000, and 2004 were closer. He ended by saying that he would "vote to respect the people's decision and defend our system of government as we know it."

Senator Schumer made similar points, but homed in on the direct assault to our democracy and our standing around the world: "What message will we send to those countries where democratic values are under assault and look to us to see if those values are still worth fighting for?" "Sadly," he said, "a small band of Republican objectors may darken the view of our democracy today, but a larger group of senators and House members from both sides of the aisle can send a message, too: that democracy beats deep in the hearts of our citizens and our elected representatives . . ."

Next up? Objector Cruz. He led his remarks with a made-for-Trump trope, noting that 39 percent of Americans believed that the election that had just occurred "was rigged."

I would later respond that the reason they thought it "was rigged" was the very reason we were there for an unprecedented vote on the Senate floor: because the President of the United States was falsely claiming the election had been rigged and his supporters believed him.

Cruz suggested *delaying* the certification of the votes—which by then had been counted and recounted, with courts across the land rejecting the false claims of fraud—in order to set up a commission to examine voter fraud. He also noted that while his objection was for Arizona, it was also about an additional five contested states (no surprise, all states that Joe Biden had won).

It was my duty to respond to Cruz, something I have done many times during my Senate career. I noted that throughout history, in the rare times there have been debates in the Senate on one individual state's votes, they have been resoundingly defeated. But here? This was unprecedented, as Cruz and his friends were planning to object to at least six states.

I thanked the Democrats and Republicans who had joined the ranks of what I called the "coup fighters." In hindsight, I was in fact the only senator to use the word "coup" before the Senate adjourned due to the invading mob. While what happened came to be known as the "insurrection," it turned out I was generally right on, and only a few minutes later everyone found out how true those words actually were.

In my remarks, I noted that if Senator Cruz wanted to improve the percentage of Republicans who believed the election was valid, maybe he should start speaking with Republican-appointed officials in Trump's own Homeland Security Department, which had dubbed the election "the safest in history," or with Attorney General Barr, who had publicly stated there was no evidence of fraud. I reminded my colleagues that eighty judges—including conservative judges—had thrown out Trump's and Rudy Giuliani's ridiculous lawsuits. I made clear that Republican officials in Arizona, including the governor, stood by the state's results.

I ended my speech by telling a story that my longtime friend Roy Blunt had shared with me. In Roy's Senate office at the time, he had a bust of a man displayed at the top of a bookcase. The unique thing about the bust? No one knows who he is. Roy did research. He went to the historians. All he could find out was that he was a cleric, but no one knew who he was. Hence, the statue is called "The Unknown Cleric."

The irony? At the time the statue was commissioned and sculpted, our nation's leaders thought this man so important that he warranted an actual statue, but today no one knows who he is.

When people visited Roy's Senate office—whether they were schoolkids or senators—he showed them the statue and told the story. His lesson? What we do here is more important than who we are.

I ended my speech with that story because I wanted to make the point that what matters is not our personal futures, not our own short-term destinies. "What matters," I said, "is our democracy's destiny. People will not know who we are a hundred years from now or two hundred years from now, but what they will know is this: They will know what we did today, how we voted today. That is more important than who we are." I ended by paraphrasing the famous quote often attributed to Benjamin Franklin: "It is a Republic, if we can keep it."

## Democracy on Fire

When I finished speaking, then-Pennsylvania Senator Toomey, a staunch conservative, spoke up in favor of upholding the will of the people, and in particular Pennsylvania's electoral votes. Arizona Democratic Senator Sinema then defended the procedure in Arizona and asked our colleagues to support the decision of the people of her state. Oklahoma Republican Senator Lankford was next, and right in the middle of his remarks—during which he was speaking in favor of the objection and stalling the count in favor of establishing a voter fraud commission—Vice President Pence was abruptly rushed out of the chamber by U.S. Secret Service agents. Senator Chuck Grassley of Iowa, who was then the president pro tem (a title that refers to the senator who takes over the Senate in the vice president's absence and since 1890 has typically been assumed by the most senior senator of the majority party), took over the presiding chair from the vice president and then gaveled the Senate to adjournment.

It all happened so fast. Right after my remarks—only about ten minutes before the Senate adjourned—my staff had approached me on the floor and whispered a warning that the mob had come down the Mall and that there were rumors that the police could not hold the line. Now there was talk that the rioters had entered the Capitol and the vice president had been taken to a secure location. The senators—who were allegedly, in security parlance, "sheltered in place"—milled around the Senate chamber, trying to figure out what was going on.

I spoke directly with the police who were in the chamber and in the hallway behind it. I always have had a good relationship with the officers in the Capitol. Some of it is personal—I enjoy talking to them. And some of it is professional—for years Roy Blunt and I had worked with them in our roles on the Rules Committee.

The police and the Senate Sergeant at Arms's Office (the historic name for the Senate-assigned security) asked me to do two things: (1) call senators who were not accounted for but were in the building so they could locate them and bring them to safety (they didn't have all their cell phone numbers); and (2) announce that the senators should stay away from doors with windows, since there were reports that the rioters who had breached the Capitol were dangerous and specifically seeking out elected officials.

I immediately yelled out to my colleagues, "Everyone, stay

away from the doors! There are reports that the rioters have entered the Capitol and shots have been fired. Stay away from the doors."

I was immediately approached by a senator who said, "Amy, stop scaring people. Stop scaring people. Don't say that."

We will let history be my witness as to who was right about that. A lot of people said things they regretted that day.

Minutes later we were told it was no longer safe to stay in the chamber and we were escorted to another room in the Capitol complex. It was during this approximate time period that one police officer, Eugene Goodman, bravely distracted the insurrectionists with nothing but a stick-shaped baton to save Mitt Romney's life. Given that Senator Romney was the only Republican to vote to convict Donald Trump at the first impeachment trial only a year before, Mitt had more than a target on his back.

When we got to the other room, it was teeming with senators and Senate leadership staff. The senators were mostly all there except for Leaders Schumer, McConnell, Durbin, and Thune (who had been taken to an entirely different location) and a few senators who had originally been in their offices or hideaways instead of on the Senate floor. I called my own staff and found out that two of them were stranded in our makeshift "war room," which was unfortunately the first room next to the main Senate doors where the rioters were entering. When the mob broke in through the Capitol doors, my staff quickly retreated to a closet in an adjoining kitchen off the room. For four hours, Tommy Walker (my longtime policy aide) and Madeline Coles (my longtime assistant), were holed up in that closet in the adjoining kitchen with nothing but dining room forks in their hands to protect themselves.

As my staff hid in the closet, fearing for their lives, the rioting mob ran wild, attacking officers both inside and outside the Capitol with shields and sticks and bear spray. Over in the House chamber, security fended off multiple violent rioters. The insurrectionists also entered Speaker Pelosi's office, looking for her and other leaders, ominously calling out their names.

At 2:14 P.M., not long after we had been evacuated from the Senate chamber, insurrectionists entered our chamber—the historic room filled with centuries-old desks where we had just been debating. Bellowing "Mike Pence is a f—ing traitor," shirtless Jacob Chansley, also known as the "QAnon Shaman," carrying a spear and wearing a horned Viking hat with his face painted red, white, and blue, climbed up to the Senate rostrum and sat down in the presiding officer's chair that Vice President Pence had occupied only an hour before. Chansley—later convicted on federal charges and sentenced to forty-one months in prison—wrote a note that he left on the Senate dais: "It's Only A Matter of Time. Justice Is Coming!"

We now know that at around this time Secret Service agents were concerned enough about the safety of the vice president and their own lives—given that it was their solemn duty to protect him at all costs—that they called their family members to say goodbye.

With all that was going on, it is understandable that there were not many officers assigned to guard the room—still an undisclosed location—where the senators were brought to "shelter in place." The Capitol Police leadership repeatedly told me to convey to the other senators that they had only a limited number of officers they could assign to the room, either inside or outside. And they didn't want the senators to leave the room—even if they felt it was safer to go to their own offices—since the police had no spare officers to protect them and they didn't even have enough officers assigned to protect them in this room as it was. It was the officers' feeling that dividing up the senators into smaller groups would make things even more unsafe. And, as I explained to some of the senators who questioned the situation, a bunch of elected officials walking around amidst an armed mob who wanted to "hang" them just seemed like a really bad idea.

As time went on, Roy and I both got updates over the phone from Leaders Schumer and McConnell, and the two of us decided to address the senators to fill them in on what we knew. First, Senator Tim Scott of South Carolina led the Senate and the assembled staff in prayer. Then Roy and I stepped up on an elevated platform in the room. I explained that we had separately spoken with Chuck and Mitch and that we were all in agreement: no matter how late it got that night, we would finish what we had started and certify the states' Electoral College votes. I noted that our number one plan was to return to the Senate chamber but we couldn't do that until it was safe. I got uniform applause when I said, "There is one thing that's going to happen for sure. These guys are in the Capitol right now. But no matter how long it takes, we will take it back and get the job done."

Roy and I then calmly divided our work into two very different and distinct jobs. The first was to keep the senators safe and in the room. The second was to try to talk some of them into consolidating their objections so that on top of an insurrection, we didn't go another twenty-four hours into the next day as was originally planned by the objectors. That would delay the outcome and only feed the conspiracy theories of the insurrectionists. While I spoke with some of the objectors, the work of talking to the Republican objectors about consolidating or dropping their objections was mainly Roy's—along with Senator McConnell's—job. I focused on keeping the senators in the room and—along with Senator Schumer—making a plan for our return to the Senate chamber.

I continued in my role as the contact with law enforcement. Several senators who weren't in the room with us needed to leave their offices because they were alone and weren't safe. Yet when the police went to get them, the senators were never sure if it was really law enforcement or rioters who had infiltrated the building. The call to Illinois Senator Tammy Duckworth, an incredible patriot who lost both her legs in a helicopter crash in Iraq while serving our country, was the most memorable one I made. I spoke with Tammy and connected her with the police commander, who reached by phone the officers who were outside her door. It was good to get Tammy out of her office and into the safer room. Roy also assisted and spoke with Senator Patty Murray and the officers who worked to bring her safely to our room from her hideaway office, which was in a particularly dangerous location off a hallway filled with insurrectionists.

At one point a police officer, his face cut up by rioters and visibly bleeding, asked me to get on the platform and announce that someone had just posted a selfie in the room on social media. The photo, according to the officer, could easily identify our undisclosed location. The officer asked me to tell the senators and assembled staff that no one should put photos of the room on Facebook or other social media platforms. He noted what other officers had told me earlier in the afternoon: they weren't certain if they had enough law enforcement left to protect us. And if the mob figured out where we were, it would—to put it mildly—not be good.

Even though I was not entirely sure who the selfie-poster was, I stood up on the elevated hearing platform that had now become our makeshift stage and addressed the assembled senators. "Someone has publicly posted a picture of themselves in this room. You know who you are," I said in my toughest former prosecutor—and more important, mom—voice.

I then pointed to the officer's cut-up face and reminded them that we were in the middle of an attempted coup and that there may not be enough officers to protect us: "Unless you want the mob doing this to you, take down that post that could lead them right to this place. No one should be putting up photos."

I felt like adding, "This isn't a photo line, this is an insurrection!"

Hours went by, during which we had TVs on around the room that showed the rioting. It was pretty somber when we all saw the insurrectionists in the Senate chamber, rifling through our desks.

Everyone waited for President Trump to tell his mob to go home. Instead Joe Biden, then the President-elect, spoke. Nearly all of us—including a good number of Republicans, many of whom had served alongside the incoming President—cheered when they saw our next President filling the void and decrying the violence.

Joe Biden wasn't the only one filling the gaping hole of leadership President Trump left that day. While Donald Trump sat in the White House dining room, watching TV, multiple members from both parties in the Senate—and, as we now know, the House—were calling law enforcement and military contacts. As was revealed on video during the January 6th House Select Committee hearing on October 13, 2022, the Democratic and Republican Senate and House leaders (located in separate rooms from the rest of us) were all making desperate calls—on their own and jointly—to the White House, the acting secretary of defense, and the acting attorney general, all begging for help to protect the Capitol, the members, and the staff.

One of the most memorable parts of the January 6th Select Committee video was Speaker Pelosi directly calling then-Governor Ralph Northam of Virginia, asking him to send in the Virginia National Guard, since there had been no sign that the Department of Defense was helping. Back in our room, the Virginia and Maryland Senators—Mark Warner, Tim Kaine, Ben Cardin, and Chris Van Hollen— were also in contact with their governors and their National Guards seeking military protection for the Capitol. Incoming Vice President Harris called me twice for updates.

In the course of the afternoon, I also had several discussions with Senator Schumer about what our options would be to finish our jobs if and when the Senate chamber and the complex were safely cleared, which was going to take longer than we thought. They had to do tests for chemicals and bombs. Given that there had been pipe bombs planted outside the Democratic and Republican Party buildings, they didn't know for certain if there were any explosives or other lethal or dangerous substances—such as anthrax—left in the Senate or House chamber or in the surrounding complex.

So this wasn't just a matter of getting the insurrectionists out, it was also about checking for what they had left behind. We discussed option B—holding the debate in the room where we were gathered—but agreed it wasn't optimal. While it was ready for cameras, it was important that we take back our chamber. I remember reminding Senator Schumer over the phone that there were a lot of people in the room, and while they were nearly all wearing masks, it was a human petri dish in there, just at the height of COVID.

As the hours went on, a few senators started to talk with me about going back to their offices. I explained that the police had not yet cleared the entire complex and that the law enforcement assessment was that it could be very dangerous. Rioters could be hiding in the hundreds and hundreds of rooms in the sprawling Capitol complex, and they all had to be cleared. Some of the rooms had been accidentally left unlocked before the insurrection started and were easily breached.

Somewhere along the way I figured out that the senators and their staffs were really hungry. I gathered some of the Senate staff and police in the room.

"We need to bring in some food for both the senators and staff or some of the senators are going to leave," I said. I noted the age of many of our members and that they needed basic meals on a regular basis. They could faint or worse and we had no idea how late in the evening we were going to be in the room.

Then someone—and I truly don't remember who it was except that it wasn't a senator—said, "Well, we can't bring in catering."

"Catering?" I said. "In the middle of an insurrection? No," I stressed, "that isn't on the table," noting that cafeteria staff and cooks and other workers were hiding all over the Capitol in fear for their lives.

"I have another idea," I said. I looked at the group and lowered my voice.

"Do you guys have keys to the Dirksen Cafeteria?" I asked.

They told me they did.

"Okay," I said, "here's what you're going to do. Since it's now safe for you to walk to the cafeteria, I need you to go in there and take some of those wheeling cafeteria trays—you know, the big ones with dividers that look like they belong in a hospital. And then go into the Dirksen Cafeteria and into those refrigerated cases where they keep the sandwiches and the salads and load up the carts."

Within thirty minutes they came back with carts of the salads and sandwiches. There was plenty for senators and staff. In fact, one senator actually asked me between bites of a many-layered sandwich how I had gotten such a great selection of items.

"You don't want to know," I said.

A few hours later we finally got the all clear and Senator Schumer addressed the room. We had good news to report to the leaders. Roy Blunt had talked through the objections with all the Senate objectors and thought he was close to getting them down to just one more state after Arizona—Pennsylvania. While House members would still be objecting to the certifications in Georgia, Michigan, Nevada, and Wisconsin, no senator would be joining them; if they had said they were going to do it before, they were withdrawing. The one exception was Josh Hawley, who still planned to object to Pennsylvania.

In any case, we knew we had a long night ahead, but at least we thought we could get the debate completed on the earlier Gosar/Cruz objection to Arizona in less than two hours, vote, and then return to the House before midnight. We would then go through the state roll call again, hear the objections to the states that didn't have a senator joining in, and when we got to the Pennsylvania electoral certification, go back to the Senate and vote. We would wait for a couple of hours to allow for more debate in the House, and then return to finish the remaining states up through Wyoming.

## Finishing the Job

When I got back to the Capitol, I talked to my staff. I had rejected any media interviews while the insurrection was going on because I felt my official responsibilities came first. "I won't do them until this is done," I said.

Now back at the Capitol, with the rioters cleared from the building, I did a live interview with Stephen Colbert right off the Senate floor. As his then-producer, Chris Licht—who went on to take the helm of CNN—later told me, it was an interview that stood the test of time. I was laser-focused on finishing our job and not letting the insurrectionists get the final word. When America woke up in the morning it had to be clear that the U.S. Senate and House had certified the Electoral College results and that the insurrection was over. They had to understand in no uncertain terms that Joe Biden and Kamala Harris had been duly certified to be the next president and vice president of the United States. I also called for prosecutions and accountability for what had happened.

Back on the floor that evening, I was still taking requests for speaking time and establishing a new speaking order. Several Republicans who hadn't been signed up to speak before the insurrection planned to speak now. They were aghast at what had happened. A number not only dropped their earlier objections (such as former Senator Kelly Loeffler of Georgia) but changed their votes to "No" on others' objections. That included Senators James Lankford and Steve Daines.

After the Senate debate we had the vote, and only six senators voted in favor of the Cruz objection (and that, of course, included Senator Cruz). Ninety-three voted no. In addition to Cruz, Senators Josh Hawley of Missouri, Tommy Tuberville of Alabama, Roger Marshall of Kansas, John Kennedy of Louisiana, and Cindy Hyde-Smith of Mississippi voted in favor of the objection.

Vice President Pence, Senator Blunt, and I returned to the House chamber with the three pairs of clerks with the mahogany boxes. Due to the foresight of a member of the parliamentarian's staff, the boxes had been removed from the Senate along with the senators when we were asked to evacuate the chamber. If left behind, those ballots would have most certainly been stolen or, more likely, burned and destroyed by the insurrectionists.

We continued through the roll call. When I read off the Georgia certifications, Trump-aligned Representative Jody Hice of Georgia objected on behalf of seventy-one fellow Republicans. He did not, however, have a senator objecting, so he had to withdraw it. The same thing happened when I read the votes for Michigan, but this time it was the infamous QAnon conspiracy theorist Representative Marjorie Taylor Greene of Georgia objecting to the Michigan votes on behalf of seventy Republicans. Again, no senator. The same thing happened in Nevada, with no senator joining the House objection.

But then it came to Pennsylvania. There the objections were led by Pennsylvania Representative Scott Perry and Senator Josh Hawley—the senator who had earlier defiantly saluted the rioters with his fist as he walked into the Capitol.

Bingo. They had a senator.

We returned to the Senate. The vote on the Pennsylvania objection was 92–7. That included some of the same senators voting in favor of the Arizona objection—Cruz, Hawley, Tuberville, Hyde-Smith, and Marshall. This time John Kennedy of Louisiana did not object, but two other senators took his place: Cynthia Lummis of Wyoming and Rick Scott of Florida.

After the vote, nearly all the senators went home—ready to be called back if needed—and the House continued to debate.

But Roy Blunt and I still had a job to do. At 3:30 A.M., the two of us and Vice President Pence made one last trip through the Capitol's corridor of power between the House and the Senate. With the young people carrying the mahogany boxes of ballots, we walked past the statues of George Washington and Abraham Lincoln and Thomas Jefferson and Rosa Parks. I thought about the fact that nearly seventy years had passed since Rosa Parks refused to give up her seat on that bus. Yet on this day—adorned with Confederate flags, swastikas, and noose symbols—white supremacists had actually tried to topple our government. As Black Capitol Police Officer Harry Dunn later told us, during the course of the riot he was called the "N-word" multiple times. With cuts and bruises, he finally collapsed in the Capitol Rotunda and said to a fellow officer, "Is this America? Is this America?"

That route—that walk—was the exact same one Senator Blunt and Vice President Pence and I had taken thirteen hours before. The first time we had led a long procession of our colleagues. There had been a sense of ceremony and celebration. But this time it was just the three of us. No other senators were there. Now it was silent. Glass was broken. Windows were taped up. Offices were in shambles. But we walked.

Sometimes when you do things in Congress, you realize later that they are really big deals but you were so caught up in the moment that it didn't feel like it at the time. This time it felt like it. We knew what that walk meant.

When we got to the House, we read through the last twelve states. After objecting to Wisconsin, the Trump-aligned Republican House members acknowledged that they had no senator who would join them in the objection.

Vice President Pence and I announced the final vote. Speaker Pelosi and I both thanked the vice president. The Senate chaplain—Chaplain Barry Black—gave a beautiful closing prayer that may have gotten lost in the archives of history, but it is worth remembering, since it pretty much summed up how everyone was feeling.

"We deplore the desecration of this building and the shedding of blood and the loss of life," he said.

Acknowledging the insurrection and its incitement, he added, "Words matter . . . The power of life and death is in the tongue . . . The price of eternal vigilance continues to be freedom's price."

Senator Blunt and I and House leaders Zoe Lofgren and Rodney Davis then signed multiple copies of the certified votes from the rostrum.

At 4 A.M., Roy and I walked back to the Senate. We stopped on the first floor to see all the damage that had been done to individual offices, including the parliamentarian's. I remember seeing one of the personal family photos of a beloved parliamentarian staff member strewn and seemingly broken on the floor. I wanted to make it better. I wanted to pick it up and put it back so she wouldn't see it like this in the morning, but I knew that everything should be preserved as evidence for the investigation.

The offices looked like crime scenes. In fact, they were.

As we left the torn-up office, I gave Roy a hug.

"See you tomorrow," he said, with his typical understatement.

Daybreak was approaching. There was one thing I knew for sure as I left Roy in the corridor. I would see him tomorrow.

And when tomorrow came, our democracy would still be there.

## "The Union Shall Go On."[43]

That "tomorrow"—as in January 7, the day after the insurrection—actually began for me just two hours after I left Roy in the corridor. That's how long I slept. The day dawned on discussions in the House of Representatives about a second impeachment proceeding against the President for inciting the insurrection. The day also marked the beginning of many federal law enforcement investigations that would lead to well over nine hundred prosecutions of the insurrection perpetrators. It also marked the beginning of the work Roy and I would do together—along with our colleagues, Homeland Security

---

43. Abraham Lincoln, 1863.

and Governmental Affairs Committee leaders Senators Gary Peters and Rob Portman—to investigate the security breakdowns at the U.S. Capitol. The following days would see the resignations of the Capitol Police chief and both the House and Senate sergeant at arms. New law enforcement leaders needed to be put in place. Families of officers who died as a result of the attack—a number of them by suicide—needed help. The police officers were not only physically injured, but so many had been traumatized by the attack, their spirits broken. Reinforcements from other police agencies as well as the National Guard were immediately brought in.

But despite all of that, as well as the additional challenge of skyrocketing COVID numbers, Roy and I had one more very important job: we needed to pull off an inauguration ceremony worthy of our country. After the insurrection, the stakes couldn't have been higher. The public's confidence in our democracy had been deeply shaken. The purpose of the ceremony was to mark the peaceful transfer of power from the previous administration to Joe Biden and Kamala Harris. It would have to be dignified, celebratory, and, yes, flawless.

Roy was both the chair of the Inauguration and the Senate Rules Committee and I was the committee's ranking member and incoming chair, but we had built up a trusting friendship and our staffs worked so well together that nothing was going to mess it up. Given the crisis the country had just gone through and the volatility of the politics on Capitol Hill, the moment called for calm, bipartisanship, and a historical understanding of the importance of the inauguration. Roy and I got it. We were more than up for it. And as we said many times to our colleagues and anyone else who asked us about the inaugural plans during those intense next few weeks, "Don't worry. We've got this."

During the days between the insurrection and the inauguration, January 20 (the day set by the Constitution for the new President's swearing-in), Roy and I received multiple requests, both publicly and privately, to cancel the planned public inauguration or to at least move it inside and convert it to a small, scaled-down event. While some people blatantly said they wanted it in a bunker, others suggested the House chamber (hmm . . . why don't we go back there again) or the Capitol Rotunda (which fit about fifty people during COVID). Some who called for a small indoor event were focused on COVID. I told them we had already significantly reduced the outdoor event and eliminated nearly everything a new president would usually do leading up to the ceremony and after it. In addition to that, no one was forcing anyone to go; we'd welcome the return of their inaugural tickets. But most of the calls received—particularly from members of Congress—were about security. They were concerned about more rioters or assassinations or killer drones above the Capitol. People were scared.

Back home, the Twin Cities' *Star Tribune* editorial board—whom I respect very much—publicly called on me to move the inauguration inside. In an editorial titled "Move Biden's Swearing-In Inside" (they weren't subtle), they noted that since the oath of office was only thirty-five words, and since there would be no parades or inaugural balls due to the coronavirus, and since the Capitol had been breached and overrun and security was of the utmost concern, there was no reason to re-create the pomp of the ceremony, which for years has been held on the west front of the Capitol, facing the National Mall and the iconic Washington Monument and Lincoln Memorial.

The editorial board was joined by many, many national commentators who raised these same points. I just disagreed. I felt it was a bad idea to move the ceremony inside. It would have meant that rioters and insurrectionists—under FBI investigation and soon to be facing Justice Department prosecutions—would have denied the incoming president a traditional inauguration. Roy Blunt felt the same way. And, most significantly, so did one other person whose opinion really mattered—in fact, mattered the most. That would be the President-elect, Joe Biden.

As I told my hometown newspaper's editorial board at the time, "Unless there is a real threat, we're not backing down. They [as in Donald Trump and the insurrectionists] should not scare us into changing the inauguration."

Of course, security was paramount. But unlike the disorganized and inadequate planning by then-Capitol law enforcement leaders for the election certification day, the security for the inauguration was run by the Department of Homeland Security, with the U.S. Secret Service taking the lead and coordinating efforts with the military and law enforcement. In the two weeks leading up to the inauguration, Senator Blunt and I were invited to attend multiple classified briefings with the heads of the agencies involved in inaugural security. We then invited the senators and House members on to a Zoom call with the agencies as well.

To our knowledge, this much member engagement on inauguration security had never happened before, but we adjusted to the circumstances with a pledge to the security leaders that we wouldn't give away their secrets. In the end we assured the members of Congress that the outdoor inauguration could be called off at any moment, subject to the views of the protective security agencies. We would never go forward if there were real security issues.

To my mind, what the naysayers at the time missed was this: taking down the ceremony was exactly what Donald Trump and the insurrectionists would have wanted. They had started their invasion on the platform where the ceremony was to occur. They had even tried to take down the two-story media tower that had been specifically designed for the inauguration and was already constructed on the grounds. They spray-painted the columns on the inaugural platform. They broke the historic windows behind the stage. They knew exactly what they were doing.

The other side of the coin? The nation badly needed to see Joe Biden sworn in as President of the United States. Americans also needed to see the leaders of both parties—from George Bush to Barack Obama—with him on the inaugural stage. They needed to see the leaders of Congress together. And they needed to see people outside politics bless the moment, which in this case included everyone from the incredible young poet Amanda Gorman to the United States Marine Band to Jesuit priest Father Leo O'Donovan and Reverend Silvester Beaman to Chief Justice John Roberts and Justice Sonia Sotomayor to Lady Gaga to Georgia fire captain Andrea Hall—who led the inauguration's Pledge of Allegiance—to Jennifer Lopez and Garth Brooks.

And for what it is worth, without the outside location we

would never have had that iconic visual of Bernie Sanders sitting by himself wearing those oversized Vermont mittens.

People yearned for normal again. They yearned for life and resurrection. All of that was very difficult to accomplish inside. In fact, with the COVID rules, it couldn't happen. And on that point, for a nation reeling from the pandemic, Americans really needed to see hope. They needed to see a new president take the reins with dignity and—yes—pomp and circumstance and patriotism. They needed inspiration.

An inauguration in a bunker just couldn't do that.

When Abraham Lincoln gave his first inaugural address in 1861 in front of the Capitol, its dome was only partially constructed, braced by ropes of steel. He promised he would finish it. He was criticized for spending funds on it during the Civil War. To those critics he replied, "If the people see the Capitol going on, it is a sign we intend the Union shall go on." And it did.

One hundred and sixty years later, we had the same obligation. We needed to show the people that "the Union shall go on."

The planning for the inauguration had actually begun over a year before. The Senate Rules Committee leaders, by law, took the lead on the inauguration, regardless of what party the president belonged to. But you can't exactly plan an inauguration without the input of the other Senate and House leaders assigned to the planning committee and without consulting with the incoming president. Beyond Roy Blunt, I had had many discussions with Senate and House leadership regarding the inauguration—including several with Speaker Pelosi and Leader Schumer. I also conferred with President Biden himself, as well as with members of his transition team.

December 8, 2020, marked the day that congressional leaders assigned to the inaugural committee all met in person for the first time since the election. Senator Blunt and I hosted the meeting in historic Senate Room 219 in the Capitol to discuss the ceremony's details. It was an interesting meeting indeed. First off, there were the participants (who were designated by law and title as members of the Joint Congressional Committee on Inaugural Ceremonies): Roy and myself, House Speaker Nancy Pelosi, House Majority Leader Steny Hoyer, Senate Minority Leader Mitch McConnell, and House Minority Leader Kevin McCarthy.

Now what could go wrong with that group assembled in one place?

The second issue? Complicating everything was the fact that the Republican leaders—one month after the election and more than three weeks after the race had been called by every network, including Fox—had not yet PUBLICLY conceded the election, because Donald Trump had not conceded the election. At the meeting Steny Hoyer offered a motion to recognize that our committee was in fact preparing for the inauguration of Joe Biden and Kamala Harris. Speaker Pelosi made the valid point that it would be helpful with the public if all the leaders acknowledged who had won. Noting that they didn't think it was the job of the committee to get ahead of Trump's legal challenges, the three Republicans voted against the resolution. While they later recognized Biden's victory, it wasn't going to happen that day.

The irony of it all? There we all were, planning the inauguration of Joe Biden and Kamala Harris. And—thankfully, of course—all the Republican congressional leaders planned to attend.

Believe it or not, it was a fairly functional meeting. Besides the obvious—that the Republicans wouldn't say who won—they were pragmatic in working with us to plan the ceremony. They knew that the speaker and I—and for that matter, Senator Blunt—were working with the Biden team on the plans. The morning of the meeting I had already spoken with Ron Klain—who the day before had been announced as Joe Biden's chief of staff—about some of the incoming administration's preferences and the need to make sure the event followed doctors' guidance.

Decisions had to be made. Invitations needed to be sent. The inaugural committee decided that day that we would follow COVID rules and require masks and social distancing. That meant a much smaller crowd and basically—depending on what the Biden team wanted to do with their designated space on the National Mall—an empty mall. The members' tickets for the event were drastically reduced to a member and a guest. The President-elect had tickets for a couple hundred guests. Foreign diplomats were designated tickets. And some former members of Congress had tickets. Basically that was it. There were those on the Hill who were not happy with the limited number of tickets, but in the end everyone seemed to understand.

Due to COVID and limits on the travel relating to it, there would be no parade. No inaugural ball (ah, the dress I never picked out). No fancy congressional lunch. And no big shindigs on the Mall the day before, although there was a delightful made-for-TV concert on the eve of the ceremony emceed by Tom Hanks.

While all of the missed events may have been disheartening, we were as resolute as ever in moving forward with a magnificent ceremony. We secured the media platform. We installed temporary replacement windows over the broken ones since there wasn't enough time to permanently replace them. And when the workers couldn't get all the spray paint off the columns they simply hid the vandalism with white paint.

Everyone rose to the challenge.

When the inaugural week arrived, the president-elect and vice president-elect kicked it off with what was truly a beautiful and meaningful display: nearly two hundred thousand flags flown in perfect rows on the National Mall to honor those who couldn't be with us. As far as the eye could see there were flags. They were solemn, but starkly beautiful; soulful, but hopeful. They perfectly captured what so many Americans were feeling.

Finally the big day came. I fielded many last-minute questions about COVID testing procedures and issues with seating, but for the most part people understood we were operating under some really difficult circumstances. In addition to the medically advised limits our inaugural committee placed on the number of attendees who could sit directly in front of the platform—in total there was room for only a couple thousand—there were also no people allowed in the long-stretching National Mall area, which for years had been controlled by the incoming administration's separate inaugural committee. In the past, the Mall would be filled with people without tickets. This time, because of COVID, the incoming administration's inaugural committee had turned the Mall space into the somberly beautiful "Field of Flags."

That all being said, nearly 40 million people (39.9 million to be exact) ended up watching the Biden-Harris inauguration from home and work, a number that Nielsen reported exceeded by 4 percent those 38.5 million who watched the Trump ceremony. (Okay, I just put that Trump number in there for fun—I know how obsessed Trump is about ratings—but it's true.)

On the day of the inauguration John and I started out by attending mass with the president and vice president and their families at Washington's Cathedral of St. Matthew the Apostle. From there we headed back to the Capitol, where Roy and I greeted the president-elect and vice president-elect and Dr. Jill Biden and Doug Emhoff and escorted them up the sweeping marble steps.

I wore my gold coat, in part because I felt it was important to remember that despite the insurrection and all the angst leading up to this day, it would be a joyous celebration of our democracy. No one was taking this day away from our country.

It turns out everyone got the same memo. They went bright. Michelle Obama looked stunning in her plum turtleneck, plum pants, and floor-length coat; Amanda Gorman—the first National Youth Poet Laureate—chose sunny yellow; Jill Biden wore an American-made jewel-toned coat and dress. Vice President Harris looked great in purple. Lady Gaga—well—what can I say? That was an amazing dress she wore—fitted navy on top with a humongous gold dove brooch, and then a voluminous, seemingly endless bright red silk skirt.

As I jokingly told my friends later, everything went so well with the inauguration except for one thing: "When

Lady Gaga and I showed up in the same dress. I had to go home and change."

To top it all off, right before the ceremony was set to begin, stunning flakes of snow descended from the bright blue sky, seemingly out of nowhere. Given that it was 42 degrees at the time, it was nothing short of magical. In fact, it was so unexpected by everyone—including the National Weather Service—that when Roy spoke he made a joke about the fact that wherever I went, it always snowed.

I was focused on one thing: we needed to convey strength and goodwill and we needed to smile. This was a moment to rejoice in the simple but grand gesture of the peaceful transfer of power in our unshakable democracy. Our nation had been through hell, first with the pandemic, and then with the insurrection. As the first speaker, it was on me to set the tone.

That's why I started off my remarks with a big smile and by noting the presence of Vice President Pence with a nod to the former presidents (Obama, Bush, and Clinton) who were on the stage. Trump—by his own decision—was not there. This would mark the first time in more than 150 years that a president had skipped his successor's inauguration.

My message? Our new president was being publicly acknowledged and anointed not just by Democrats, but by Republican leaders as well. I also mentioned the attendance of members of Congress, Supreme Court justices, and "a whole bunch of Bidens."

As the sun brightly shone on the stage and the flags flew in a brisk wind on the National Mall, I called the peaceful transition of power "a conveyance of a sacred trust." And I said this about the significance of the day:

Two weeks ago, when an angry, violent mob staged an insurrection and desecrated this temple of our democracy, it awakened us to our responsibilities as Americans. This is the day when our democracy picks itself up, brushes off the dust, and does what America always does. We go forward as a nation under God, indivisible, with liberty and justice for all.

I further noted that we must pledge "never to take our democracy for granted" and that we were celebrating a new president who vowed to "cross the river of our divides to a higher plane."

I also took pride in the fact that we were celebrating Kamala Harris, the first African American, first Asian American, and first woman to ascend to the position of vice president. "When she takes the oath of office," I said, "little girls and boys across the world will know that anything and everything is possible."

After I was done, Lady Gaga came to the stage in that stupendous patriotic dress and belted out the words of our national anthem. She memorably and forcefully gestured to the standing flag when she came to the line "Gave proof through the night *that our flag was still there.*"

Goose bumps. Yes, we had come through the night. And yes, the flag was still there.

But it wasn't all oohs and aahs. I had a job to do. After our speeches, Roy and I were effectively the emcees. I returned to the podium a number of times. First, to introduce Justice Sotomayor, who administered the oath of office to our new vice president. I also introduced Chief Justice Roberts, who administered the oath to the President. When I introduced

Chief Justice Roberts, I noted that the sun was shining on the new President and that it was the first time in American history that J.Lo (who had just sung "This Land Is Your Land" and "America the Beautiful") was the warm-up act to a Chief Justice.

One of the more amusing—and terrifying—parts of the ceremony for me was that because of COVID, there was no one really managing the speakers and program on stage. Few people were allowed on the platform because of the social distancing rules. Yet someone was supposed to walk to my seat and escort me up to the podium each time I spoke. After the first time, I quickly realized that this wasn't happening. I had a handwritten piece of paper (known in D.C. lingo as a "tick tock") with the order of the speakers in my pocket. I took the paper out of my pocket over and over again. I kept watch over it to the minute. Honestly, my job at that moment felt closer to being an emcee at a Rotary Club for a Tuesday morning ham-and-eggs breakfast than being the host of an internationally viewed inauguration for the President of the United States.

One sad result of my self-directed emceeing was that in several of the major published inaugural photos, while the crowd was gazing ahead, I was looking down. My eyes were never on my phone—even though it may have looked like they were—but instead I was constantly scanning the crumpled paper containing the order of the program. I had to make sure the right people were getting up on stage when they needed to, and that included me.

It all came to a crescendo right after Joe Biden had taken the oath of office. The United States Marine Band played "Hail to the Chief." The new President waved to the crowd and I came to the podium again. Why? According to the notes I had been given, he and I were to wait together for the twenty-one-gun salute and then I was to officially introduce him as the President of the United States. That's when he would give his speech.

The President and I stood together. We waited and we waited and we waited for the sounds of the gunfire. Not only did we not hear the gunshots twenty-one times, we didn't hear them once. We kept waiting for the "Voice of God" to announce the salute.

Instead a booming voice over the loudspeaker announced that the crowd should sit down.

I kept standing. The crowd started to look confused.

Finally I said to the new President, "They were going to do the twenty-one-gun salute."

He said, "I know."

I said, "Maybe it was canceled."

He said, "I better sit down."

I went over to Roy. He didn't know either. It was on my tick tock. I showed him.

Finally someone came over and said, "So sorry, the twenty-one-gun salute got canceled late last night because some people thought it might scare people at home after the insurrection."

"OMG," I thought, "this is so pandemic fog–like! They just forgot to tell me, not to mention the new President!"

Instead I said, "Thanks for letting me know."

I immediately went to the podium and did my job. Smiling and pretending like nothing had happened, I said, "Ladies and gentlemen, the moment we have all been waiting for" (well, that was sure right, both metaphorically and in the moment). I further noted that it was "my honor to be the *first* person" to officially introduce the next President of the United States, Joseph Biden.

The best part was that afterward tons of people asked me about the delay. Some people were really scared because they thought I was privy to a security threat; a reporter on one of the networks had even raised that possibility. Others thought it was an issue about the exact time a new president can address the nation. Another theory? An audio problem. My favorite? One senator told me he thought I had to wait for a commercial break!

No one guessed the truth, that pandemic programming problems didn't just happen on botched family Zoom calls or virtual class reunions. Someone just forgot to tell me—and the President—that the official program had changed.

Joe Biden gave a strong speech that day.

"This is America's day," he declared, "this is democracy's day . . . America's been tested anew, and America has risen to the challenge."

It was an uplifting speech and a stark contrast from Donald Trump's dark portrayal of America four years before on that same platform.

Joe Biden thanked his predecessors for being there and gave a shout-out to President Carter—then ninety-six—whom he'd spoken to the night before. He acknowledged the loss of lives to COVID. He addressed "the rise of political extremism, white supremacy, and domestic terrorism" that we "must confront and we will defeat."

The main focus of the speech was unity. The new President asked every American "to join [him] in this cause," adding that in America, "better angels have always prevailed."

He ended with words from the song "American Anthem": "America, America, I gave my best to you."

Garth Brooks then took the stage to reinforce the President's inaugural theme with a heartfelt rendition of "Amazing Grace."

"I once was lost, but now I'm found."

Finishing to strong applause, Brooks tipped his black cowboy hat to the new President and hugged or shook hands with everyone in sight, including George Bush, Bill Clinton, Barack Obama, and Mike Pence. Neither Roy nor I knew what song Garth Brooks was going to sing, and when Roy returned to the podium, he thanked Brooks and spontaneously reminded the crowd of the moment when President Obama sang the very same hymn at the Emanuel AME Church in Charleston, South Carolina, during his stirring 2015 eulogy for Reverend Clementa Pinckney.[44]

And if all of that wasn't emotional enough, we ended the ceremony with Amanda Gorman, who, at age twenty-two, was the youngest inaugural poet ever. Jill Biden had invited Gorman to write and present the inaugural poem after seeing her read her poetry at the Library of Congress.

Amanda Gorman simply radiated goodness. She had written the poem—"The Hill We Climb"—in the weeks in between the insurrection and the inauguration.

---

44. Reverend Pinckney had been gunned down and killed on June 17, 2015, along with eight of his parishioners, during their Wednesday-night Bible study at the church.

It was an honest and beautiful tribute to our nation.

She began by asking the question on so many Americans' minds:

> When day comes, we ask ourselves, where can we find
> light in this never-ending shade?

Line by line, she answered that question. She first acknowledged what had happened and where we were:

> Somehow we weathered and witnessed a nation that isn't
> broken, but simply unfinished . . .
> And so we lift our gaze, not to what stands between us,
> but what stands before us.

Then, on the very platform where the insurrectionists had—just two weeks before—sprayed paint on the marble columns near her podium and broken the windows behind her, she gave the nation both wise guidance and hope with these closing words:

> But while democracy can be periodically delayed, it can
> never be permanently defeated . . .
> For there is always light, if only we're brave enough to see
> it, if only we're brave enough to be it.

Wow.

The pandemic, the losses, the attack on the Capitol—it was all just the backdrop now. Because up front and center was twenty-two-year-old Amanda Gorman, the very embodiment of the youth and vitality of our country at its best, imploring us to be brave enough to be the light.

She definitely met the moment, and in doing so she helped us to meet it too.

You start where you are. That's what we did that day. We had a new president and vice president and we gave them an inauguration that lived up to America's promise. That was our hill to climb that day. And we made it to the top.

# 6

# Trials and Tribulations

Life Lesson: *"We can never tell what is in store for us."*
—President Harry Truman

## Governing

Whoever thought it was going to be easy to govern our country in a post-Trump presidency with a 50/50, split-down-the-middle Senate, please raise your hand. Seriously, do it now.

Here's the score:

When Joe Biden took the oath of office on that beautiful blue-sky day, no one thought it was going to be easy. The country was still divided. Our politics were still corrosive. The pandemic was still raging. Americans could not even agree on whether to follow the advice of doctors to get through it. In a number of states, by the end of 2021, after the vaccine had been readily available for some time, nearly one-half of the people eligible refused to even get the shot.

Beyond the politicization of the vaccines and the misinformation about their side effects, there were other issues. Given the speed at which the vaccines had to be developed and distributed, that was not unexpected. But in the polarized partisan environment in which we live, every issue and every error would be put under one big magnifying glass. Setting expectations was important.

When the Pfizer and Moderna vaccines arrived in late 2020, it was hard to get them out immediately. And there were naturally production, delivery, and workforce issues. Getting minus-90-degree vaccine storage freezers—which just happened to require a temperature colder than Antarctica in the winter—into the middle of rural Texas or, for that matter, the Iron Range of Minnesota, was never going to be easy. And while the vaccines greatly improved the survival rates of those who chose to get the shots—including seniors and people with serious medical conditions—older people and those who were ill to begin with could still die from the virus even after being vaccinated.

With the support of Congress, the Biden administration took on the vaccine distribution issue with a vengeance, and put in place a professional team—led by former Obama budget czar Jeff Zients—to oversee it. By the fall of 2022, with ever-changing variants and a million Americans dead, an astounding 224 million people—or nearly 68 percent of the U.S. population—had finally gotten fully vaccinated, with 79 percent receiving at least one dose. The best figure? Per the CDC, approximately 90 percent of Americans over eighteen have gotten at least one dose. People seemed to eventually get the message, especially when they had an unvaccinated loved one die of the virus or its complications.

By 2022, U.S. COVID death and hospitalization rates had greatly decreased. Yet, during that same year, major pandemic-related economic and supply chain issues continued to rock the world, greatly aggravated by Russia's illegal invasion of Ukraine. No country was immune from the virus.

In a global, interconnected economy, a COVID lockdown in China or missing parts in Canada could easily halt production in North Carolina and reduce the availability of everything from SUVs to sofas. And as we all learned in high school economics, when supply goes down and demand goes up, prices will inevitably increase.

Corporate price gouging—a problem predating the pandemic—got worse as energy and pharmaceutical companies seized the moment and charged exorbitant prices. The international shipping conglomerates, for example, made tons of money off the backs of American consumers, manufacturers, and farmers by charging excessive rates for shipping containers (pricing them at an average of four times what they were asking for pre-pandemic). With unbelievable chutzpah, the shippers even refused at times to fill empty containers with American exporters' products, choosing instead to quickly leave American ports and return to Asia with containers full of air to fulfill more orders abroad. These practices—one of the major factors contributing to our pricing and supply chain problems—allowed the shipping conglomerates to rake in a record $190 billion in profits in 2021, a whopping sevenfold increase over the previous year.

The shipping issue was the impetus for successful legislation that I led in 2022 with two South Dakota Republicans, Senator John Thune and Representative Dusty Johnson, and Representative John Garamendi, Democrat of California. In June of 2022, when President Biden signed our bill into law to rein in the conglomerates' price gouging, we were surrounded by consumer groups, port authorities, manufacturing CEOs, and the head of the American Farm Bureau Federation. That's not a group that usually gets together for an afternoon at the White House, but that's how big a problem it truly was. And, based on year-end 2022 data, since our bill passed, rates have significantly declined!

Another factor that wreaked havoc on our economy? Workforce shortages. The lack of workers was (and is) a major contributing factor to inflation, supply chain disruptions, and, depending on your location, limited or nonexistent provision of services. There are many reasons for the worker shortages: (1) we've tragically lost tens of thousands of workers to the virus; (2) during the course of the pandemic, many older workers took early retirement; (3) young people, yearning for more flexible work situations and virtual work environments, have not always returned to traditional jobs; (4) child care—which was already hard to come by and afford before 2020—has been even more difficult to find and pay for during and after the pandemic, leading fewer parents to return to the workforce; and (5) frontline workers—particularly in the health-care and assisted-living professions—have been burned out by long and difficult hours and have left their fields for other less taxing professions. In total, so many people left the workforce during the latter half of the pandemic that the era has been rightfully dubbed "the Great Resignation."

All told, by mid-2022 (while the number may decrease in the future due to economic conditions) over ten million jobs remained open in the U.S., with two million openings in the education and health-care sectors alone. As I once told Secretary of Labor Marty Walsh, "when Sven and Ole's Pizza in Grand Marais, Minnesota, can only open four days a week with no lunch service, you know we have a workforce problem."

While increased wages, private sector incentives, and

private and public apprenticeship and training programs have encouraged more people to return to the workforce, Washington's (and by this I really mean Republicans') longtime refusal to act on immigration reform—something I've long championed—further constrains our country's ability to fill jobs.[45] In fact, U.S. immigration declined from the Census Bureau's annual projections of a million new immigrants a year to below three hundred thousand in 2021.

Russia's brazen invasion of Ukraine and the rightful decision by Europe and the U.S. and our allies across the globe to respond with severe sanctions on Russian exports and businesses also created major short-term shocks to the economy, including escalating global fuel prices, exacerbated by the actions of the international oil cartel OPEC, whose members include Russia, Iran, and Saudi Arabia. Leaders across the world correctly predicted that energy prices would most likely go up as a result of the coordinated sanctions, and that's why allied countries immediately started looking for alternative energy supplies and ways to assist people so that they could better afford increased heating costs.

Along with the vast majority of Democrats and Republicans in Congress, I supported the sanctions against Russia, as well as later actions to expand them. I had visited Ukraine on several occasions, including with Senator John McCain

---

45. Several times during the last fifteen years we have been close to passing immigration reform. Yet each time, despite bipartisan support, our work has been blown up by the right wing. These legislative efforts include a comprehensive 2007 George Bush bill stopped by Senate Republicans, an Obama-era effort that passed the Senate but was stymied by House Republicans, and a bipartisan Senate bill that was produced by a "gang" of senators (including me) only to be stopped by the Trump administration.

seven weeks after Donald Trump had gotten elected but before he had been sworn into office. Along with Senator Lindsey Graham, McCain and I spent New Year's Eve of 2016 on the Russian front lines in southeastern Ukraine, including stops in Mariupol and Shyrokyne with then-Ukrainian President Poroshenko. I went again right before the 2022 war started with a bipartisan group of senators to meet with President Zelenskyy to pledge our support to him and his people, and then again with Senator Rob Portman in August 2022 in the midst of the war to meet again with Zelenskyy and his defense minister. My interest in the region was grounded in both local and national interests. First, Minnesota is home to sixteen thousand Ukrainian Americans. Second, I had serious concerns about Vladimir Putin's continual global aggression and his disdain for democracy. If he had been allowed to run roughshod over a neighboring sovereign country with little consequence, there would have been no end to what he did next. We had to respond and support the people of Ukraine against the invasion and the unimaginable war crimes and atrocities committed against complete and utter innocents, men, women, and children alike.

But ultimately—no matter the circumstances or how good the explanations—Americans were still caught up in a whirlwind of pandemic workforce transition, rising prices, and random and incredibly frustrating shortages of goods and services. While workers' wages rightfully increased, the pandemic-related supply chain issues, the price gouging, the lack of workers, and the Russian invasion of Ukraine all contributed to an increase in the cost of living. Any inflationary pressure brought on by government spending—by that I mean appropriations designated by Congress during both administrations to respond to the pandemic—would have been eliminated or greatly reduced if congressional Republicans (and yes, a few Democrats) would've been open to overturning the most egregious of the Trump tax cuts. That included targeted tax increases aimed at the wealthy (as in major corporations and those households making over $400,000 a year). In other words, we could have made (and still can make) those changes to both bring down costs for people and pay down the debt.

In the end, the 2022 Inflation Reduction Act—supported entirely by Democrats—was paid for mainly by some increased corporate tax rates. But Republican resistance still meant that the basic Trump corporate tax rates stayed in effect. Many business leaders had assumed the rates would have been increased to somewhere in the neighborhood of 25 percent when President Biden took office, after they had been decreased to a 21 percent flat rate under Donald Trump. Before the Trump tax cuts, the corporate tax rate was upward of 35 percent. Every point increase above 21 percent could have meant another $100 billion every ten years to either pay down the national debt or help American taxpayers afford things like housing and child care.

As has been widely acknowledged, the Federal Reserve was slow to respond to inflation, believing at the time that it was a temporary situation. In June of 2021 I attended a small meeting with a few members of the Joint Economic Committee with the Federal Reserve chair, Jerome Powell, someone I respect. We specifically pressed Powell on the inflation issue. Concerned about the workforce issue, I further asked him about the economic impact of the lack of workers. By 2022 the Fed—which I view as an important tool of U.S. economic policy, having been in Congress during the 2008–

2009 downturn and having seen firsthand the stabilizing effects of the Fed's fiscal policy decisions—changed course and started increasing interest rates to rein in inflation.

Meanwhile, our task in Congress—and President Biden's in the White House—was to immediately deal with the pandemic's continual stress on our health-care system and economy, while simultaneously taking on our country's long-term challenges, which had either lain dormant or gotten worse during the Trump administration. These included ever-worsening climate change; immigration reform; income disparity; health-care costs; tech policy; corporate consolidation; child care and family leave; affordable post-secondary education; gun safety; and the protection of civil rights—from voting to privacy to criminal justice reform to reproductive freedom.

Our country's reputation around the world had also been badly tarnished during the Trump years, and it was on Joe Biden and his diplomatic and security teams to reset our relations around the world to deal with two major threats: first, a tyrant in Vladimir Putin who seemingly knew—and knows—no limits; and second, an ever-expanding Chinese sphere of influence that had—and has—significant implications for the U.S. economy.

In addition, in the Mideast there were ongoing Israeli/Palestinian issues, the withdrawal of troops from Afghanistan, and a dangerous escalation of Iran's nuclear capabilities. Donald Trump's ill-fated decision to take us out of the Obama-era nuclear agreement with Iran and other nations made things decidedly worse, not better. The agreement was not perfect, to be sure, but once it had been entered into, getting out of it made inspection and monitoring of Iranian nuclear facilities even more difficult and lessened any potential U.S. leverage.

Another issue confronting the Biden administration from the start? Overlaying all of these crises was a depleted and demoralized federal workforce, one that lost much of its mojo during the Trump administration. There were an untold number of early retirements and resignations during the Trump years, and thus the Biden administration began its term with thousands and thousands of unfilled positions, particularly in the State Department, the Justice Department, and at the Environmental Protection Agency. Add to that the pandemic and the Great Resignation, and it was harder than ever to steer the ship that is the federal bureaucracy.

Finally, when Joe Biden took office our country was more politically divided than ever. This was caused in part by the fact that our citizens increasingly rely on completely separate silos to obtain their news and political information, whether it's Fox News or MSNBC or algorithm-driven Facebook pages. But the divide was also exacerbated by the vitriolic rhetoric and anger of the Trump era. Finding common ground—which has always been my approach to solving problems was, and is, much harder than it was even a decade ago.

I saw for years how rank partisanship—pushed to the brink by a glut of dark-money spending—increasingly tainted our work in the Senate. It has become more and more difficult to reach across the aisle to tackle our nation's toughest problems and find solutions. That's why I did not go into the post-Trump era naive about how hard it would be to take on our enormous challenges. I just thought—and I continue to believe—that we can and must meet them, no matter how difficult the obstacles may be.

I knew that given Democrats' and Republicans' close

numbers in Congress, we would not be able to confront all of our challenges at once. Some would need to be tackled sooner, and some, unfortunately, would likely need to be taken on later. I also knew that delay would inevitably lead to dashed hopes and numerous disappointments, since expectations for the new administration were so high. The jobs we ultimately got done sooner—like investing big-time in broadband and finally taking on climate change and lifting the ban on negotiating prescription drug prices for seniors— were monumental and a blast to get over the finish line. The ones that still remain to get done—from bringing down costs on everything from housing to child care, to training our workforce and passing immigration reform, to protecting voting rights and codifying reproductive freedom into law, for example—are motivators for going to work every day, and never, ever giving up. There's just too much at stake.

But even I never predicted the extent of the trials and tribulations that would come our way in 2021 and 2022. Some we handled really well, and some—due in large part to the incredible partisan constraints on our politics, the dark-money spending, and archaic Senate rules—not so much.

## Mr. Phil E. Buster

One time a few years back I was in the car with a young state staffer. I was late to a meeting. As I ran out of the vehicle, I turned to him and said quickly, "When I get back remind me that I have to make a call to D.C. about the filibuster."

An hour later I was back in the car and there was one of the staff member's signature Post-it Notes stuck on the dashboard. He would conveniently use the Post-its—in a rainbow of colors—to remind me to make upcoming calls as we drove around the state. This time the Post-it read "Call Mr. Phil E. Buster in D.C."

Not familiar with the crazy ways of Washington, that is exactly what he thought I had said.

That's a true story. He and I had a running joke about it for years.

I start this discussion about our current American policy challenges with a nod to the enormous obstacles created by that guy—Mr. Phil E. Buster. We are the only democracy in the world that demands 60 percent of the vote of lawmakers to pass major policy reforms. Under the current Senate rules, senators can prolong debate—without even having to speak—and stop an actual vote on a bill unless sixty or more senators invoke something called "cloture" to end the debate. Without the sixty senators to end the debate (and thus end the faux filibuster), there will be no vote.

As Massachusetts Senator Henry Cabot Lodge once said over a century ago, "To vote without debating is perilous, but to debate and never vote is imbecile." In other words, with today's requirement that there be sixty votes to allow for serious consideration of any major bill, we basically exist in a perpetual state of "failure to launch." In a deeply divided country with an outsized percentage of representation in the U.S. Senate given to people living in small states (for instance, California, population 39,185,605, has two U.S. senators, the same as Wyoming, population 581,075), it is hard to imagine that in this era we could ever get to the magic number of sixty Democratic senators. And so long as the Republicans continue to vote in lockstep on key procedural votes, major legislation will only rarely be unleashed from the filibuster. Progress will be blocked on a range of key policies that may even garner support from 60 to 80 percent of the public.

It is important to note that the filibuster is not part of the U.S. Constitution. As Adam Jentleson, who served as deputy chief of staff for former Leader Harry Reid, recounts in his book *Kill Switch*, the filibuster was also not part of the original Senate rules and was not even used until 1837. When Thomas Jefferson—who, as vice president during John Adams's presidency, presided over the Senate—wrote *A Manual of Parliamentary Practice for the Use of the Senate of the United States* in 1801, it contained no reference to the filibuster. It did, however, have a lot to say about "Order in Debate" and decorum. "No one is to disturb another in his speech by hissing, coughing, spitting, speaking or whispering to another; nor to stand up or interrupt him," Jefferson wrote of the expected Senate etiquette while a person was speaking in the chamber.

It was Senator John C. Calhoun, of South Carolina, who first notoriously used the filibuster procedure to delay legislation in the 1840s. As the decades went on, other segregationists seized on the procedure to prevent civil rights legislation from advancing and becoming law. Fast-forwarding to the way it works today, the Senate minority can essentially halt debate and delay or stop votes on nearly all legislation. That way of doing business is inimical to the Framers' intent, with Article I, Section 1 of the Constitution—which sets up the country's legislative bodies—saying nothing whatsoever about the "filibuster" and stating only, "All legislative Powers herein granted shall be vested in a Congress of the United States, which shall consist of a Senate and House of Representatives."

The use of the filibuster—now in the hands of Senate Minority Leader Mitch McConnell—has gotten worse and worse
over the years. Of the thousands of times it has been used in
U.S. history, half of those have occurred in just the last twelve
years. The filibuster has truly turned into an albatross, a procedure with a highly discriminatory history that too often stops
our country from moving forward to face the difficult issues of
the modern age. The filibuster means that things just sit, mired
in the Senate swamp, which by the way is the actual name of a
grassy knoll located right in front of the Capitol.[46]

I say all this knowing that using a simple majority vote
in the Senate could well lead to some things passing that I
don't agree with, just like what happens in the House. My
response? There are two other players here—the House and
the President—that you need to pass bills.

My other response? In a filibuster-free Senate, at least
senators would own their decisions and we would stop trying
to fit major policy responses into a host of strange filibuster
exceptions carved out over the years to meet the demands of
previous eras, as opposed to the era we actually live in.

That's really both the most hilarious and saddest part
about our current situation (if you are up for gallows humor).
In the past, senators would creatively enact exemptions to the
filibuster to keep up with the times or serve what they felt
were the nation's best interests. Even Senator Robert Byrd—a

---

46. Biographers of the late Senator Ted Kennedy, of Massachusetts, described the "Senate Swamp" in 2015: "a patch of ground in front of the Senate side of the East Front of the Capitol that was often used for press events."
Nick Littlefield and David Nexon, *Lion of the Senate: When Ted Kennedy Ral-
lied the Democrats in a GOP Congress* (New York: Simon & Schuster, 2015),
p. 321.

staunch defender of Senate rules—once said that "certain rules that were necessary . . . must be changed to reflect changed circumstances." Yet now an out-of-whack Supreme Court has thrown out decades of established precedent—including *Roe v. Wade*'s protection of women's freedom to make decisions on reproductive health care—but we in the Senate, because of those who defend the filibuster at all costs, cannot respond legislatively due to an antiquated rule put in place before women could even vote. How messed up is that?

The advantage of getting rid of—or at least reforming—the archaic sixty-vote requirement? At least people could no longer hide behind the cloak of "Well, we just don't have sixty votes." And for the most part, when the stars are aligned, it would actually allow our country to move forward to pass legislation that would be in sync with both the public's wishes AND the public interest.

As Senator Byrd once acknowledged, there is well-established history for change and reform to the filibuster procedure. Throughout Senate history, there have been more than 160 exceptions carved out to the threshold, which comprise some of the biggest subjects of legislative debate as well as the smallest. In fact the sixty-vote threshold used to be higher, but it was changed in 1975 from sixty-seven to sixty votes, a change led by my late mentor Walter Mondale.[47]

---

47. In his autobiography, Walter Mondale wrote that "[a] sixty-vote cloture threshold was a big victory" because it made "it easier to round up votes for cloture." As the former vice president and Minnesota senator emphasized of his time—and the benefits of reducing the necessary threshold—in the Senate: "You could tell a colleague that you had, say, fifty-eight votes and absolutely needed his or her vote to get to sixty." Walter F. Mondale (with

The current 160 exceptions—which require only a majority fifty-one-vote margin—range from confirmations for nominees, "reconciliation" (think taxes and spending), the disapproval of arms sales, and compensation plans for victims of space and nuclear accidents. Additionally, time and time again the majority in the Senate has also changed the rules in other ways to help pass important legislation, such as the Natural Gas Policy Act and the funding of the Selective Service System.

The best way to see the utter unfairness of how the filibuster has currently evolved is this: while it takes only fifty-one votes to approve a Supreme Court Justice—note the approvals of Gorsuch, Kavanaugh, and Coney Barrett—it would take sixty votes to enact into law the very policy (as in *Roe v. Wade* rights) that six justices overturned with their conservative majority *Dobbs v. Jackson Women's Health Organization* (2022) decision. In other words, after nearly fifty years, three justices who were confirmed with just over *fifty* votes—and a few of their friends who were already on the nation's highest court—overruled the *Roe* precedent and changed the lives of millions of women. We can fix it—but because of the filibuster, only with *sixty* votes.[48]

---

David Hage), *The Good Fight: A Life in Liberal Politics* (New York: Scribner, 2010), pp. 121–132.

48. Even if you want to blame former Majority Leader Harry Reid and Democrats for making the initial change to the fifty-one-vote threshold vote for non–Supreme Court judges, expanded on by then-Majority Leader Mitch McConnell to include Supreme Court justices, the fact is, this is where we are today.

It makes no sense—none whatsoever.

Or how about this? It takes only fifty-one votes for tax-and-spend policies, so any policies we want to enact into law on critical subjects like immigration reform or environmental protection *must* involve either taxing or spending in order to avoid the sixty-vote requirement. Rather than voting on the best immigration policy or the best environmental policy, we are forced to fit the policies into a "tax and spend" framework in order to get the votes necessary to do anything.

And it gets weirder. While it takes sixty votes to pass any laws or regulations that don't involve taxing and spending, it takes fifty-one votes to overturn them under the Congressional Review Act (which has been used to overturn twenty rules), and again, only fifty-one votes to put the justices on the Supreme Court who strike them down.

Here's another example of the hypocrisy: caps on insulin prices under Medicare were given a green light by the Senate parliamentarian under the reconciliation rules for the recently passed Inflation Reduction Act. But younger and middle-aged people are still out of luck. Based on a Senate Republican motion that resulted in a parliamentary ruling that extending the Medicare insulin caps model to the rest of the population was "out of order," younger Americans can't enjoy the same insulin pricing caps that all seniors can now take advantage of. Thus, due solely to obsolete Senate rules, seniors are protected from insulin price increases, but for everyone else, you're on your own.

I believe that if we don't make some changes to the Senate rules in the very near future, we will be forever hampered in our ability to protect the right to vote and to respond to some of the biggest problems the world has ever faced. The rules must be changed to allow us to vote either for or against legislation on a timely basis as well as to more quickly approve a president's appointees for important posts. When half the posts in the U.S. government remain vacant for years as they await Senate confirmation, it makes it very difficult for our country—regardless of who is president—to have an effective and functional government.

So that's the procedural backstory behind the tales you are about to hear. Be assured the names have not been changed to protect the innocent (or the guilty). These stories are all from the 117th Congress—as in the years 2021 and 2022. They are good and bad and, yes, at times completely ridiculous. But unless you understand the archaic system in which we function—or should I say *dys*function?—in the U.S. Senate, it makes it hard to grasp two things: (1) why we can't quickly pass things when 60 or 70 or even 80 percent of the American people are with us (like an assault weapons ban, or codifying abortion rights into law); and (2) how extraordinary a feat it truly is when we get something done.

That happened in the last six months of 2022. We actually got things done. It happened, mind you, after a full year and a half of mindless Senate floor drudgery—which mainly featured day after day and week after week of procedural votes on nominees for everything from the Export-Import Bank to the U.S. Court of Claims.

Yet suddenly—seemingly out of nowhere—a switch went on (and it wasn't a kill switch). Some of the success was the result of months of negotiation and comity across the aisle. Some of it was due to the keen and relentless leadership of Senator Chuck Schumer and our Democratic Senate leadership team, Republican leadership on certain bipartisan issues, as well as that of Speaker Nancy Pelosi and President Biden, his Chief of Staff Ron Klain, his experienced and respected cabinet members, and the White House staff, including Steve Ricchetti, Louisa Terrell, and Reema Dodin. Some of it was just plain bare-knuckles politics and good fortune. We were, as they say, in the right place at the right time. But whatever it was, it was exhilarating to be part of it. We didn't do everything by any means, but we did good. And, just as every pundit had counted us out in the 2022 midterms, our "doing good" was in part understood and recognized by the voters. We were up against a lot of headwinds, but the fact that we walked into the election armed with results and accomplishments mattered.

## The Good

Elizabeth Warren was wearing a hoodie.

Through the thirty-six hours of voting to pass the most consequential climate legislation of our time—starting on August 6, 2022, running through the night, and ending on the afternoon of August 7—Elizabeth had on that hoodie.

Our Democratic bill—titled the Inflation Reduction Act by Senator Joe Manchin—had been painstakingly negotiated by Senator Schumer and Senator Manchin for months, and nearly every Democratic Senator, including myself, had contributed in some way to the final product. Its provisions included the most significant step we had ever taken toward saving our planet, by committing to reduce our nation's greenhouse gases by 40 percent by the year 2030. It also reduced the debt by $238 billion, after the Republican tax cuts of 2017 (most distinguished by their giveaways to the wealthy) had increased the deficit by an estimated $1.9 trillion over eleven years. In addition, our Inflation Reduction Act took on the pharmaceutical companies by allowing Medicare to negotiate for less expensive prescription drugs for our nation's seniors, something I had been championing for years. Although the agreed-to prescription drug provision was much more narrow than I would have liked, my years of work leading the effort to lift the ban on Medicare negotiation—something that had been practically written into law by the pharma companies themselves twenty years before—would finally pay off for the American people. And for their sake, I vowed it would be the beginning and not the end when it came to drug price reductions.

And through it all, Elizabeth wore that hoodie. Now, she wasn't wearing it in any conventional manner, that's for sure. It was worn tucked under a pseudo–suit jacket, which was actually more like a warm-up suit, but it passed for a jacket on C-SPAN. The look was honestly so unique that one Minnesotan who had tuned in to watch the proceedings called to inquire.

"Is Elizabeth Warren wearing an airport neck pillow under her jacket?" he asked.

"No," I said, "of course not," adding with some irritation, "She's wearing a hoodie and it looks just fine."

Now the better question is this: Why? Why this wardrobe choice for a woman better known for her traditional jewel-toned suit jackets and black pants?

First off, it was practical. It can get freezing in the Senate chamber. And, second, when you are working to pass a bill that simultaneously takes on the pharmaceutical industry, the biggest corporations in the country, fossil fuel, and every member of the Senate Republican caucus, you want to be comfortable.

Yet Elizabeth's hoodie was nevertheless an interesting fashion choice in the U.S. Senate—a workplace that for years had kicked women off the Senate floor for having the audacity to wear anything different. That included until very recently an unwritten but enforced policy that mandated that women wear nylons.

The mandatory-nylons requirement unceremoniously ended in the summer of 2009, when my dear departed friend Senator Kay Hagan of North Carolina rebelled. On a hot, sweltering Washington, D.C. day, Kay walked through the hallowed halls leading into the Senate chamber, surrounded by marble statues of every former male vice president from Teddy Roosevelt to Richard Nixon. She walked past the gold-framed portraits of Senators Daniel Webster and Robert La Follette and straight into the Senate chamber, all while wearing—*gasp*—a suit with bare legs. In her most charming southern accent, Kay Hagan told the Secretary of the Senate that she came from the South and knew what to wear in hot climates, and it wasn't nylons.

A new precedent—*thank you*, Kay—was established.

But the nylons were nothing compared to the capped sleeves. Here's looking at you, Claire McCaskill.

You see, one day Claire—the former Democratic senator from Missouri who first got elected to the Senate in 2006 (the same year I did)—was presiding over the Senate from the elevated President's desk. She was wearing a very nice nearly sleeveless black dress that she later told me she'd worn to a close friend's funeral in Missouri. A few minutes into her presiding time, the floor staff sent her a note and asked her to either put on a jacket or leave. Not having a jacket that day, she got kicked off the Senate floor, replaced by a male senator, and was asked to put on some sleeves.

That really happened.

But fast-forwarding to what I will now call—with some obvious sarcasm—the "new age" of the Senate (better known as that glorious time period in which I've chaired or have been the ranking member on the Senate Rules Committee), things have changed for the better. I've advocated for a significantly more practical and dare I say modern regime. This has included my work with Roy Blunt to update the sexual harassment rules in the Senate. I've pushed to increase the number of statues and paintings of women and people of color in the Capitol so that when kids visit the building they can both learn its history but also see themselves in our halls of government.[49] I also successfully pushed to allow senators' babies on the Senate floor (OMG—yes, Senator Tammy Duckworth, you patriot, you can bring your six-week-old baby on the floor with you). And finally, I championed wardrobe updates, including the allowance of Senator Sinema's many fashion-

---

49. The Capitol currently has more than two hundred historical statues. Only sixteen are women and only thirteen are people of color! Susan Collins and I recently passed a bill allowing for two new statues: former Supreme Court Justices Ruth Bader Ginsburg and Sandra Day O'Connor. In 2022 we voted in a bust of Thurgood Marshall. Next up? Harriet Tubman.

forward outfits,[50] tennis shoes for comfort, and yes—from time to time—hoodies.[51]

Getting approval for babies on the Senate floor was by far the most fun. And it wasn't easy. Tammy Duckworth—the Democratic senator from Illinois who lost both of her legs in a helicopter crash serving our country in Iraq—came to me before the birth of her second daughter to seek permission to bring her soon-to-be-born baby to the Senate floor in the event there were late votes or she had to keep the baby on a feeding schedule.

"No problem," I said.

Months later, Tammy was, well, even more pregnant (surprise!), and I had encountered all kinds of passive resistance. Apparently the senators had allowed a dog on the floor once, but no kids.

---

50. Note that at her request I advocated for Senator Sinema to be able to wear sleeveless dresses on the Senate floor. And if anyone remembers the infamous furry pink stole she wore at her swearing-in, I feel personally responsible for that. You see, after I had gotten the Senate's male leaders to sign off on the "radical" idea that women's bare arms could grace the Senate chamber in perpetuity, I reported the positive news back to Kyrsten and made a minor suggestion. I suggested that for the first day of our new bare-arms regime—her actual swearing-in—wearing a jacket or a wrap in addition to the sleeveless dress would be a nice touch. She came up with a better idea!

51. While the senatorial wardrobes and the family policies may have gone modern under my watch, I have admittedly been less successful in making other changes. Like why, for instance, are the only drinks allowed on the Senate floor for the past hundred-plus-whatever years milk and water? At some point some senator was able to successfully advocate for and spice it up with *sparkling* water, since that did not exist in the horse-and-buggy days. But why not coffee, especially since we often end up voting through the night? And why can't we use laptops? These are some of the many questions new senators inevitably ask me to ponder late in the evening from my perch in the back row of the Senate floor.

I finally took to humor. When Senator Orrin Hatch told a group of reporters, "Maybe it's okay to have this baby on the floor, but what if we have ten babies on the floor," I responded, "We *already* have ten babies on the floor." (That happened.)

Then, after sitting behind several senior male senators at a classified briefing and tapping them on the shoulders and asking them in a loud whisper if it was true they had a problem with breastfeeding (red faces all around), I finally channeled Dr. Seuss and came up with a jingle to make my point:

> *She's not going to change the diaper on the floor;*
> *She won't be breastfeeding by the door.*

> *She's not going to change the baby in the House;*
> *She'll be as quiet as a mouse.*

> *She won't burp the baby at work;*
> *Stop being such a jerk.*

Bingo. That worked. We passed the rules change. And one day during a close vote, the fifty-year-old veteran wheeled herself onto the Senate floor with six-week-old Maile Pearl on her lap. Tammy made sure the baby was all decked out in a little green suit so as to not violate the Senate dress code. The reporters oohed and aahed from the gallery above. Many were tearing up.

I was sitting with Mitch McConnell.

"This is the moment," I said.

"What do you mean?" he asked.

"This is the moment when you and I and Chuck and Roy

go down and greet the baby. Since I made this change as an ode to the modern era and you agreed to it, we may as well own it."

"In all my years campaigning," he said, "I've never kissed a baby."

"I don't think that needs to happen," I said. "You just need to greet the baby."

And he did.

But I digress.

I loved Elizabeth's hoodie that night. I loved it because it was an hour-by-hour reminder of just how truly absurd our situation was. The U.S. Senate, once known as the world's greatest deliberative body, has devolved into a place where the minority party can avoid getting to a vote on an actual bill or major issue by simply refusing to give the sixty votes that would allow the bill to move forward.

And then (as was the case with the Inflation Reduction Act) the political party trying to pass the bill resorts to the fifty-one-vote threshold of the procedural morass called "reconciliation." That then means that the opposing party can again challenge multiple provisions of the bill before the parliamentarian by claiming that the proposal doesn't fit into the historical "it must involve taxing or spending" limits placed on "reconciliation" by one former West Virginia senator, Robert Byrd. Byrd, while admittedly one of the lions of the Senate, has now been dead for well over a decade.

After weeks of wrangling over what Robert Byrd would rule allowable under the reconciliation rules if he were still alive (a phenomenon known as the "Byrd bath"), the bill can be given the green light only by the parliamentarian. That's when the bill (minus any provisions ruled out in the Byrd bath) gets called up for a vote. The opposing minority party can then put forth a slew of endless partisan amendments—known as "poison pills" or "messaging amendments"—just to make the other side look bad. These amendments—all of which must most likely be voted down in order for the bill to pass—are proposed not in a good-faith effort to foster further debate, but for later use in negative political ads.

That's the highway pileup we were in on the evening of August 6, 2022. We trudged through the night, voting over and over again on amendments put forth by the likes of Rand Paul and Ted Cruz. We were completely at the mercy of the minority party, with the Republicans forcing us to take part in the modern-day death march known not-so-fondly as "vote-a-rama." Both sides had used this technique before, but over the years it was getting worse.

During those two days in August, the Republicans were using the Senate procedures to throw up any roadblock they could find. They feigned earth-shattering dismay that Senate Democrats had the audacity to use the fifty-one-vote-threshold "reconciliation" procedure to pass the bill. Yet what choice did we have? Not one of them—much less ten—would vote for it, or for that matter make any significant commitment to do anything about climate change.

One of the ironies here is that our colleagues seemed to forget that back in 2017—only four years before—the fifty-one-vote "reconciliation" was the exact same procedure they had used to pass the Trump tax cuts that had significantly cut taxes on those making over $400,000 per year. It was the same procedure they used to reduce the corporate rate from a maximum of 35 percent to a flat rate of 21 percent.

And never mind that our purpose of reducing greenhouse gases and bringing down pharmaceutical prices seemed a wee bit loftier than the just-mentioned Republican tax cuts, which greatly benefited the very rich and big corporations.

But the Senate Republican leaders had decided that the best way to beat us in November's midterm elections and to increase their base's interest in those elections was to throw a bunch of seemingly embarrassing amendment votes at our members. The strategy also had the virtue of both slowing the process down and potentially breaking the deal that had been negotiated. The amendments included ones purposely crafted and designed to try to make us look bad on a variety of subjects from immigration to public safety. With the elections only three months away, they hoped the votes could tear down the credibility of our candidates in key battleground races across the country.[52]

They knew that we had to vote all of their amendments[53] down to keep the deal whole and pass the bill.

---

52. These amendments were actually child's play compared to the ones they required us to vote on in 2009 when we passed the Affordable Care Act. Those included ones about convicted sex offenders using Viagra and voting down a mobile mammogram van. Why? Any change to the Affordable Care Act from the House version would have made it unpassable. Back then, just like this time, we hung together, rejected all the "gotcha" amendments, and got it done. And the Affordable Care Act—or as we are glad to call it, "Obamacare"—has provided health-care coverage to more than twenty million people.

53. In addition to the Republican amendments, we had to defeat a few Democratic amendments that so many of us agreed with, including a bill Bernie Sanders and I led to expand the number of drugs negotiated under Medicare. Bernie had every right to bring up that amendment, and I sat with him for half an hour afterward, bemoaning the process and the outcome. He

The other even more devious strategy that August eve? It was always possible one of our members might faint or fall over or wouldn't be able to handle the "death march" with no sleep. Losing one of the senators—even for a few of the amendment votes—would mean we would lose the deal. Many members of our caucus had gotten COVID and missed votes in the weeks leading up to the vote-a-rama. Two of them—though in good health now—had had strokes only months before. Several had had cancer. Senator Leahy was in a wheelchair due to breaking his hip just a few weeks before. And Senator Feinstein was eighty-nine—not exactly the ideal age for pulling an all-nighter.

As the votes ground on, it became obvious that in a 50/50 Senate, one of our members could simply get sick or be temporarily too exhausted—based on being awake for thirty-six hours straight—to vote.

In the end it was about physical endurance (or what game theorists might call "a game of chicken"). You could never sleep more than twenty minutes at a time—in an uncomfortable chair or on the floor, or on a couch if you were lucky. We were in survival mode. Elizabeth wasn't the only one in comfort gear for that thirty-six-hour block. By the morning my colleague Tina Smith was sporting a Nordic fleece jacket. Senator Sinema was wearing her signature jeans jacket over her brightly colored dress, and tennis shoes (sorry, Robert C. Byrd) were the norm for both men and women.

On the afternoon of August 7, the Senate Republicans

---

wanted to make the point, a valid one at that. I wanted to pass the ultimate bill. I pledged to keep working with him to get more done on Medicare negotiations as well as reducing drug prices for non-Medicare recipients.

finally gave up. They agreed to rolling a number of their final amendments into one vote so we could finish the amendment votes and get to a vote on the final passage of the historic bill.

And there it was, the final vote: fifty to fifty.

We did it. We defeated every gotcha amendment and everyone was still in one piece for the final vote to pass the bill.

Kamala Harris entered the chamber, broke the tie, and we won.

Staff members were crying. Senators were crying. The victory was sweet.


## More Good


But that vote on August 7, 2022 was far from the only victory that summer. From June on we passed not only the Inflation Reduction Act, but also the bipartisan gun safety bill, the bipartisan semiconductor chips and science bill, the bipartisan burn pits bill to protect our veterans, my bipartisan shipping bill to bring down costs for American businesses and consumers, and the resolution allowing Sweden and Finland into NATO.

The NATO resolution was up for a vote the very same week as the Inflation Reduction Act. And I had the good fortune of giving my Senate floor speech in favor of the expansion of NATO membership immediately after Republican Senator Josh Hawley addressed the chamber. He was the only senator who planned to cast a "no" vote, and it was frankly a lot of fun to respond to his remarks. With the Swedish and Finnish ambassadors and Scandinavian military leaders looking down from the gallery, I refuted his points.

"Perhaps the senator from Missouri hasn't been to these

countries," I noted, channeling Scandinavian bravado (if there is such a thing). "Our nation, and my state of Minnesota in particular, share a special bond with Finland and Sweden."

I made the case that adding the two nations to NATO would not only be good for the security of the two countries, one of which (Finland) shares an 830-mile-long border with Russia, but that their inclusion was also a net gain for NATO, given the two nations' strong commitment to peace and stability and their defense capabilities. I added that Finland had already exceeded 2 percent of its budget on military spending and that Sweden had recently ramped up its defense spending as well.

Shortly after I finished the speech, I got a note of thanks from the President of Finland.

All in all, a good day.

One bipartisan bill—the PACT Act—which helped our veterans who had gotten sick in Iraq and Afghanistan after being stationed next to burn pits, also garnered a lot of attention. I had introduced one of the first bills on the burn pit issue back in 2017 with Republican Senator Thom Tillis of North Carolina. We called it the Helping Veterans Exposed to Burn Pits Act—and for good reason. Brian Muller was the husband of Amie Muller, a thirty-six-year-old Minnesota veteran who had died of pancreatic cancer after being stationed next to one of the most notorious burn pits in Iraq, leaving behind not only Brian but also three beautiful young children. Brian came to me that year and asked me to take on the issue on his family's behalf.

"It makes me really mad," Sergeant Amie Muller had said in June 2016, just a month after learning that she had

Stage 3 pancreatic cancer. "I inhaled that stuff all day, all night. Everything that they burned there is illegal to burn in America. That tells you something."

Our initial bill to pass a burn pit research "Center of Excellence" with the VA was passed into law in 2018, followed by another bill I passed in 2019 with Senator Dan Sullivan of Alaska to evaluate service members for burn pit–related illnesses. But it ultimately took years of work by many senators and House members, as well as veterans' groups, to gain the broad bipartisan support necessary to pass comprehensive coverage legislation to help our veterans who had been exposed to toxic substances. Veterans' Affairs Committee chair Jon Tester and ranking member Jerry Moran led the way and reached an agreement.

On July 27, 2022, the bill was set to be passed in the Senate for a second time after some minor changes to the text in the House. All the veterans' groups were there in advance to celebrate its passage. Then, that afternoon—the very same day Senators Schumer and Manchin announced the surprise agreement on the Inflation Reduction Act—the Republicans, in a surly mood over that announcement, reversed their original votes on the PACT Act and voted it down. At first, they argued it was because of the change in the House. But the reason they gave for voting it down was actually in the original bill they had already voted for!

In any case, Jon Stewart—the former host of *The Daily Show* who has been a stalwart in his support of 9/11 first responders and veterans—went viral with his mince-no-words comments against the Republicans' move. The veterans and their family members slept on the U.S. Capitol steps, including Minnesotan Amanda Barbosa—whose husband, former army helicopter pilot Rafael Barbosa, had gotten seriously sick with cancer after being stationed next to two different burn pits in Iraq and Afghanistan. The first night the vets and family members slept on the steps, I went over and hung out with Amanda. She was an incredible advocate not only for her husband, but for our country.

A few days later, we passed the bill.

Other bipartisan victories were not as dramatic but nevertheless incredibly important. The semiconductor chips and science bill—led by Leader Schumer and Republican Indiana Senator Todd Young (with some major work by Virginia Senator Mark Warner)—passed in July and was heralded for both economic and national security reasons. The number of chips made in the U.S. has plummeted to 12 percent of our supply, down from 37 percent in the 1990s. The bill's major investment will allow our country to manufacture its own sophisticated chips for everything from cars to cell phones.

There were other victories as well. Due to the dogged persistence of both President Biden and his esteemed counsel Dana Remus, as well as Judiciary Chair Dick Durbin and the rest of the Judiciary Committee Democratic senators (Senators Leahy, Feinstein, Whitehouse, Coons, Blumenthal, Hirono, Booker, Padilla, Ossoff, and myself) we confirmed new judges for federal vacancies at a groundbreaking pace, including, of course, new Supreme Court Justice Ketanji Brown Jackson.

The major Biden infrastructure bill was signed into law in November of 2021 thanks to a bipartisan group of senators. That bill included a version of my and Majority Whip Jim Clyburn's major broadband legislation. The Postal Reform Act—essential for the continuing viability of our economy—

was signed into law in April of 2022 thanks to the methodical work of House members Carolyn Maloney and James Comer and, in the Senate, of Homeland Security chair Gary Peters of Michigan and ranking member Rob Portman of Ohio. And, as noted earlier, the shipping bill I led with Republican Senator and Minority Whip John Thune and Representatives John Garamendi and Dusty Johnson to reduce costs and fix supply chain issues passed in June of 2022.

The landmark Respect for Marriage Act—led in the Senate by my colleagues Tammy Baldwin, Kyrsten Sinema, Rob Portman, and Thom Tillis—passed at the end of 2022, protecting marriage equality. Also at the very end of 2022, we came together to pass the previously mentioned Electoral Count Reform Act, a bill I was proud to shepherd through the Senate.

Last, but certainly not least, there was the gun safety legislation.

As Americans, we've seen gun violence cut short far too many lives: from domestic violence disputes that escalate to murder, to suicides that leave families shattered, to shootings at bus stops and street corners, to the mass shootings that have turned hundreds of stores, concert venues, places of worship, and schools across our country into crime scenes and places of mourning.

There were nearly three hundred mass shootings in the first half of 2022, including the tragic massacres in Buffalo, New York, and Uvalde, Texas, which killed a combined thirty-one Americans in just ten days. Among the dead in Buffalo were a seventy-seven-year-old substitute teacher, a loving wife who was picking up groceries for her husband in a nursing home, and a father who dropped in to grab a surprise birthday cake for his three-year-old son.

In Texas, the Uvalde community lost nineteen children and two teachers to an eighteen-year-old madman who had purchased an assault weapon on the internet. Seeing photos of the fourth-grade kids who had been killed was heartbreaking. There they were in their sports uniforms, their first communion dresses, and their green Converse sneakers with a heart on the right toe. There were even photos of the kids holding awards they had won that very morning. It was a chilling reminder of just how quickly an assault weapon in the hands of a deranged murderer can turn a normal day at school, or a visit to a movie theater, or a neighborhood Fourth of July parade into a day of horror and carnage.

But the reminder was hardly needed. In the twenty-three years since Columbine, we have seen headline after headline detailing mass shooting after mass shooting. Towns like Aurora, Newtown, San Bernardino, Squirrel Hill, El Paso, and Highland Park have become synonymous with the nation's epidemic of gun violence—and our country has grown all too familiar with the sights of makeshift memorials, as well as the often-hollow calls for "thoughts and prayers" from politicians.

I will always remember going to the White House with a number of other senators right after the school shooting in Parkland, Florida. I was seated directly across from then-President Trump and next to Vice President Pence. I kept the piece of paper where I wrote a hash mark down every time Trump said that he was for universal background checks—not once, not twice, not three times. NINE times. And then what happened? A few days later, he met with the NRA and folded.

After years of disappointments, it would have been easy for

those who have advocated for change to our gun laws to give up hope. But they didn't. Even in the wake of no action after Sandy Hook, Parkland, and Las Vegas, they never gave up. But those two mass shootings in Uvalde and Buffalo—both by eighteen-year-olds using AR-15s—somehow broke the dam. Maybe it was those photos of the Uvalde kids. Maybe it was the white supremacism motivating the murderer in the Buffalo mass shooting. But somehow the world changed. Americans who had previously stayed silent joined activists from gun safety groups like Everytown, Moms Demand Action, Giffords (as in the group founded by former Congresswoman Gabby Giffords), and the Brady Campaign to call for immediate action. Actor Matthew McConaughey—who had grown up in Uvalde—and his wife, Camila Alves, spent days with the families of the murdered kids and came to Washington to meet at length with Democrats and Republicans alike. When McConaughey pounded his fist on the White House podium as he passionately called for action and "responsible gun ownership," he was expressing the pent-up frustrations of the vast majority of Americans.

Against all odds, we had a breakthrough in the Senate. Senator Chris Murphy of Connecticut—whose Senate career had been intensely shaped by the Sandy Hook Elementary shooting, which took place just weeks before he was sworn into office—sat down with Senator John Cornyn of Texas, a staunch conservative with an A+ rating from the NRA, and the two of them did what all of us are sent to Washington to do: they worked together to find common ground. Along with Senators Sinema, Tillis, and many others, they forged a compromise that had eluded Congress for far too long.

That compromise—opposed by the NRA—included my legislation to close the boyfriend loophole, something I had first introduced way back in 2013.

As the former Hennepin County attorney, I saw the toll of domestic violence. Every year, more than six hundred American women are tragically shot to death by intimate partners. Half of those cases involve dating partners. But under federal law, a person in a dating relationship could get convicted of domestic abuse and then go out and buy a gun the next day, just because they weren't married to their victim or they didn't have a child together. It had become known as "the boyfriend loophole."

Fighting to close the boyfriend loophole was a lesson in persistence. When I first introduced the bill in 2013, I had just one cosponsor, Senator Mazie Hirono of Hawaii. But the more I talked to my colleagues, the more people were willing to get on board. By 2015, we had five cosponsors, including a Republican, former Senator Mark Kirk of Illinois. Congresswoman Debbie Dingell then took up the legislation in the House. By 2017, we had thirty Senate cosponsors, and when I reintroduced the bill in 2021, I was joined by thirty-eight senators.

As previously explained, while the boyfriend loophole provision had been included in the House-passed Violence Against Women Act Reauthorization Act back in 2021, it got cut out of the version that ultimately passed the Senate. This new bipartisan gun safety legislation was our first real shot to close the loophole, and I worked with Senators Murphy and Cornyn to get it done.

In the end, the Senate and the House ultimately came together to pass the comprehensive legislation based on the Senate agreement that not only included the closure of the boyfriend loophole, but also more thorough background checks for people between the ages of eighteen and twenty-one, major investments in mental health, and support for states in their efforts to pass and implement red flag laws—also known as extreme risk laws—to basically allow someone to petition for judicial intervention to temporarily remove guns when someone is in a crisis situation. The bill passed the Senate by a vote of 65–33, with fifteen Republicans supporting it. And—along with so many others who had never given up on passing a federal gun safety bill—I was honored to sit in the front row at the gathering on the White House lawn to celebrate the bill's passage with President Biden and Vice President Harris, both of whom had long advocated for change.

Was it progress? Absolutely. Is our work done? Absolutely not.

A few weeks after the Uvalde and Highland Park, Illinois, Fourth of July parade tragedies, I met with a Robb Elementary ten-year-old survivor named Caitlyne. With tears streaming down her cheeks, she told me how she had hid with classmates behind her teacher's desk in her Uvalde, Texas, fourth-grade classroom that May morning, listening to the mass slaughter of nineteen fellow fourth-grade students— including her best friend, Jackie—and their two teachers just across the hall. Caitlyne eventually crawled out a window to get to safety. She showed me pictures of Jackie and five other fourth-grade friends she lost that day and told me what an assault weapons ban would mean to her.

The sad truth is that Caitlyne and the hundreds of kids from Robb Elementary are going to carry the scars of that day for the rest of their lives. You can't recover from a thing like that—you can only learn to live with it. I don't know how anyone could look in her eyes and conclude that passing an assault weapons ban is anything less than imperative. I promised Caitlyne that I would keep fighting—for her, for her friends, and for all Americans.

## The Bad

One of the most self-aware moments you can have as a leader—whether it be in politics or any other occupation—is when you realize the plain truth that someone else can do it better than you. It's a gift when you can recognize that no matter how prepared you are, no matter how much research and earnest work you have put into making your case or memorizing your presentation or giving your speech, someone else can capture the moment too. They just do it better.

That happened to me one hot day on the street in front of the U.S. Supreme Court steps. I had just given a speech on voting rights in front of a big crowd. The speech was good. Maybe it was even a little better than that. Our collective cause to pass federal voting rights legislation was necessitated by the 2013 conservative Supreme Court ruling in *Shelby County v. Holder* that struck down major parts of the Voting Rights Act. The urgency of our legislative efforts on voting rights was also due to a slew of recently enacted state laws that were making it harder for so many people to vote.

That day at the voting rights rally, I was followed by a preacher. That preacher just happened to also be a U.S. senator. In his booming voice, Reverend Raphael Warnock, then the brand-new senator from Georgia, gave all of us a master class on how you can take a complex subject and—using sim-

ple, straightforward language—really make it mean something. He got up to the podium, paused, looked wisely out
at the crowd, and emphatically summed up in one sentence
what the rest of us had taken hours to say: "*Some* people don't
want *some* people to vote."

"*Some* people don't want *some* people to vote." Everything
else that day was blather. Senator Warnock had boiled it all
down to one simple truth. After Joe Biden had won the presidential election with a whopping seven-million-vote margin
and Senators Warnock and Ossoff had flipped the Senate in
their come-from-behind victories in the runoff in Georgia
on January 5, 2021, leaders in the Republican Party had figured out that their party's leader (as in Donald Trump) and
their message (as in divisive) just wasn't working.

But instead of changing their policies or their candidates to
better sync up with the public, they decided that their best path
forward was to try to change their voters. That meant making
it harder for people who voted in the 2020 election to vote
again in 2022 and beyond. That meant purging voter rolls.
That meant limiting drop-off ballot boxes. That meant making it harder and more complicated to vote by mail. That meant
trying to get rid of fifteen years of highly successful same-day
registration in Montana. Or enacting a new law in Iowa to cut
the period of early voting by nine days and close polls an hour
earlier on Election Day. And that meant limiting the runoff
period in Georgia and basically outlawing voter registration
during that time. Given that seventy thousand Georgians had
registered in the time period leading up to the Senate runoff
in 2021, why not—they decided—make that impossible to do?

That's what they did.

We had already seen this playbook. All kinds of cases

were brought by Trump and his allies leading up to the 2020 election, for the sole purpose of eliminating voters or at least making it much more confusing to vote. Then we all witnessed the post-election lies and the attempts to pressure local and state election officials to change the results. Then there were the slates of fake electors, culminating in the assault on the U.S. Capitol on January 6th—an actual insurrection aimed at stopping our democracy by force.

But it didn't stop there. What Trump's supporters couldn't accomplish with bear spray, batons, and flagpoles they tried again with voter suppression laws. Over four hundred bills to restrict voting were introduced in almost every state in 2021. Sadly, over thirty bills have passed.

And then there was the dark money. Republicans, led by Mitch McConnell, fought campaign finance reform for years and refused to even pass the DISCLOSE Act long championed by my friend Senator Sheldon Whitehouse—a straightforward bill supported by every Democrat in the Senate that would have required major dark money contributions to be reported. Then they used the current laws' loopholes—created of course by years of conservative court decisions—and injected record amounts of dark money into the 2022 midterm elections. A dark money group captained by Leonard Leo—who for years had influenced the Supreme Court selection process with boatloads of dark money—received a record $1.6 billion donation to spend against Democratic candidates in the midterms. With no limits or even disclosures, Democratic candidates who had been ahead or tied until August in states like Wisconsin and North Carolina fell behind in just a few weeks shortly after the onslaught of negative ads the dark money bought. Yes, countervailing outside independent expenditures were made to help Democratic candidates, but in the end the truth remains: Democratic elected officials keep trying to stop the dark money and the Republicans stop us every time.

The way I look at it is this: to quote former Republican Senate Leader Bob Dole, "No first-class democracy can treat people like second-class citizens."[54] That's why in the past both Democratic and Republican secretaries of state and legislative leaders united in their support to both maximize voter turnout as well as put sensible campaign finance disclosure rules and limits in place. The McCain/Feingold campaign finance law of 2002 was strongly bipartisan. The Voting Rights Act of 1965 had originally passed with bipartisan support, and it was reauthorized several times. The Fannie Lou Hamer, Rosa Parks, and Coretta Scott King Voting Rights Act Reauthorization and Amendments Act of 2006 passed the U.S. Senate 98–0 without a single dissenting vote, and President George W. Bush signed that legislation into law, specifically pledging to cheers of applause: "My administration will vigorously enforce the provisions of this law, and we will defend it in court."

But today bipartisan support for voting rights and campaign finance reform has taken a bad turn. State-by-state attempts to suppress the vote are rampant. And the constant federal court litigation to allow for more dark money to pollute our elections is against every tenet of our democracy.

Over the years I—along with many others—came to the conclusion that the only fail-safe way to protect the freedom

---

54. Joe Biden recalled this quote when he spoke in memory of Bob Dole at Dole's funeral.

to vote and the right to free and fair elections without the scourge of dark money was to enact clear minimum federal standards for voting, along with campaign finance and disclosure rules.

As the chair of the Senate Rules Committee, I held a number of hearings through 2021 and 2022 on election issues, including the DISCLOSE Act. During the summer of 2021 I took the committee on the road to Georgia, holding its first field hearing in decades. Over the years I traveled to a number of states and held forums and events on voting rights, including in my neighboring state of Wisconsin. In the spring of 2021 the Rules Committee marked up—which means voting on a bill after which in this case was a slew of amendments—a major voting rights bill (appropriately named the For the People Act) led by Jeff Merkley in the Senate and John Sarbanes in the House. I held a marathon markup on the bill, made many changes, and got it up for a vote the day before my dad died and in between my cancer surgery at Mayo and radiation. Those were a difficult few days.

While the For the People Act deadlocked in committee along party lines, the tie vote would allow Leader Schumer to call the bill to the floor. In the Democratic caucus we had nearly every Democrat cosponsoring the bill. While we did not have the key support of Senator Manchin, he had been a cosponsor of nearly identical legislation in the past.

Then the talks began. A group of us, which included Senator Schumer and me as well as Senators Manchin, Merkley, Padilla, Kaine, King, Tester, and Warnock—met for months to negotiate a new bill. By the end of the year we announced the Freedom to Vote Act, which I led in the Senate. It was a good, strong bill. It included campaign finance disclosure provisions; minimum standards for voting registration and drop-off boxes; and some basic rules for mail-in balloting.

I was joined by every member of our caucus on the bill, and Joe Manchin signed his name as a cosponsor on the dotted line.

Okay, we really don't have dotted lines on bills, but you get the drift.

Given the Senate rules, we needed sixty votes to pass it. And while Senator Murkowski had signaled an interest in supporting some version of the John Lewis Voting Rights bill, which would have restored certain portions of the Voting Rights Act, there was zero Republican support for even minimum federal vote-by-mail, voter registration standards, or dark money contribution and expenditure disclosures.

Thus, our only hope to stop the vicious voter suppression efforts and finally do something about rampant dark money campaign spending was to reform the filibuster by at least creating an exemption to the archaic filibuster rule for the purpose of passing voting rights/campaign finance reform legislation. There was a good argument for doing this, in light of the fact that our very democracy was at stake.

We worked for weeks to get our colleagues on board on a limited filibuster exception. In the end, we fell short because two of our colleagues—Senators Manchin and Sinema—announced that they would not make any exceptions to the filibuster. And since voting rights clearly did not fall under the "tax and spend" rubric of the fifty-one-vote reconciliation procedure discussed above, the voting rights bill fell short of the sixty votes necessary to get past the filibuster.

It was a hard and very disappointing end to our efforts.

But in looking back at all of it, I have no regrets. We fought as hard as we could to pass the bill, with the country's leading civil rights groups at our side, but in the end, we just didn't have the votes.

Losses in the Senate are tough to take, but there are always lessons—and one has to take solace where one can and remember that the fight is never over.

First, the lengthy negotiations had produced a good, strong bill that will stand the test of time for another day. We spent a lot of time building a coalition of support for the bill, and that coalition remains.

Second, we educated ourselves and the American public on what was going on in the states, which was helpful not only for civic reasons, but also allowed state officials a bigger window into the national efforts. As democracy was clearly on the ballot in the 2022 midterms, our unsuccessful effort to reform voting rules helped set the stage for our candidates: with so many election deniers on the ballot, our earlier work allowed our party to make the case that our leaders were in sync with so many Americans when it came to upholding our democracy.

Third (and this may have been the most important reason), we set the stage for filibuster reform for the future. Our colleagues learned the filibuster's racist history, and they came to see the Swiss cheese, arbitrary nature of its exceptions and loopholes. A full forty-eight of them voted for the exception to pass all-important voting rights legislation.

Fourth, we educated ourselves on the specific problems related to the Electoral Count Act of 1887 and later worked with our Republican colleagues to fix it.

Those were the silver linings (if you could call them that). But it still really hurt the day it failed.

And sadly, voting rights wasn't the only example of a bill that had strong public support but failed because of the filibuster.

When the infamous leaked Alito opinion in the *Dobbs* case rocked the political world in May of 2022, many legal experts thought it was going to be "cleaned up," and that the actual Supreme Court opinion would never be so extreme. In fact, a *Saturday Night Live* skit that aired shortly after the leak mocked Justice Alito mercilessly for citing a thirteenth-century English treatise as one of the proof points for overturning *Roe* in the leaked draft decision. The *SNL* crew noted with brilliant sarcasm that by grounding his initial draft decision in the Middle Ages, Alito took us back to "that profound moment of moral clarity, almost a thousand years ago, which laid such a clear foundation for what our laws should be in 2022."

Ridiculing the backward nature of the Court's leaked analysis, the *SNL* skit referenced the medieval practices in place at the time, which included a ban on pointy shoes and the burning of women at the stake, and pondered that the ultimate punishment for the "crime" of seeking to terminate a pregnancy could well be putting a woman in a boat and letting her "sail to the end of the earth," where she would surely fall off the edge and be eaten by the giant turtles who were holding it up.

The skit concluded, "No need to update [our abortion laws] at all," since "they nailed it back in 1235."

In the end, as macabre as it all sounded, the truth was in fact stranger than fiction. *Roe v. Wade*—the law of the land for nearly fifty years—was completely and unconditionally overturned. As I said immediately after the opinion was finally issued on June 24, 2022, "We knew they would take us back to the '50s, we just didn't think it would be the *1850s*."

Republican governors and legislatures whose laws didn't immediately "trigger" an abortion ban immediately tried to outrace each other to their respective state capitols to see who could be the first to enact the strictest law, with several of the proposals not even including exceptions for rape and incest. A Texas law, which had already been passed before the *Dobbs* decision was issued, created a "bounty hunter" vigilante situation in which private citizens could get money for turning in women seeking abortions. Bills were introduced to stop medication-induced abortions, a common method in today's world.

Other legislators introduced post-*Dobbs* legislation to criminally prosecute those who aided a woman to seek reproductive health care in another state. More bills were introduced to both civilly sue and criminally prosecute doctors and other health-care workers who either performed abortions or advised patients of their rights in other states. Even Uber and Lyft drivers became worried about potential liability for rides they might give women seeking health-care services.

Immediately the horror stories unfolded. An initial story that a ten-year-old girl was raped, got pregnant, and was denied an abortion in Ohio started circulating. Major news organizations—including the *Wall Street Journal* editorial board—dismissed the story, alleging that there was no evidence that the girl even existed. Then days later an Ohio criminal complaint against the rapist was filed. The story was undeniably true. The girl had been sent to Indiana, a state in which the abortion ban was not yet in effect, where Dr. Caitlin Bernard, a physician affiliated with Indiana University, performed the procedure. The attorney general of Indiana then started investigating the doctor. The school stood by her. News organizations had to admit they were initially wrong and the story was true.

And that was just the first month.

Back in the Senate, the women leaders of our Senate leadership team—Patty Murray, Debbie Stabenow, Tammy Baldwin, Elizabeth Warren, Catherine Cortez Masto, and I—started meeting among ourselves and with Senator Schumer about our response. While we knew we didn't immediately have the votes to overcome the sixty-vote threshold of the filibuster to codify *Roe*, we did have a few pro-choice Republicans on our side, including Susan Collins and Lisa Murkowski.

Yet we also knew that there were not enough pro-choice Republican senators to even get close to the sixty votes we would need to pass a law to protect reproductive freedom, something the House did in July after the *Dobbs* decision was issued. We were also well aware that the upcoming election could result in more Democratic senators who would be willing to vote for an exception to the filibuster to codify *Roe* into law.

That was most likely our best path to stop the chaos and protect women's rights, although if the House flipped Republican (which eventually *barely* happened) we would not be able to get it through in the next session of Congress.

In the meantime, we kept our message simple: women—not politicians—should have the freedom to make their own decisions about their health care. And they didn't want Ted Cruz in the waiting room. Okay, I added that second part.

Only two months after the opinion was issued, fourteen states had already banned or severely restricted abortion, including states with large populations like Ohio, Missouri, and Texas.

Voters across the country responded. In a completely unexpected referendum on abortion rights in Kansas—in which the proponents of an abortion ban did everything in their power to confuse the voters by having the vote occur in August and in a way that was procedurally complicated—more than 540,000 voters turned up to vote on the side of protecting the right to an abortion. The referendum failed by 18 percentage points. In a stunning turnout of pro-choice voters, more people voted on the side of reproductive rights in Kansas than had voted IN TOTAL during the last midterm election primary.

The day after the Kansas vote, I recalled the nearly two-decades-old book about the conservative swing of voters in Kansas entitled, *What's the Matter with Kansas? How Conservatives Won the Heart of America* (2004).

My answer to "What's the matter with Kansas" now?

Nothing. Absolutely nothing.

*Washington Post* humorist Alexandra Petri best summed up the Sunflower State's surprising election results in a satirical column entitled "Whoops, we forgot women could still vote."

Aimed at the proponents of the abortion ban, she wrote, "So this is a little embarrassing, but we may have gotten so carried away trying to pass abortion restrictions that we sort of forgot women could still vote.

"Oops. Our bad."

In addition to the straight-out referendum of the Kansas

vote, August congressional special elections, including a Democrat's victory in a race that was less close than had been predicted in New York's Hudson Valley, as well as the victory for a Democratic congressional candidate in Alaska—Mary Peltola defeated Sarah Palin—revealed that voters were in fact appalled by the extremism of the Republican Party's position on abortion rights.

Now in order to truly assure that young women of my daughter's generation will not have fewer rights than their moms or grandmas we have to reform the Senate filibuster. Yet at the time of this writing, even after the "red tide" defying results of the 2022 midterms in which Republicans barely took control of the House and Democrats held the Senate, it still does not appear that we have the votes to get an exemption from the filibuster. And even if we did, we couldn't clear a codification of *Roe* through the Republican-controlled House. As the battles will continue to be fought on a state-by-state basis, I have no doubt reproductive rights will be a major issue in the 2024 federal elections when we will have yet another opportunity to win control of Congress.

But what we know for certain now is that when we consistently fail to act on issues that garner 70 to 80 percent of the public's support—from codifying *Roe v. Wade*, to an assault weapons ban for eighteen-to-twenty-one-year-olds, to passing sensible immigration reform, to making sure presidents (regardless of party) have their appointees in place so they can run the government—then something has to give.

Also notable about federal inaction: outside spending facilitated by conservative Supreme Court decisions is utterly and completely out of control. The fact that the pharmaceutical companies have had such sway over the members of Congress that they could first write into law a ban on Medicare negotiation for less expensive drug prices, and then stave off efforts to change it for decades when 88 percent of the public wanted it lifted, is just one of many egregious examples. But it happened.

And it is equally hard to believe that as of August 2022, the Big Tech companies had spent more ad money than any other political group ON ANY ISSUE against my bipartisan bill to simply put some basic rules of the road in place when it comes to self-preferencing their own products over those of small businesses and others. When I got my bill with Senator Grassley through the Senate Judiciary Committee on a 16–6 bipartisan vote—after an eighteen-month bipartisan House Judiciary Committee tech investigation by my friends Democrat David Cicilline and Republican Ken Buck and after numerous hearings on tech competition issues in the Senate—it was the FIRST tech bill addressing competitiveness to ever be passed out of a Senate committee!

Yet Google maintains a 90 percent market share for search engines. Apple and Google have a duopoly when it comes to app stores. Amazon has blatantly ripped off other companies' products based on nonpublic data and has a habit of flagrantly using information it has garnered from its algorithms to develop and promote its own products against those that advertise on its site all the time. And Facebook is, well, Facebook. Except it changed its name to Meta in the middle of all the mess.

Tech monopolies' dominance and bullying cries out for action for the simple reason that capitalism doesn't work when a few companies can dominate access to markets. Yet time and again, trillion-dollar tech companies use their monopoly profits and power to target my colleagues on both sides of the aisle with ads that basically threaten them if they dare to take any action. The contributions? Yes, they can roll in the money. The lobbyists and lawyers? Yes, they outnumber me 2,800 to 2 (as in I have only two antitrust lawyers on my staff). But the ads? Over 120 million dollars and counting—on national networks and local stations across the country—and that doesn't even include the internet ones that no one can track.

Every day I go to work I feel like I am bringing a small Swiss Army knife to a well-equipped, armed battlefield where trillion-dollar-company CEOs routinely visit with senators and their hordes of lobbyists and on-contract "experts" spread false rumors about me and the legislation on a minute-by-minute basis.

A great democracy cannot function with this kind of bias. The only way we get around it is by acting and showing they don't own us.

And if we really want to even the playing field? As noted above, pass campaign finance legislation including the DISCLOSE Act to shed light on who is giving and receiving dark money and pass a constitutional amendment to overturn the U.S. Supreme Court's *Citizens United* case, which severely limited campaign finance rules.

But in the end, the most straightforward solution is to put people in office who are willing to vote the courage of their convictions and listen to the people of this country.

Even if you lose an election over it, at least you can leave your office knowing you did the right thing.

If that sounds naive and Pollyannish, why else do you run for office if not to leave this world a better place?

# The Hope

Barack Obama was once asked, at an April 30, 2009, White House press conference, what he had accomplished in his first hundred days in office. At the time, he had inherited a cratering economy that was bleeding jobs. He was dealing with an H1N1 flu virus that was spreading across farm country. He was trying to make good on his number one priority to get a health-care bill passed. There were multiple crises every day in Iraq, Afghanistan, Iran, and North Korea. And, earlier in the month, a U.S.-flagged cargo ship called the *Maersk Alabama*—whose crew included twenty-one Americans, including Captain Richard Phillips—had been hijacked by four Somali pirates in the Indian Ocean. The standoff ended when Navy SEAL snipers killed three of the captors, a fourth having already surrendered.

When asked how he balanced all of it, this is what President Obama said:

> "I would love a nice, lean portfolio to deal with. But that's not the hand that's been dealt us. And every generation has to rise up to the specific challenges that confront them. We happen to have gotten a big set of challenges, but we're not the first generation that that's happened to. And I'm confident that we're going to meet these challenges just like our grandparents and forebearers met them before."

Running this country has always been a lot. It's never, as President Obama acknowledged, been "a nice, lean portfolio." But, fast-forwarding to the 2020s, there is something that has gotten much harder since Obama's time, and certainly since the times of the presidents who governed before him. What feels different now is the distrust that has been sown in our citizenry when it comes to believing in those they have elected to govern this great nation.

While I remain proud of the things we have accomplished in recent years, like so many Americans I am also frustrated when things don't get done or just, well, take too long. As someone who spent thirteen years in the private sector before going into government, I am always up for better governing. That's why I relentlessly focus on getting results and forging compromises and performing oversight and holding people accountable. I also want quicker nomination processes and confirmations for federal appointees, regardless of the president's party. There should at least be expeditious up-or-down votes on nominees so people's lives aren't held hostage for months—even years—at a time.

Better governing and getting things done is why I am also so focused on campaign finance reform. I believe that outsized and oversized spending actually stops us from doing the things we are supposed to do. Elected officials get afraid that voting a certain way—even when they want to—will hurt them in their next election. Why? Because if the interests affected by the vote have money, they will most likely spend it against the member in negative ads.

And one more thing that could really change the game when it comes to getting big-ticket things done and holding senators accountable in Washington? Getting rid of, or at least reforming, that much-overused relic of the past: the

Senate filibuster. While I do not question that we can get through immediate crises—like financial meltdowns, earthquakes, hurricanes, pandemics, locusts, etc.—within our existing system, my concern is that without procedural reform we will never get ahead of these crises.

Despite the workforce shortage, for example, with millions of jobs unfilled, it will be very difficult to enact comprehensive immigration reform without a procedural change to the Senate rules and of course a change in the current House politics. It will be extremely challenging to get the tax reform we need, to both get a handle on the debt and pay for items like assisting families with child and elder care. Passing tech legislation or antitrust reform or a host of other measures we need to respond to the complex economic issues of our time are made much harder because of procedural constraints. And we will never truly protect our rights in this democracy—a system people cherish so much that they voted in record numbers even during a public health crisis—without setting into law some basic rules to protect us, from voting to privacy and beyond.

Yet through all of this, I still remain a glass-half-full—and not half-empty—person. That's because every day when I go to work, I pledge to myself that no matter how bad things may seem, I will continue to embrace the "Happy Warrior" approach of former vice president and former Minnesota Senator Hubert Humphrey. I ground myself in the belief that it is an honor to serve our country (in his words, this "great American experiment in democracy") with (again in his words) "joy and without apology."

Why try to go for the positive at a time when negative sells? That part is really straightforward. Our pluses as a nation are huge. We live in a beautiful country that is known for its entrepreneurial spirit. We invent things. We export things. We see the world's endless possibilities.

We have a diverse and amazingly interesting country. Our citizenry's mix of racial and ethnic backgrounds is unparalleled. Our country's historical willingness to share the American dream with new generations of immigrants has led to centuries of economic expansion. The strong, scrappy work ethic of those who come to this country to start a new life for themselves and their families has produced awe-inspiring companies, new ideas, and cool products. At last count, 148 of United States Nobel laureates came to this country as immigrants, and over 40 percent of our Fortune 500 companies were founded by immigrants or their children. Immigrants don't diminish America. They are America.

Ours is also a country that fiercely thrives on freedom. In the 2022 elections many predicted that Americans—having suffered through three very tough years of a pandemic, supply chain issues, and inflation—would simply take their fundamental freedoms for granted when casting their ballots. That turned out to be wrong. So many American voters— and in particular women—clearly understood the implications of the United States Supreme Court's reversal of nearly fifty years of reproductive freedom. Other voters—including many independents and moderate Republicans—simply refused to vote for MAGA election-denying candidates. In the end, the notion that a "red wave" led by Trump-endorsed candidates would sweep through the 2022 political landscape was brought down by independent-thinking Americans who care deeply about our democracy and our constitutional freedoms.

As noted by Senate Majority Leader Chuck Schumer,

our candidates were also able to point to a "blue wave of accomplishments"—many of them bipartisan—achieved under Democratic leadership. While supply chain and cost-of-living issues stemming from the pandemic and the war in Ukraine had hit nearly every country in the world, we had clear proof points that Democrats never stopped doing the work for the American people. Sometimes we were successful. Sometimes we were not. But our goals and policies were the ones most often in sync with the needs of the American people.

Finally, our candidates were really good. It was public knowledge that several excellent candidates Republican leadership tried to recruit in 2022 simply didn't want to run. They just couldn't stomach the cynicism and extremism of the MAGA wing of the Republican Party, a force that continued to show its strength during the January 2023 House speaker election.

And while there were clearly moderate Republicans and even conservatives like Liz Cheney who were willing to stand up to Trump, many of them didn't run or lost their elections. That being said, there were some that did make it through, including my friend Lisa Murkowski, Republican of Alaska, who actually ended up endorsing Mary Peltola, the Democratic House candidate who ran against Sarah Palin.

And predictably, despite all the negativity of the 2022 election cycle, I once again sought out the joy. I accompanied our Minnesota candidates at door knocks and phone banks and canvassing events throughout our state. It all culminated in a four-day bus trip right before what turned out to be a very positive election. Our governor, Tim Walz, and the rest of our statewide ticket won, and we flipped the state Senate and kept the House.

And then there was the rest of the country. I remember the glee of former space shuttle commander and now Arizona Senator Mark Kelly as he flew me in a small plane from one event to another over the incredible wide vistas and red rocks of his home state. Our destination was the way-too-narrow mesa that is the Sedona airport. Just as we took off Mark turned to me and said, "FYI, I've never actually flown a civilian before in this plane . . . and the Sedona airstrip? It's pretty tough. Lots of wind. They call it the USS Sedona for a reason. It's kind of like an aircraft carrier in an ocean of rocks."

Of course it was the smoothest landing ever (always a good idea to catch a ride with a space shuttle commander). Mark went on to fly that plane to victory, going to every corner of his state, red or blue. He handily won his re-election.

I accompanied my friend Maggie Hassan and her husband and daughter on visits to small coffee shops and sports bars, munching on tater tots with Patriot fans in Nashua. The always-impressive Governor Laura Kelly of Kansas—a state that Trump won by 15 points in 2020—invited me in for an event in Kansas City. She ended up winning by a 2-point margin.

I got to pair up with secretary of state candidates in Arizona, Nevada, and Colorado, who, like so many of their Democratic counterparts across the country, put it all on the line for democracy and won their races. I spoke at exhilarating party events in Georgia and Michigan and Pennsylvania and New Hampshire. And for the incredible candidates I campaigned with that didn't make it—Judge Cheri Beasley in North Carolina, Lieutenant Governor Mandela Barnes in Wisconsin, and Congressman Tim Ryan in Ohio—I still look back at their campaigns with a smile. They showed such strength. They were in it for the right reasons.

And most memorable of all? The in-your-face resilience of John Fetterman as we did a Q and A at a brewery in Chester County, Pennsylvania, a few days before his debate. Neither political smears nor stroke recovery could overshadow the joy of his one-of-a-kind campaign. Talk about never giving up in the face of a major life challenge!

One useful measure of candidates regardless of party? Do they tap into our hopes? Do they tend to look for the good or the bad in people? One of the things that stands out about America, of course, goes way beyond politics: we tend to look for the good. We are by nature an optimistic bunch.

And that's why every so often—against all odds, through all of the muck and the noise—we keep our eyes on the good and we in fact DO good and get things done, even in Washington, D.C. That's what happened in Congress during the summer of 2022. That's what happened, in part, during the elections that followed that fall. That's the joy of politics.

# Afterword: Redemption

Life Lesson: *"America might be the greatest song the world has yet to hear."*
—BONO, FULBRIGHT DINNER, MARCH 31, 2022

This is supposed to be the conclusion of this book. But in politics—as in life—there is never really a conclusion when you are still in the middle of it.

In March of 2022 I attended the annual Fulbright Prize dinner in Washington, D.C. It was a memorable evening because it was one of the first big in-person gatherings in Washington since the beginning of the pandemic. There we were, all dressed up, and we finally had a place to go. The honoree was Bono, the celebrity rock star who never rests on his laurels and instead uses his time and clout to do the hard work of persuading people in power to invest in curing diseases and repairing the world. I'd met him a few times and hung out with him and his friends once in a bar in Munich (a story for another day), but I didn't go into this particular event expecting a big speech. By the time I left, my friend Senator Mark Warner took me aside and said, "I think we just heard the best speech ever."

Bono's theme? "America might be the best song the world has yet to hear."

His point? Our song is just not done yet.

Actually, none of our songs are done yet.

I write this in January of 2023, in the aftermath of the midterm elections, a volatile hellscape of a campaign season featuring election-denying candidates, billions of dollars in outside money and negative ad buys, and the return of Donald Trump rallies and his post-election announcement for president. Yet somehow—at least on the day I am writing this—our democracy has prevailed. There are still people of goodwill on both sides of the aisle trying to do the right thing. There are still people in the Senate who understand that courage is not always about standing by yourself and giving an angry speech to an empty Senate chamber. Courage is whether you are willing to stand next to someone you don't always agree with for the betterment of this country.

For months leading up to the midterm elections, Americans watched in horror as extreme right-wing MAGA candidates threw truth out the window, tried to shutter the rule of law, and callously dismissed and laughed at acts of political violence. And then right before the election, the husband of the speaker of the House, Paul Pelosi, got bludgeoned with a hammer in their own home in the middle of the night. The guy who did it was a psychopath, a man whose anger was fueled by reading far-right, virulent, bigoted online posts, many of them directed at Speaker Pelosi herself. "Where is Nancy?" he shouted in the middle of the night, parroting the words used by insurrectionists on January 6th. That's when a lot of people who had been trying to pretend everything was normal realized the truth: things just aren't normal.

And after the midterms, when the election for speaker in the House of Representatives went to fifteen separate votes, it became abundantly clear that the MAGA forces were more than eager to disrupt the People's House. There appeared to be no limit to what concessions they would demand.

When threats against members of Congress have exponentially increased and threats against judges and their court staff have more than tripled in four years, we know we have a problem. And when one out of six local election officials has reported personal threats against themselves and/or their family, and more than 50 percent of Americans had an election denier on the ballot in 2022, things are clearly way out of whack in our democracy.

So why pick this particular moment in time to write a book about "joy" in politics? As in how Pollyannish, how dumbheaded, how completely naive can you actually be?

I wrote this book because I believe that it is on all of us— as citizens, as elected officials, as people who simply want to pass on a better world to our kids and grandkids—to look for the good and do it. We must—as Amanda Gorman reminded us when she read her poem under that perfect blue sky of the 2021 inauguration—"find light in this never-ending shade." That means being honest about not just our country's shortcomings, but also our strengths. Generations of our fellow Americans gave us their all, adding up to, in Bono's words at the Fulbright speech, "246 years of inching and crawling towards freedom, sometimes on your belly, sometimes on your knees, sometimes marching, sometimes striding . . . to uphold the ideal of democracy."

I figure it is on all of us to continue that march, the long strides and, yes, the "inching and crawling," to uphold the ideal of democracy.

As this book has documented, like all Americans, my last few years didn't go as planned. In my case, I lost a presidential primary, almost lost my husband to COVID, lost my dad, lost my sense of well-being after learning I had breast cancer, and, at times—as so viciously captured on January 6th—nearly lost my faith in our collective ability to move forward as a nation.

I wrote this book not for the purpose of lamenting each and every setback, but to rejoice in the comebacks. To remind my fellow Americans that, as the visiting preacher Reverend Dr. Claudette Anderson Copeland said at Reverend Raphael Warnock's church in Atlanta, "you START WHERE YOU ARE," not where you were in the past or even where you thought you'd be before your life veered off what you thought was your well-planned path.

On the bad days, I remind myself of the amusing story I recalled in chapter 2 of this book about the ever-optimistic Paul Wellstone—the beloved former senator from Minnesota. One late afternoon after suffering a public defeat on a bill on the Senate floor, he walked into his offices grumbling and mad about the loss. He then saw his staff—who'd watched it all unfold before their eyes on TV—with their heads down, glum as could be. Without missing a beat—and with full awareness of the irony of it all—he gruffly called out: "Where's the JOY in this room? Where's the JOY?"

Let me answer that today.

On my personal journey over these last few years I've managed to find plenty of joy. Despite the loss in the presidential race, what a privilege it was to travel the country and make my case and test the limits. The people I met and the young staff and volunteers who believed in our cause were awe-inspiring. And then to endorse Joe Biden and help him win the election was a privilege, not a chore.

Political resiliency, like resiliency after any life challenge, can best be measured by how you deal with setbacks. Do you try your best to move on and look for the good and a new mission? Or do you retreat, miring yourself in dark thoughts, revenge, and pity? As recounted in these pages, I have had a front-row seat to learning resiliency from the best of the best.

John McCain—a mentor who would always make sure I got my due respect from a roomful of male foreign leaders in whatever country we were visiting—lost a major presidential race. Instead of living a life of regrets, he immediately—and at times merrily—sprang back into action, leading the charge on foreign affairs issues from his post in the U.S. Senate. He battled his brain cancer to the end, returning to the Senate many times after his diagnosis, including to cast his famous thumbs-down vote against the Trump administration's and his Republican colleagues' attempt to bring down the Affordable Care Act, also known as Obamacare.

John McCain—former Vietnam War POW, someone who continually dealt with the aches and pains and limitations that came with being tortured for over five years in captivity—taught me that it is the big stuff that matters. My last visit with him came in his dying days at the beautiful ranch he and Cindy had built, his view overlooking an oasis of a creek filled with wildlife set against the red rocks of Sedona. We reminisced about the trip we'd taken the year before to a number of Eastern European countries bordering

Russia. During that trip, on New Year's Eve in the middle of a snowstorm in the Donbas region, the former President of Ukraine gave McCain a Ukrainian-made machine gun as a token of his country's appreciation for McCain's support for Ukraine's democracy in the wake of Russia's repeated invasions of their sovereignty. The gift, as well as the Ukrainian-made pistols the former President had given Senator Lindsey Graham and me[55] that night, had been allegedly and under-standably "confiscated" by the U.S. military accompanying us on the trip pursuant to various ethical and safety rules. Re-calling the importance of that shared moment on the world stage, but also remembering the humor of many parts of the trip, John whispered to me with a glint in his eye, "Whatever happened to my Ukrainian machine gun? I'm still looking for it."

As our visit ended, he grew too tired to talk. As a part-ing gesture, he pointed to the words in one of his books: "Nothing in life is more liberating than to fight for a cause larger than yourself." Those were the last words John McCain shared with me.

Then there was Walter Mondale—renowned vice pres-ident to Jimmy Carter and former Minnesota senator—whom we also lost, a few years later. Like McCain, Mondale suffered a major electoral defeat when he ran for president against Ronald Reagan. I learned a lot from Walter Mondale

---

55. On stage, Ukrainians had given John the machine gun and Lindsey a pistol. I was the last to be given a gift, and when they came across the stage with a flat box, I knew it was something different. When I opened it, it turned out to be two daggers. McCain later found the whole thing so amus-ing that he told them it was sexist, and a few hours later they handed me a pistol just like Lindsey's.

as both a college intern in his office and a partner at his law firm, where for a few years I also served as his aide. Mondale was the first to encourage me to run for the Senate and gave me advice at every stage of my career since college. But the most amazing gift he gave me was the gift of resilience.

Because you see, it wasn't just the decency Walter Mondale displayed on the national political stage that made him stand out. It was the dignity he brought home with him in the wake of defeat.

It was not easy for the former vice president to run against Ronald Reagan, knowing that most people were predicting that Reagan would win. And it wasn't easy for him to come out of retirement and run for the Senate after we lost Paul Wellstone.

And finally, it was far from easy for Walter Mondale to continue his work while caring for and losing both his beloved wife, Joan, and their daughter, Eleanor, through heartbreaking illnesses.

None of it was easy. But when saddled with enormous setbacks, Fritz didn't stand down, he stood up. He didn't crawl under his desk or hide from public view, he simply found a different way to serve.

He went from being driven around with tons of Secret Service agents and meeting with world leaders and negotiating international treaties to going into a local grocery store, shopping on his own, and happily ending his visit with a long engaging talk about Mideast peace with the high school kid at the checkout counter.

Being humble meant it was much easier for him to be resilient. Being grounded meant that no matter how high he had risen, there was always a place to come home to.

I have always been blessed to have a place to come home to, a state and a family that I love so much. For nearly everyone, the pandemic years have been marked by missed events, lost friends and family, and many sorrows. But for some of us, these years have also involved unexpected and unplanned time with family. Seeing our daughter make her way in the world of work and enter law school as happy and purposeful as any parent could hope for has been pure joy. Someone once shared an old adage: "You're only as happy as your least happy child." When you only have one, that's a lot of burden on her shoulders, but Abigail has done it with great aplomb and somehow balanced being a duty-bound kid of a politician with fiercely holding true to her own life, views, and mission.

As explained throughout this book, any words to describe my husband just feel too clichéd to put in writing right now. Rock? Tried before. Soulmate? OMG too much. Let's try this: He's the guy who everyone wants to sit with at dinner because he listens, he's funny, and he's kind. All those qualities are in short supply in our politics today. Not a step on my political journey would have been—or is—any fun without John. Without him, I would have missed a whole bunch of the joy. Who else can I look to at the end of the day after grueling Senate floor debates or political speeches and say, "Did that guy really say that to me?" or "You know what I really wanted to say back but I didn't?" John has shared in my biggest dreams and my hardest losses, all while being an extraordinary teacher, husband, dad, and son.

In the middle of all of this, of course, we lost my dad. While his magnificent mind was riddled with Alzheimer's in his closing years, he was still joyful. He told tons of amusing stories from his various perches: a patio lawn chair, a couch in the assisted living family area, on his bed sitting upright in his brightly decorated room, the walls filled with photos of the people he adored and the treks he had taken from Nepal to Tanzania to Peru.

How he loved to tell stories. And some of them were even true. "Okay," I remember explaining to the nursing assistants one morning, "I know he's focused on this today, but he really didn't have breakfast with Isaac Newton."

The remarkable thing about my dad was that he knew he was dying for months. He had always been a believer. He loved going to church. He led religious trips to Israel. He was proud of his Catholic roots while nevertheless becoming a Lutheran after his divorce from my mom and before his second marriage.

To see someone who had been so incredibly ambitious, such a master of words, slip away with late-onset Alzheimer's was, yes, very sad. But the joy? It was there in his irascible spirit and faith in God that guided him through the end. He had literally climbed some of the world's highest mountains. But he had also descended into the lowest of valleys during his yearslong struggle with alcoholism.

In his later years—after a successful recovery and hundreds of meetings—he could no longer venture out to his Alcoholics Anonymous group or morning Bible study. Instead, members of his AA and Bible groups would come to him in the assisted living facility. Per their accounts, he would sometimes look around the communal living area and note with a smile, "I've been sober for years now, but you couldn't get a drink around here anyway."

My dad's story was one of redemption. That was his joy.

Now during those same few months we knew we were

losing my dad, I found out I had breast cancer. There's no sugarcoating it: there isn't a lot of joy in a breast cancer diagnosis. And there's certainly no joy in the surgery's and radiation's aftermath, with assorted—but not unexpected—hot flashes and various other medical challenges. Yes, there were the devoted doctors and nurses and my friends and family who were there with me every step of the way. There was the gratitude and lessons learned that you should never take anything or anyone for granted (something we all learned during the pandemic). But most of the joy in that time of healing came from knowing that by making the diagnosis public, I could help others.

In working on the final draft of this book, I made some phone calls to people I had written about or featured in stories to check out the facts. I had never spoken to or met Melissa of Maple Grove, Minnesota, the woman who sent me an unsolicited letter about how the public disclosure of my diagnosis of breast cancer had motivated her to go in for a long-delayed cancer test. In the brief letter (which is included in chapter 1), she explained that she found out she had stage 2 breast cancer and was in the course of getting treatment. But when I called her to ask her if it was okay to use the letter and feature her first name, I had no idea what the outcome of her treatment was.

The most bizarre part was that when I called her she actually answered the phone from the waiting room of a suburban breast cancer clinic, where she was calmly awaiting her first mammogram checkup after her cancer surgery and treatment. While I still have never met Melissa in person, I pictured her that day in her clinical gown tied in the back, in the slippers they give you to wear, with a cup of coffee in her hand.

Both Melissa and I decided that the timing of my call was a positive sign. I asked her to call me back with the results. A few days later she did. She was 100 percent good.

"Okay, God," I thought, "I get it and you don't have to make it so obvious. I did something good."

That joy in doing good should be the lifeblood of our democracy. For citizens—smack out of this pandemic, just as we are emerging from our million-plus COVID silos—getting involved in that democracy and nurturing our politics couldn't be more important.

When it comes to my own work I have realized that through all the sludge, muck, and mudslinging of politics, there is still the one thing that keeps drawing me back, the one thing that has grounded me. It is our democracy. That's why I so loved Bono's speech.

The touchstone of Bono's talk was what was happening in Ukraine, where, as he described it, Ukrainians were "actually living, actually dying, for the ideal that is freedom."

Ukraine in many ways defined my own work in 2022. First there was the obvious: I went there and championed the cause. I visited with President Zelenskyy three times during the last year, twice in his home country and once at the Munich Security Conference, where he bravely traveled to ask for the world's help. Everyone had counted him out. But he defied them all. He went to the Kyiv street corner the first night of the invasion and said three simple words: "We are here."

As Bono described it, Ukrainians have been mustering everything they have to preserve their freedom, meeting and exceeding President Zelenskyy's courage and call to fight back:

"Shopkeepers making Molotov cocktails . . . ballet dancers wearing combat gear . . . Freedom in Ukraine means people who don't want to take up arms taking up arms."

And Bono's speech went beyond the international to also thanking our own public servants here at home who "toil away" in the conference room trenches, writing the laws and reading the documents and legalese, doing the not-always-glamorous work of our own democracy.

I think about that a lot.

I think about my Senate colleagues and their staffs—both Democrats and Republicans (and yes, three Independents)—crafting bills late into the night and painstakingly working to reach agreement on amendments. I think about the White House and agency staff doing the same and responding to all kinds of crises. I think about brave Republicans, like Liz Cheney and Adam Kinzinger and Jeff Flake, who put their whole careers on the line just to buck Donald Trump and stand up for our Constitution and our country. I think about my constituents, reading the news, asking me detailed questions about complex issues of war and peace and health and tax policy. When I need any inspiration, I conjure up the images of the veterans gathering at the memorials, the volunteers at the food banks, the young people protesting injustice, the workers working extra shifts or extra jobs just to pay the rent and put food on the table for their families.

As time goes on I continue to gravitate toward issues and causes where the critics and special interests are so loud, but where the people who I am standing up for are either silenced or suppressed by the big guys with all the power. The

Afghan refugees, so many of whom bravely stood with our country. I figure they deserve an advocate. The people who can't afford prescription drugs while the Big Pharma companies bring in mountains of money. The people who want to vote but struggle with state barriers put in place for the sole purpose of making it harder for them to do so. The small newspapers and radio stations struggling to stay afloat just to report the high school football scores and the latest actions of the local city council, all while the major tech companies rake in billions of dollars and use their content at will. The small businesses squeezed out by monopolies. The people of Ukraine—the underdogs invaded by a nuclear and military superpower—who stood up just when everyone had counted them out.

"Be nice to your mom this weekend," my husband once told my daughter. "She has the biggest companies the world has ever known up against her and she's been banned from Russia."

But the point is in a democracy, we can do these things. We can make our case, and we can make progress. But only if we cherish that democracy and fight for it.

So I'll end this with Bono and the greatest speech you have probably never heard of:

America . . . America is a song to me. I caught the melody line early, when my life needed saving. [As a] teenager in Dublin, America's song came on the radio like a surge of static electricity, knocked me out of my bed, knocked me out of my head. You know, the song sounded like Elvis. It sounded like Bobby Dylan, sounded like Aretha Franklin,

sounded like Johnny Cash, Joey Ramone, you know?
It sounded like Jack Kennedy, Bobby Kennedy.
Sounded like King. Bob Dylan sounded like the
Declaration of Independence—with a harmonica
and guitar.

I grew up in Dublin . . . we looked to America,
we had a big crush on you all. And we saw a country
with its own long-running arguments, its own
injustices. We knew this promised land wasn't always
keeping to that promise. We knew America wasn't
living up to all its ideals, but the fact is America had
ideals.

. . . I love this song called AMERICA. I love it.
I love it.

Can you still hold that tune? I ask you as both
fanboy and critic.

Yes, you can. Of course you can.

So that's how I go forward—with a deep love of our
country and the realization that our work is never done. Not
everything turns out as we want, but there are still many
paths ahead. But most of all I go forward with joy, with a
spring in my step, to a tune that's not yet finished.

# Acknowledgments

You can't write a book about joy in the midst of a pandemic, a cancer diagnosis, a presidential primary defeat, an insurrection, and the ever-present bare-knuckles politics of Washington, D.C. without having a whole lot of people keeping you joyful and resilient along the way. So as always, the first thank you goes to my husband, John, who read every word of this book and corrected at least 150 typos and grammar errors and (this is putting it as positively as possible) "bad turns of phrase." Okay, he would double that number to three hundred.

During this past year, John, a law professor at the University of Baltimore School of Law as well as an adjunct at Georgetown Law, had a heavy course load and taught Civil Procedure, Legal Writing, Administrative Law, Torts, Contracts, and two Capital Punishment seminars. In his words, he could be a law school unto himself. He also published two books. But somehow, someway, he was always there for me both in Minnesota and in Washington. There would not have been much joy on the campaign trail, the hiking trail, or just in life in general without my husband.

Our daughter, Abigail, is now a law student herself and is just an awesome person, as well as a stand-up comedian on the side. I hope one day twenty or thirty years from now she will be able to go back and read these pages and find solace in the fact that you can go through—in her words—"a lot" and still come out the other side. Thanks for her review of the book as well as her pointed comments on photos (as in, "you CAN'T use *that one* Mom").

This book truly wouldn't have happened without St. Martin's Press and George Witte—editor and poet extraordinaire. George and St. Martin's were willing to publish a book that wasn't really your typical political autobiography. George also had to deal with the fact that the politician (gasp) actually wrote the book *herself*! The team at St. Martin's understood the theme and purpose of the project and let me run with it. Also thanks to my superb agent, Bob Barnett, who was great through the whole process, as well as many others at St. Martin's, including Brigitte Dale, Laura Clark, Tracey Guest, Gabi Gantz, Lizz Blaise, Susannah Noel, and Lena Shekhter. And while I didn't have a ghostwriter, I did have in Sarah Muller a fantastic researcher and fact-checker who is a really good writer herself. What outstanding work you did, Sarah. Thanks!

There were a number of friends who read parts of this book and gave me useful suggestions (some of which I actually took). Dana Remus, former White House counsel, read the entire book and gave me many helpful ideas, as did my way-back friend Sara Grewing. One of the main prosecutors on the George Floyd case, Jerry Blackwell, read the relevant portions of chapter 4 of the book with his usual eye for detail. Now he's a federal judge! My friend and former Missouri Senator Roy Blunt gave me helpful changes to the book's section on the inauguration. Gianrico Farrugia, M.D.—the head of Mayo Clinic—as well as Dr. Karthik Ghosh of Mayo, made sure I was at least close to accurate in my medical descriptions.

Mandy Grunwald, who has been giving me sage political advice since I first ran for the United States Senate, provided her usual never-mince-words-yet-be-very-constructive thoughts about the book. One of my earliest and fondest memories of Mandy is when I was first running for the Senate and she asked—in preparation for the Senate race—to see the TV ads I had run in my previous county attorney campaigns. After reviewing the ads, which consisted of thirty seconds of black-and-white still shots and accompanying somewhat stilted voice-overs, she called and said, "I need to see the real ads, not just the demos!"

I responded, "Those *are* the real ads!"

Separate and apart from the book, I want to thank all the staff from my U.S. Senate campaigns as well as the entire crew from the presidential campaign, which included many, many full-time staff and volunteers working in our Minnesota headquarters and in field offices throughout the country. I know the stories in chapter 2 will bring back happy (and sometimes amusing) memories that would never have even happened without our devoted staff. You know who you are, and I am so proud of what we did together. Thank you.

Justin Buoen managed my presidential campaign and is one of my closest advisers. He has played a leadership role in every one of my campaigns since he started working with me on parades right out of college in 2004. I thank him for that as well as for so much more.

I want to specifically mention the leaders of our Amy for America policy team, which included the inimitable Brigit

Helgen (my former chief of staff and longtime political adviser), Rosa Po (my former deputy chief of staff who is now at the White House), Tommy Walker (my former legislative assistant and Rules Committee election expert, now at the Small Business Administration), Tom Sullivan (my former deputy chief of staff and now one of the top advisers to Secretary of State Tony Blinken), and Noah Rayman (my former policy adviser and speechwriter, now chief of staff at Empire State Development).

Our fantastic communications team included—among many other talented people—Tim Hogan, Carlie Waibel (now principal deputy assistant for Public Affairs in the Defense Department), Nate Evans (who went on to be my deputy chief of staff and now is the spokesperson and communications director for the U.S. Mission to the United Nations), Christina Freundlich, Digital Director Alli Peters, and photographer Cameron Smith (who is now at the White House and vice president's office taking all kinds of great photos).

On the political, field, and finance sides of the presidential campaign we had tons of good people, but here are some of the leaders who were either there with us from the beginning or played key roles later in the campaign: Julia Kennedy, Elise Convy, Natalie Shaw, Kieran McCarney, Edwin Torres, Enid Swaggert, Kimberly Hunt, Mike McLaughlin, Lucinda Ware, Mia Mayberry, John Davis, Scott Merrick, Marina Negroponte, Angela Kouters, Cameron Miller, Megan Nashban Kenney, Tina Stoll, Ashley Martens, Morgan Brown, Anjan Mukherjee, and Kendall Witmer. And in a category unto her own, the amazing Lauren Dillon, who went on to become my deputy chief of staff in the Senate office.

On the operations side, thanks to the incredible Heidi

Kraus Kaplan and her team, which included (at various times) Nicole Greenberg, Madeline Coles, Asal Sayas, Mitch Perry, Greg Swanholm, Francisco Hardacker, Hannah McDonald, and Grace Waltz. I had many hours in the car and on the phone with this talented group, and they were so good but also—just as importantly—a lot of fun.

Our outside advisers included Fred Yang, Roy Temple, Andi Johnson, Jay Howser, Pete Giangreco, and Annie Levene. All of them were wonderful to work with.

Then there is my staff in the Senate who work so hard every day. Given the focus of the book, I wanted to especially thank those who got us through the pandemic and the insurrection and managed to pass a whole bunch of important bills along the way. Our state office team has been led over the last few years by Erika Nelson, Jodi Niehoff, Ben Hill, Elizabeth Ebot, and, of key note, Clara Haycraft—our deputy state director—who for fifteen years has led a group of passionate constituent service advocates. Clara and her team were literally a lifeline for Minnesotans throughout the pandemic.

On the D.C. side of our office, our staff were—and are—important lifelines to our constituents in a different but equally important way. They passed the bills that kept the country afloat and continue to focus on legislation that—in the words of Paul Wellstone—"improves people's lives." I particularly want to thank Lizzy Peluso, who has served in multiple leadership roles with both my office and the Rules Committee I chair; Elizabeth Farrar, my former counsel and legislative director and now staff director of the Rules Committee; Hannah Hankins, who, along with Lizzy, led the office through both the presidential campaign and the first year of the pandemic before taking the job as communications director to

Barack Obama; Lindsey Kerr, who, after serving in various key roles in our office, led the Rules Committee during the inauguration; Devan Cayea, who led the operations side of our office for many years; Keagan Buchanan, our chief counsel, who leads our amazing judiciary team, which includes all our antitrust work; Jane Meyer, our communications director who has become an expert in, well, just about everything; Lauren Santabar, our very cool legislative director; Kate Leone, who was Harry Reid's former counsel during the passage of the Affordable Care Act and has led our Steering Committee for the past two years, following in the footsteps of Laura Schiller who went on to be chief of staff to Secretary Pete Buttigieg. There are also two people I especially want to mention and thank for their specific work during this period: Doug Calidas—my economic policy adviser, legislative director, and then chief of staff, who successfully shepherded through the all-important Save Our Stages bill, and Baz Selassie—my deputy legislative director, who drafted and negotiated the shipping bill to help bring down rates for farmers and others. How much fun did Baz and I have at the White House bill-signing ceremony in which I took pictures of him with a number of presidents (as in, their portraits) . . . not to mention the White House china. And last but *never* least, thanks to Jack Hostager, Lizzie Haskell, Olivia Lee, Blair Mallin, Savanna Peterson, and Lydia Hubert-Peterson for the enormous help keeping me prepared, on time, and where I was supposed to be during these past few years of busy legislative action.

By virtue of the fact that in chapter 1 of this book I ran through the entire roll of the U.S. Senate, I will not acknowledge all my colleagues one by one. But I did want to thank my Minnesota colleague Tina Smith for her long and trusted friendship, as well as our entire Minnesota delegation to Congress past and present (Democrats and Republicans in the House and Senate) who I have worked with so well in so many different ways for years. That includes Al Franken (now on the road with his very funny "The Only Former U.S. Senator Currently on Tour Tour"), Mark Dayton (Minnesota's former senator and governor), Tim Walz (Minnesota's current governor and former congressman for Minnesota's First District), and Norm Coleman, who served with me during my first two years in the Senate. We also have a great group of Minnesota statewide and legislative leaders who have my profound respect. And finally, our longtime and highly effective DFL Party chair and vice-chair, Ken Martin and Marge Hoffa.

I do want to mention the Senate leaders on both sides of the aisle, including our Democratic leadership team led by Majority Leader Chuck Schumer. That group includes Dick Durbin, Patty Murray, Debbie Stabenow, Elizabeth Warren, Mark Warner, Bernie Sanders, Tammy Baldwin, Cory Booker, Catherine Cortez Masto, Joe Manchin, Brian Schatz, and myself. A team of rivals, yes, but it has worked. On the other side we have Mitch McConnell, John Thune, and several other Republican leaders, and it is my hope that we can continue to pass bipartisan bills just as we did over the past Congress.

Now, in 2023, it might be more than a little harder in the House.

And what a job Speaker Pelosi, Leader Steny Hoyer, and Majority Whip Jim Clyburn did in getting all of this work done in 2021–2022, as well! I look forward to working with them and the new House leaders: Minority Leader Hakeem

Jeffries, Minority Whip Katherine Clark, House Democratic Caucus Chairman Pete Aguilar, and the other new House leaders in the years to come.

Each chapter of this book features people who got me through a tough time and to the other side. I've already mentioned the people I've worked with on the campaigns and in the Senate, but I also want to thank those who kept me going on the personal—and medical—side as well, most of whom were mentioned already. That includes the Mayo Clinic nurses and doctors mentioned in chapter 1 as well as those who work at the Piper Breast Center in Minneapolis. Thanks to Mayo orthopedic surgeon Dr. William Truesdale for fixing my hip (twice). And finally, thanks to the incredible group of doctors and nurses at Inova Mount Vernon Hospital who cared for John when he had COVID, including our friend and infectious disease doctor, John Symington (the husband of my college roommate Meg Symington).

The people who cared for my dad during the last years of his life were simply lovely and loving. They include the staff at Meridian Manor in Wayzata, The Waters in Minneapolis and finally—during the last and hardest two years—Emerald Crest in Burnsville. Mark Hanson, my dad's best friend, his pastor, and the former presiding bishop of the Evangelical Lutheran Church in America, was at my dad's side throughout his life, and especially those last few years. What was amazing about Mark was that he was also—at the same time and at the same place—caring for his beloved wife, Ione, who also has Alzheimer's. My sister Meagan and my dad's good friends, including Rod Wilson (who kept all my dad's financial records), Doug Kelley, Bob Fisher, Barbara Schmitt, Jim Cavanaugh, Randy Furst, Gary Eichten, Kjell Bergh, and

Jeri Nelson, were so loyal, as was his AA group and Tuesday-morning Bible study group.

The United States Capitol Police officers who—at great cost to themselves personally—protected us on January 6th and beyond are a daily inspiration. Thanks to our staff and Senator Blunt's staff who worked on the Electoral Count Act and the inauguration as well as those who worked for Roy and for Senator Gary Peters, Chair of the Homeland Security Committee, and former Senator Rob Portman, who served as ranking member. Together we drafted an important Senate report about what went wrong on January 6th from a security standpoint with recommended security changes at the Capitol. We are pleased that many of the changes have already been implemented.

Finally, my constituents. Resilience isn't something you are just born with. You learn it from watching people pick themselves up after difficult times. Minnesotans are a hardy bunch, and I have met and worked with so many strong people who work every day just to make a better life for their families. I am privileged to know those who worked the front lines during the pandemic and those who refused to be brought down by its isolation.

And when it comes to democracy? My state repeatedly bests the rest of the country on voter turnout. Representing people with high expectations for their elected officials is a good thing. It makes you rise to the occasion. And when that happens and you get stuff done for people? That is the joy of politics.

# Index